The pos,
States depenc
and religious
relationships e
spheres of Am
by non-Cathol
religious reviva
of Church and
reform, and par
of Catholic imr

The positic
the second ha
examined by
the rights of
American life
has come wh
legally certair

There are
to avoid the
religious life
that for most
America Ror
faith of a r
Catholic mir
Gradually, fir
and then with
peoples, the C
they are abou
lem of the
been easy fo
for the Scotc
of religion
speaking ir
was the to
has been c
nationalisr
with som
in the stat
The recc
America
religiou
cept has
immigr

ABOUT THE EDITOR

Rev. Thomas T. McAvoy, C.S.C., is an authority on the history of the Catholic Church in the United States. He is the author of *The Great Crisis in American Catholic History, 1895-1900* (1957), *The Catholic Church in Indiana, 1789-1834,* and *A History of the Catholic Church in the South Bend Area,* and is co-author of *A History of the United States.*

In addition to his duties as Head of the Department of History and Archivist at the University of Notre Dame, Father McAvoy is also managing editor of *The Review of Politics,* a quarterly journal primarily interested in the philosophical and historical approach to political realities.

A native of Tipton, Indiana, Father McAvoy took his undergraduate work and received his master's degree at Notre Dame. He was awarded a Ph.D. by Columbia University in 1940.

ROMAN CATHOLICISM

and the

AMERICAN WAY OF LIFE

EDITED BY

THOMAS T. McAVOY, C.S.C.

UNIVERSITY OF NOTRE DAME PRESS • 1960

© 1960
University of Notre Dame Press
Notre Dame, Indiana

Library of Congress Catalog Card Number 59-14100

IMPRIMI POTEST

Theodore J. Mehling, C.S.C.
Provincial

NIHIL OBSTAT

Edward D. O'Connor, C.S.C.
Censor Deputatus

IMPRIMATUR

✠ Leo A. Pursley, D.D., LL.D.
Bishop of Fort Wayne

September 5, 1959

Preface

This volume needs a brief introduction, partly to explain its title and partly to explain the purpose of the essays that have been here collected.

The title refers to the general problem faced by the Catholic minority in the United States during the second half of the twentieth century. This is not the place to argue whether minority is the proper characterization of the Roman Catholics in the United States. But whether one calls these Roman Catholics a minority or just a church they have a bond of unity that differentiates them from non-Roman Catholics. There have been times since Europeans and others came to that part of the North American continent which we now call the United States when the right of Roman Catholics to remain and to enjoy civic privileges has been questioned. I believe the time has come when these civic privileges are not only legally certain but generally granted. But the social arrangements and the religious relations between American citizens are generally not the subject of legislation. As a matter of fact the Constitution forbade the establishment of a religion in the United States. Consequently the social and religious position of Roman Catholics in the United States in this second half of the twentieth century will depend upon the natural sequence of events in the social and religious realms. These social and religious relationships do expand over into the political and economic spheres of American life, but these political and economic results of the religious life of American Catholics are the concern of this volume only by accident.

Most of the essays in this volume are the product of two symposia held at Notre Dame under the auspices of the Department of History and the Faculty Seminar in American Civilization. The essays in the

iii

first half of the volume deal with the general position of Roman Catholics in the United States. The first group of these essays deals with the general religious situation in the United States at the start of the second half of the twentieth century. The second group deals with some particular factors that affect the position of the Catholic minority in the nation. The third group deals with some of the more important problems being faced by the Roman Catholics in the United States at this time. In the second half of the volume the essays discuss one of the more pressing problems of the Catholic minority in the United States at the present time, the adaptation of the immigrant Catholic to the American scene.

There are certain facts that are the justification for both the symposia and also the present volume. In the first place, Catholics are well aware that for most of the history of English-speaking North America, Catholicism has been the religious faith of a minority. In the colonial era and the era of the American Revolution and the foundation of the United States, that minority never ceased to exist but never had a constituency large enough to have much weight in the political, social, or economic life of the country. Gradually in the nineteenth century, first with the Irish and German immigrants and then with immigrants from many other non-English countries, the Catholics increased in number until they became about one-fifth of the population. In the meantime the differences of language and customs that existed between these non-English and the Anglo-American Catholics disappeared, just as they disappeared between the other non-English but Protestant immigrants and the native people of English abstraction. The problem of the Americanization of the immigrant has been quite easy for the English immigrant, and fairly easy for the Scotch and Irish immigrant, insofar as a change in religion was not involved. For the non-English-speaking immigrant the old language was the tool for culture and for them Americanization has been complicated. Consequently, the main problem of the Americanization of the Roman Catholic immigrant as of any other European should not then be a question of religion but one of language and custom. However, in the mists of modern nationalism in Europe, including of course, that of the British Isles, religion was closely bound up with the language and culture during the past three hundred years. The giving up of these foreign nationalisms has, therefore, involved parting not only with some customs, with the language, but a change in the status of religion in the lives of the immigrants. The recognition that religion is not national in our American way of life and the adjustment of the religious life of the immigrant according to this concept has been a problem not only for the non-English immigrant but for the English immigrant as well.

The twentieth century with its acceptance of an American way of life together with the near cessation of corporate immigration from Europe has brought about the recognition, at least in the newer generations, that these people whom well-meaning Americans have called foreigners have now become Americans. There is a problem both within and without these immigrant groups of reconciling the religious life of the American people with the changing American way of life — just as the social and economic way of life which they or their parents experienced in the villages or cities of Europe, Africa, or Asia has been changed to fit into the American scene. To complicate matters, in the meantime even the American scene has been shifting in the atomic world. But such changes take time and call for thinking ahead. These essays are intended to help in that thinking ahead about an existing problem and the future America. In presenting these essays under one cover, I have no serious apologies for their incompleteness. Primarily these essays are not planned to give a rounded solution to any problem. At no time have the contributors been asked to hold or to achieve any definite purpose or theme. Since the problems are treated in the theater of American life I have invited Jewish and Protestant writers to contribute to the discussion, although those most interested in these problems are the Catholics themselves. For the same reasons these essays differ in intensity and in form, but I think that each writer has something worthwhile to contribute to the study of American Catholicism and the American Way of Life. I am sure that each one hopes that his statements will add to the understanding of these problems, and to worthwhile solutions to some of the apparent difficulties.

THOMAS T. McAVOY, C.S.C.

Notre Dame, Ind.,
April, 1959.

Table of Contents

vii

Part I

ROMAN CATHOLICISM IN TWENTIETH-CENTURY AMERICA

The Present Position of Religion in America

WILL HERBERG*

I. Religion and Culture
in Present-Day America

I

Whatever may be true about the religious situation, it certainly
cannot be doubted that religion is enjoying a boom of unprecedented
proportions in America today. Well over 95 per cent of the American
people identify themselves religiously, as Protestants, Catholics, or Jews
— an incredibly high figure by all available standards of comparison.
The proportion of Americans who are church members — that is,
actually on the rolls of the churches — has nearly doubled in the past
half century; in the last twenty years indeed, church membership has
been increasing twice as fast as population. Church and synagogue
attendance is rising rapidly, Sunday school enrollment is rising even
more rapidly, and religious giving has reached a formidable figure,
even allowing for the inflationary devaluation of the dollar. Interest
in religion and religious thinking is widespread on all cultural levels.
Whatever the criterion of religiousness we take — and by religiousness
I mean the "externals" of religion, using this term in a neutral sense,
without prejudice — we cannot escape the conclusion that we are today witnessing an upsurge of religion without precedent in recent times.

But it is a curious kind of religion. The very same people who
are so unanimous in identifying themselves religiously, who are joining
churches at an accelerating rate, and who take it for granted that
religion is a "very important" thing, do not hesitate to acknowledge

*Dr. Will Herberg is Professor of Judaic Studies and Social Philosophy at
Drew University. He is the author of *Judaism and Modern Man: An Inter-
pretation of Jewish Religion* (1951) and *Protestant-Catholic-Jew: An Essay in
American Religious Sociology* (1955), as well as editor of *The Writings of
Martin Buber* (1956).

that religion is quite peripheral to their everyday lives: more than half of them quite frankly admit that their religious beliefs have no influence whatever on their ideas in economics and politics, and a good proportion of the remainder are obviously uncertain. The very same people who distribute the Bible in vast quantities, largely by voluntary effort, are unable in their majority to give the name of one single book of the New Testament, and the showing is not very different when you take the Bible as a whole. The very same people who, four out of five, say they regard Jesus as divine, when asked to name the most important event in all universal history, place the Christ-event — the birth or crucifixion of Christ — fourteenth on the list, tied with the Wright brothers' invention of the airplane: the Number 1 event, almost without exception, is given as Columbus' discovery of America.[1]

This is the problem: America is in the grip of a great religious boom, that is obvious; yet equally obvious, though not so easy to establish by facts and figures, is the continuing "trend toward secularism in ideas," to use Professor Handlin's phrase[2] — it is really a trend toward secularism not only in ideas, but in attitudes and values as well. This is the problem: the religiousness of a secularist society, the "strengthening of the religious structure in spite of increasing secularization."[3] Thinking through this paradox will take us a long way toward understanding the present religious situation in this country.

II

The best approach to the problem, I think, is to try to understand something of the role that religious belonging plays in the social structure and functioning of contemporary America. I well recognize that religion has its transcendent dimension, which escapes all external scrutiny and analysis; but I am deliberately limiting my inquiry at this point to those aspects that are subject to such scrutiny and analysis, and I think that these aspects are significant in the total picture. What, then, is it that strikes one about the new function of religion in the life of the American people today? It is, I think, that religion, in its tripartite form of Protestant-Catholic-Jew, is rapidly becoming

1. Data illustrating both sides of the contemporary religious situation will be found in Will Herberg, *Protestant-Catholic-Jew: An Essay in American Religious Sociology* (Doubleday, 1955), esp. chaps. I, IV, and V.

2. Oscar Handlin, *The American People in the Twentieth Century* (Harvard, 1954), p. 222.

3. Marshall Sklare, *Conservative Judaism: An American Religious Movement* (Free Press, 1955), p. 39.

the primary context of self-identification and social location in present-day America. Let us see what this really means.

By and large, since the latter part of the nineteenth century at any rate, Americans have tended to identify and locate themselves in terms of race, ethnicity, and religion. "When asked the simple question, 'What are you?'," Gordon W. Allport has noted, referring to certain recent researches, "only ten per cent of four-year-olds answer in terms of racial, ethnic, or religious membership, but 75 per cent of nine-year-olds do so" [4] — and the percentage is even higher for adults. "Race" in America today means color, white vs. non-white, and racial stigmatization has introduced an element of caste-like stratification into American life. For white Americans, ethnicity (immigrant origin) and religion have been, and remain, the major sources of pluralistic diversity, and therefore the major forms of self-identification and social location. But the relation between the two has changed drastically in the course of the past generation, and it is this change that provides a clue to the new role of religion in American life.

As long as large-scale immigration continued, and America was predominantly a land of immigrants, in the days when "the immigrants were American history," as Handlin puts it,[5] the dominant form of diversity, and therefore the dominant form of self-identification, was immigrant ethnicity. The always interesting question about a new family moving into the neighborhood — "What are they?" — was regularly answered in terms of ethnic-immigrant origin. Religion was felt to be an aspect of ethnicity, a part of the ethnic heritage, recent or remote. The enthusiasts of the "melting pot" were eager to eliminate these diverse heritages as quickly as possible; the "cultural pluralists" were determined to perpetuate them; but both alike moved within a pluralism based substantially on ethnicity, ethnic culture, and ethnic religion.

Within the past generation, the picture has been radically transformed. The stoppage of mass immigration during the first World War, followed by the anti-immigration legislation of the 1920's, undermined the foundations of immigrant ethnicity and the immigrant ethnic group with amazing rapidity; what it did was to facilitate the emergence of third and post-third generations, with their characteristic responses and attitudes, as a decisive influence on American life, no

4. Gordon W. Allport, *The Resolution of Intergroup Tensions*, p. 7.
5. Oscar Handlin, *The Uprooted: The Epic Story of the Great Migrations That Made the American People* (Little Brown, 1951), p. 3.

longer threatened with submergence by the next new wave of immigration. Within the threefold American scheme of race, ethnicity, and religion, a shift took place, a shift is taking place, from ethnicity to religion as the dominant form of self-identification — as the dominant way of answering the question, "What am I? how do I differ from 'one man's family'? where do I fit in in the totality of American society?" Ethnic identifications and traditions have not disappeared; on the contrary, with the third generation, they are enjoying a lively popularity as symbols of "heritage." But now the relation between ethnicity and religion has been reversed: religion is no longer an aspect of ethnicity; it is ethnicity, or rather what remains of it, that is taken up, redefined, and expressed through religious identifications and institutions. Religion, or at least the tripartite differentiation of Protestant, Catholic, and Jew has (aside from race) become the prevailing form of defining one's identity as an American in contemporary American society.

Keeping this in mind, we can begin to understand one of the most striking facts in the religious history of this country during the past half century — the transformation of America from a *Protestant* country into a *three-religion* country.

Writing just thirty years ago, Andrè Siegfried described Protestantism as America's "national religion," [6] and he was largely right, despite the ban on religious establishment in the Constitution. Normally, to be born an American meant to be a Protestant; this was the religious identification that in the American mind quite naturally went along with being an American. Non-Protestants felt the force of this conviction almost as strongly as did the Protestants; Catholics and Jews, despite their vastly increasing numbers, experienced their non-Protestant religion as a problem, even as an obstacle, to their becoming full-fledged Americans: it was a mark of their foreignness. (This was true despite the much esteemed colonial heritage of both Jews and Catholics, since it was not the "old American" elements in these two groups that influenced American attitudes, but the newer immigrant masses.) In the familiar Troeltschean sense, Protestantism — not any one of the multiplying denominations, but Protestantism as a whole — constituted America's "established church."

This is no longer the case. Today, to be born an American is no longer taken to mean that one is necessarily a Protestant; Protestantism is no longer the obvious and "natural" religious identification of the

6. Andrè Siegfried, *America Comes of Age* (Harcourt Brace, 1927), p. 33.

American. Today, the evidence strongly indicates, America has become a three-religion country: the normal religious implication of being an American today is that one is either a Protestant, a Catholic,
or a Jew. These three are felt to be, by and large, three different
forms of being religious in the American way; they are the three "religions of democracy," the "three great faiths" of America. Today,
unlike fifty years ago, not only Protestants, but increasingly Catholics
and Jews as well, feel themselves, and are recognized to be, Americans
not apart from, or in spite of, their religion, but because of it. If
America today possesses a "church" in the Troeltschean sense — that
is, a form of religious belonging which is felt to be involved in one's
belonging to the national community — it is the tripartite religious
system of Protestant-Catholic-Jew.

This transformation of America from a Protestant into a three-
religion country has come about not because of any marked increase
in Catholics or Jews — the Protestant-Catholic ratio has remained
pretty well the same for the past thirty years, and the proportion of
Jews in the general population has probably been declining. It has
come about, as I have suggested, through the emergence of a stabilized
American third generation, which is able to set its mark on American
life because it is no longer threatened with dissolution by recurrent
waves of mass immigration.

The immigrant generation, and this is true of all immigrant nationalities, established itself in America as an ethnic group with an
ethnic culture, of which the ethnic language and the ethnic religion
were generally the most significant elements. For the first, the immigrant generation, religion was part of ethnicity; for the Italian immigrant, in other words, his Catholicness was part of his Italianness;
for the Jewish immigrant, his Judaism, his Jewish religion, was part
of his *Yiddishkait,* his ethnic culture. You remember the movie
"Marty." You remember how Marty brings home the girl Clara to
introduce her to his mother. His mother is a good church-going Catholic, but what is the question she asks about Clara? Not "Is she
Catholic?," but "Is she Italian?" Why? Because to the mother, the
first-generation immigrant, if she's Italian, then she's Catholic, and if
she's Catholic without being Italian, it doesn't do any good anyway!
This is the outlook on ethnicity and religion characteristic of the immigrant generation.

The second generation is in a very different position. The second generation is marginal — "too American for the home and too foreign for the school," in Marcus Hansen's celebrated phrase. It is doubly alienated, belonging to two communities but at home in neither, torn away from the old moorings and not yet anchored in the new reality. The second generation responds to its marginality in a number of ways, but by and large it may be said that what the second generation wants most of all is to get rid of its foreignness and become American. This obviously influences its attitude to religion. Just because in the immigrant home, in which the second generation grows up, religion is understood to be a part of ethnicity, to be a part of the immigrant foreignness, the second generation takes a negative view of religion, sometimes breaking with it entirely, usually retaining an uneasy connection, mixed with hostility and embarrassment. The second generation — and that holds true for every immigrant group in America — is characteristically the least religious of American generations.

But now comes the third generation. The third generation — and with it we must include the post-third generations that have arisen on American soil — is again in a very different position. It is at last American, securely American, secure as any American is in his Americanness. But it is faced with a new problem, the problem of defining its identity. Ethnic identifications will no longer serve, as in one way or another they served the first and second generations. What then? — how is the third generation to answer the question, "What am I? how do I differ from 'one man's family'? where do I fit in the totality of American society?" In an effort to define its social identity — without which no tolerable life is possible — the American third generation goes in search of a "heritage." In a sensational reversal of earlier attitudes, the third generation seeks a "return." Some two decades ago, Marcus Lee Hansen, studying not Italians or Jews on the east coast, but Scandinavian Lutherans in the Midwest in the twenties and thirties, expressed this reversal in a classic formula: "What the son wishes to forget, the grandson wishes to remember." [7] The "son," constituting the second generation, wishes to "forget" because he wants so passionately to get rid of his foreignness; the "grandson," belonging to the third generation, wishes to "remember" because he needs a "heritage." But what of the grandfather can the grandson "remember"? — what of his grandfather's legacy can he take over

7. M. L. Hansen, *The Problem of the Third Generation Immigrant* (Augustana Historical Society, 1938), p. 9.

and use for the purpose of giving ....mself a "heritage" and defining his identity? Not his grandfather's nationality, language, or culture; the American pattern of assimilative acculturation obviously makes that impossible. But the grandfather's religion is a very different thing: America not only permits, it even encourages, the perpetuation of one's religious diversity and distinctiveness without danger to one's Americanness. Of course, it is not the grandfather's religion as the grandfather would have recognized it; it is the grandfather's religion brought up to date and Americanized. But it serves; and so religion becomes the characteristic symbol of "heritage" for the third generation, and its return to its heritage becomes a return to religion. With Catholics and Jews, the process, however complex, is relatively unambiguous. With Protestants, however, there is a double movement: on the one side, a return to ethnically associated religion, as among Lutherans; on the other side, because of the confusion, blurring, and growing meaninglessness of denominational lines, a "return" to Protestantism rather than to any particular group within it as a form of religious identification. William H. Whyte's account, in *The Organization Man,* of the emergence of the United Protestant Church in Park Forest, Ill., a story which could be duplicated in so many other suburban communities, well illustrates this pattern of development; but even where denominational affiliations are still maintained, the basic identification is still Protestant, especially among the younger people. And so a three-religion America has emerged, an America in which being a Protestant, being a Catholic, and being a Jew are the three recognized alternative ways of being an American.

A word of caution is necessary. It should not be imagined that just because America has become, or is becoming, a three-religion country, all ethnic or religious group tensions are at an end. Anti-Semitism runs deeper than any merely sociological analysis can penetrate, and even on the sociological level, the new tripartite system would, for the time being at least, seem to make almost as much for the exacerbation as for the alleviation of intergroup tensions. Anti-Jewish manifestations are, for the moment, at a low ebb, but Protestant-Catholic antagonisms appear to be growing sharper. This accentuation of Protestant-Catholic tensions seems to me to be very largely a reflection of the painful transition period through which we are passing; there is every reason to hope that with the stabilization of the new situation, these hostilities too will abate. Yet we should not overlook the fact that the new system of tripartite coexistence is bound to raise its own problems and breed its own tensions with which we will have to cope in the time to come.

III

What has the transformation of America from an ethnic into a religious pluralism, and concomitantly from a Protestant into a three-religion country, meant so far as the status and character of religion in this country are concerned?

Very obviously, it has made for a boom in religious belonging. To have a "name" in American society today — to have an identity, to be able to answer the question "What am I? where do I belong?" — means increasingly to identify oneself in religious terms, as Protestant, Catholic, or Jew. These are three alternative ways of being an American. This is eminently true of the burgeoning suburban sector of American society, least true in the rural areas, and measurably true in the older urban centers. It is certainly the over-all pattern of American life. Obviously, such self-identification in religious terms engenders a new sense of belonging to one's religious community; obviously, too, it impels to institutional affiliation, characteristically expressed in terms of concern for the children: "We have to join a church (or a temple) for the sake of the children." There is profound sociological wisdom in this remark, though its theological implications may be dubious. "The church," Oscar Handlin points out, "supplies a place where the children come to learn what they are" [8] — what kind of Americans they are. The mechanisms of other-directed conformity to which David Riesman has called attention serve to give religious belonging the compelling power it is acquiring in the pattern of suburban "sociability," but the new role of religion in this process is the result of the more basic factors I have tried to indicate in my remarks on the third generation and the transformation of America into a three-religion country.

Just as Americans are coming more and more to think of being a Protestant, being a Catholic, and being a Jew as three alternative ways of being an American, so they are coming to regard Protestantism, Catholicism, and Judaism, the "three great faiths," as three alternative (though not necessarily equal) expressions of a great overarching commitment which they all share by virtue of being Americans. This commitment is, of course, democracy or the American Way of Life.

8. Oscar Handlin, *The American People in the Twentieth Century*, p. 222.

It is the common allegiance which (to use Professor Williams' phrase) provides Americans with the "common set of ideas, rituals, and symbols" through which an "overarching sense of unity" is achieved amidst diversity and conflict.[9] It is, in a sense far more real than John Dewey ever dreamed of, the "common religion" of Americans.

Let me illustrate this point with two texts borrowed from President Eisenhower, who may, I think, be taken as a representative American really serious about religion. "Our government," Mr. Eisenhower declared shortly after his election in 1952, "makes no sense unless it is founded in a deeply felt religious faith, *and I don't care what it is.*"[10] It is the last phrase which I have emphasized — 'and I don't care what it is' — to which I want to call your attention. Of course, President Eisenhower did not mean that literally; he would have been much disturbed had any sizable proportion of Americans become Buddhists, or Shintoists, or Confucianists — but of course that never entered his mind. When he said "I don't care what it is," he obviously meant "I don't care which of the three it is — Protestantism, Catholicism, or Judaism." And why didn't he care which it was? Because, in his view, as in the view of all normal Americans, they "all say the same thing." And what is the "same thing" which they all say? The answer is given to us from the current vocabulary: "the moral and spiritual values of democracy." These, for the typical American, are in a real sense final and ultimate; the three conventional religions are approved of and validated primarily because they embody and express these "moral and spiritual values of democracy."

Let me drive this home with the second text from President Eisenhower. In 1948, four years before his election, just before he became president of Columbia, Mr. Eisenhower made another important pronouncement on religion. "I am the most intensely religious man I know," he declared. "Nobody goes through six years of war without faith. That does not mean that I adhere to any sect. (Incidentally, following the way of all flesh, he was soon to join a "sect," the Presbyterian.) A democracy cannot exist without a religious base. I believe in democracy."[11] Here we have the entire story in a single phrase: I believe in religion because I believe in democracy! Pre-

9. Robin M. Williams, Jr., *American Society: A Sociological Interpretation* (Knopf, 1951), p. 312.
10. *New York Times,* December 23, 1952.
11. *New York Times,* May 4, 1948.

cisely the same conviction, though expressed in a rather more sophis-
ticated manner, was affirmed by an eminent New York rabbi not long
ago. "The spiritual meaning of American democracy," he declared,
"is realized in its three great faiths." [12] Similar statements, I assure
you, could be found in the pronouncements of spokesmen of the other
two religious groups.

What I am describing is essentially the "Americanization" of religion in America, and therefore also its thorough-going secularization.
This process is not a recent one. It began for Protestantism some time
after the Civil War and proceeded apace in the latter decades of the
nineteenth century. Sidney Mead's brilliant description of this trend
is particularly relevant.

> What was not so obvious at the time (he writes) was that the
> United States, in effect, had two religions, or at least two different
> forms of the same religion, and that the prevailing Protestant ide-
> ology represented a syncretistic mingling of the two. The first was
> the religion of the (Protestant) denominations which was com-
> monly articulated in terms of scholastic Protestant orthodoxy and
> almost universally practised in terms of the experimental religion
> of pietistic revivalism. . . . The second was the religion of the
> democratic society and nation. This. . .was articulated in terms
> of the destiny of America, under God, to be fulfilled by perfecting
> the democratic way of life for the example and betterment of
> mankind. [13]

With remarkably little change — something would have to be said
about the waning of scholastic orthodoxy and the new forms of pietis-
tic revivalism — these words could stand as a description of the current situation. What is new, what is crucially new, is that this is no
longer true merely of Protestantism; it is becoming more and more
true of Catholicism and Judaism as well, precisely because Catholicism
and Judaism have become American, integral parts of the three-religion America. In this, as in so many other respects, their Americanization has meant their "Protestantization," using this term to describe
the American Protestant ethos, so at variance with classical Protestant
Chrisian faith. With the loss of their foreignness, of their immigrant
marginality, these two religious groups seem to be losing their capacity

12. Rabbi David J. Seligson, quoted in *New York Times,* March 25, 1956.
13. Sidney E. Mead, "American Protestantism Since the Civil War. I. From
Denominationalism to Americanism," *The Journal of Religion,* vol. XXXVI,
No. 1, January 1956, p. 2.

to resist dissolution in the culture. In becoming American, they have apparently become American all the way.

We are now, I think, in a position to penetrate the apparent paradox with which we initiated this discussion, the paradox of the religiousness of a secularist society. How can Americans be so religious and so secularistic at the same time? The answer is that for increasing numbers of Americans religion serves a function largely unrelated to the content of faith, the function of defining their identity and providing them with a context of belonging in the great wilderness of a mobile American society. Indeed, for such a purpose, the authentic content of faith may even prove a serious handicap, for if it is Jewish or Christian faith, it carries a prophetic impact which serves rather to unadjust than to adjust, to emphasize the ambiguity of every earthly form of belonging rather than to let the individual rest secure in his "sociability." For this reason, the typical American has developed a remarkable capacity for being serious about religion without taking religion seriously — in which respect he is not unlike sinful human beings of all ages. His ideas, values, and standards he takes from what is so often really his ultimate commitment, the American Way of Life. He combines the two — his religion and his culture — by making the former an expression of the latter, his religion an expression of the "moral and spiritual values of democracy." Hence his puzzling pro-religious secularism, his secularistic religionism, which, looked at more closely, does not seem so puzzling after all.

IV

From the standpoint of the man of faith, of the man who takes his religious tradition seriously, what does the picture of religion in contemporary America add up to? No simple or unequivocal answer can be given.

On the one hand, the emergence of religion as a vehicle of American belonging has made for a breakdown of anti-religious prejudice. One of the most striking features of present-day American culture is the complete absence of an Ingersoll or a Darrow, of the "village atheist" on a national scale, or for that matter, except here and there, even on a village scale. Contemporary Americans, especially the younger generation, simply cannot understand the militant atheist of yesterday; he is so remote from their mentality as to be hardly credible. The breakdown of anti-religion has contributed toward the new openness to religion that is so obvious today. Yet the religion that emerges is only too often a religiousness, or perhaps a pro-religiousness, without religion, without serious religious content, conviction, or commitment. There is great danger, as one Jewish leader recently put it, that our church or synagogue cards may hide from us the basically secularistic character of our religion. There is even danger that with the rapid spread of a contentless religiousness, the very meaning of religion in its authentic sense may be lost for increasing numbers.

There is also a positive side to the "Americanization" of religion, which sees in Protestantism, Catholicism, and Judaism three forms of being religious in the American way. To the degree that this is felt to be true, the stigma of foreignness is lifted from Catholicism and Judaism, and from such ethnic forms of Protestantism as the Lutheran. There is a new freedom and tolerance, and at least the public equality of the "three great faiths" in American life. No one who remembers what misery the taint of foreignness once brought, and what a formidable obstacle it constituted to the preservation and communication of the "non-American" faiths, will fail to be grateful for this development. But it has been purchased at a heavy price, the price of embracing an idolatrous civic religion of Americanism.

I want to express myself here very clearly, and I will do so by speaking to you as Catholics. I recently lectured to the entire student body of a well-known Catholic girls' college. In the course of my remarks, I confronted them — not in such a way as to put them on their guard, of course — with Christopher Dawson's celebrated question: "Are you Americans who happen to be Catholics, or Catholics who happen to be Americans?" Almost with one voice the girls answered, "Americans who happen to be Catholics. . ." You appreciate the significance of the question and the answer. The question really means: "Is your ultimate allegiance and your ultimate community the Universal Church, or is it the American nation?" The answer of the girls indicated that they normally thought of themselves as primarily Americans, but of course as Americans of the "Catholic kind," just as some of their friends were Americans of the "Protestant kind," and still others Americans of the "Jewish kind." Let me assure you that I have received the same kind of response from other Catholic groups — lay groups, that is — and from Protestant and Jewish audiences as well, when the question was put to them in their own terms.

What does that mean? It means that we have in America an invisible, formally unacknowledged, but very potent religion — the religion of democracy, the religion of the American Way of Life — of which the conventional religions are felt to be more or less adequate expressions. Americans do not put it that way, in just so many words, but that is how they feel and behave. In effect, this means that they participate in an actual civic religion, very much like the civic religion of the Roman Empire in early Christian times. The authentic relation between religion and culture is subverted, of which the civic religion is the sanctification, is idolatrized by being made ultimate, which means divine. Judaism, and Christianity in its two forms, become subordinated to the culture and tend to lose all sense of uniqueness, universality, and special vocation. To the man of Jewish or Christian faith, this divinization of the American Way — even if he acknowledges, as I do, the American Way to be one of the best ways of life yet devised for a mass society — must appear as abhorrent as the ancient civic religions appeared to the Jew or Christian of those days, in spite of the fact that our own civic religion is not officially established, overtly promulgated, or enforced through persecution.

It is not without significance that this conversion of democracy, or the American Way of Life, into the "common religion" of Americans has been given explicit formulation by a number of secularist-minded philosophers, such as Horace M. Kallen, who proclaims the "democratic faith" to be, for its "communicants" — the words are Kallen's — 'the religion *of* and *for* religions, . . . all may freely come together in it." [14] What Kallen here states explicitly — the title of his article is "Democracy's True Religion" — is implicit in the ethos of American life and finds expression in many of its social and cultural, as well as religious, patterns. No wonder that Dean Sperry introduced his survey of religion in America with the words: "The honest critic of American affairs must therefore face the possibility that the true religion of his is not that of Protestant, Catholic, or Jew, but is rather a secular idolatry." [15]

The American conviction that "religion is a very good thing" — this may be taken as the second article in the American religious creed; the first is belief in God, and the third, and last, is that all really American religion is either Protestant, Catholic, or Jewish — the American conviction that religion is a very good thing, I say, means that religion is taken seriously and is endowed with a vigor and vitality that amazes foreign observers. But it also means that religion is thoroughly "func-

14. Horace M. Kallen, "Democracy's True Religion," *Saturday Review,* July 28, 1951.
15. W. S. Sperry, *Religion in America* (Macmillan, 1946), p. 19.

tionalized," that is, converted into a tool for secular purposes. It is made to serve the sociological function of providing a form of identification and a context of belonging in a world of other-directed "sociability"; of this we have already spoken. But it is also made to serve the psychological function of conferring, on the one side, reassurance and "peace of mind," and on the other, a sense of power and achievement through "positive thinking." It is not our purpose to examine this aspect in any detail, but one thing should be noted. Just as religion on its sociological side seems to function best if it is unembarrassed with content, so religion on its psychological side easily comes to mean a contentless faith. In the one case, it may be said that Americans are religious about religion; in the other, that they have faith in faith. I appeal to you to take this description with the utmost seriousness. So eminent a religious leader as Daniel Poling quite simply describes his own conviction about faith in these words: "It was back in those days that I formed a habit which I have never broken. I began saying in the morning two words, 'I believe.' Those two words, with nothing added, . . . give me a running start for my day, for every day." [16] Another religious leader, not a Protestant, puts it this way: "The storehouse of dynamic power on which you may draw, is *Faith.* Not religion, . . . not God, but *FAITH.*" [17] And an advertisement in a New York paper of three eminently respectable churches is headed: "When Faith Alone Protects." In the entire ad neither God nor Christ is so much as mentioned. Church-going is recommended with the argument: "There are times in your life when faith alone protects. We all reach these times in hours of crisis which dot life's span. Regular church attendance helps you build your own personal reserve of faith." [18] What is this but picturing God as a great cosmic public utility, and religion or church-going as a way of charging one's storage battery of faith for use in emergencies? It is hardly necessary to point out that this faith in faith, this religion of religion, is just as idolatrous as faith in a stock or stone or the religion of magical self-salvation.

Americans crave security; they are bewildered and uneasy even in their prosperity. Americans crave personal power and achievement;

16. Daniel Poling, "A Running Start for Every Day," *Parade: The Sunday Picture Magazine,* September 19, 1954.

17. Louis Binstock, *The Power of Faith* (Prentice-Hall, 1952), p. 4.

18. Advertisement of three Episcopal churches, *New York Herald-Tribune,* April 15, 1955.

they are frightened at the great heteronomous forces of a mass society which threaten to grind them into nothingness. Americans crave sociability; they are terrified at the prospect of being lost in the crowd. But most of all they crave reassurance about their goals and values, which they feel called into question and threatened on every side. And so they have fashioned their religion to serve these purposes by turning it into a man-centered cult of "peace of mind," "positive thinking," and American belonging. The religion that has emerged was bitingly described by Richard Niebuhr, speaking of latter-day Protestantism, two decades ago: "A God without wrath (brings) men without sin into a kingdom without judgment through the ministrations of a Christ without a cross." [19]

V

This is a picture of the religious situation in the United States today, but it is only a partial picture. There are other and more authentic stirrings of faith abroad, especially among the younger people on the campuses and their somewhat elder contemporaries in the suburban communities. These stirrings, fed from deeper sources, express themselves in different degrees on the various levels of interest, concern, and commitment, but everywhere the signs are unmistakable. Recent surveys have documented it,[20] and the report of the Student Council of Harvard University issued in February 1956 under the title of "Religion at Harvard," along with like expressions of student opinion on other campuses, may be taken as significant manifestations. This type of religious revival is very different, in its origins and in its expressions, from the religiousness we have been describing; it looks to religion not for "peace of mind," the "power of positive thinking," or the comfort of adjustment and belonging, but for some outlook, perhaps even commitment, that will illumine the meaning of existence and give one the resources to preserve authenticity of being in a world poised at the brink of nothingness and trying to save itself by an increasingly rigid conformism. This deeper kind of faith combines with the mass religiousness of the American people in various ways, but

19. H. Richard Niebuhr, *The Kingdom of God in America* (Willett Clark, 1937), p. 193.
20. See esp. the report of the study of campus attitudes toward religion conducted by the Rev. James L. Stoner, director of the University Christian Mission of the National Council of Churches of Christ in the U.S.A., *New York Times,* October 22 and 24, 1956; cp. also Will Herberg, "The Religious Stirring on the Campus," *Commentary,* March 1952.

the distinctive thing about it is that it fights shy of institutional embodiment and involvement. This constitutes a very real problem, for a religiousness without a firm institutional framework of tradition and doctrine is bound to degenerate into eccentricity, sentimentalism, or intellectual dilettantism. And in fact something of the sort seems to be occurring here and there, although usually what happens is that the stirrings of faith aroused in the "open" period of campus and immediate post-campus life are overwhelmed and dissipated by the overpowering force of American mass religiousness. What the final outcome will be, as these two very different types of religious revival meet and confront each other, it is still too soon to say. Only the future can tell what the deeper stirrings of faith, wherever they may arise, will amount to and what consequences they will hold for the American religion of tomorrow.

But even the more dubious forms of American religion should not be written off entirely. Even in this ambiguous structure, there may be elements and aspects — not always those, incidentally, that seem most promising to us today — which could in the longer view transform the character of American religion and bring it closer to the traditions of faith it claims to represent. Nothing is too unpromising or refractory to serve the divine will. After all, the God who is able to make the "wrath of men" to praise Him, is surely capable of turning even the superficialities, inadequacies, and perversities of contemporary religion into an instrument of His redemptive purpose.

WINTHROP S. HUDSON*

II. Protestantism in Post-Protestant America

Of all the symbols of nineteenth-century America, none was more characteristically Protestant than the Chautauqua Institution which Theodore Roosevelt described as the most American thing in America. In similar vein he declared that he "would rather address a Methodist audience than any other audience in America," for "the Methodists represent the great middle class and in consequence are the most representative Church in America." These random comments of a former president serve to highlight the dramatic shift in the religious complexion of the United States that has occurred during the past fifty years. In 1900 few would have disputed the contention that the United States was a Protestant nation, so self-evident was the fact that its life and its culture had been shaped by three centuries of Protestant witness and influence. But fifty years later so drastically had the situation changed that when Arnold S. Nash wrote the introductory chapter to a symposium *Protestant Thought in the Twentieth Century,* he gave it the title "America at the End of the Protestant Era."

To say that the United States has entered a post-Protestant era is not to deny that much of American culture is still informed by a distinctly Protestant ethos, nor is it to contend that Protestantism is no longer a factor in the shaping of American life. It is simply to affirm that the United States has become a pluralistic society in which Protestantism has ceased to enjoy its old predominance and near monopoly in the religious life of the nation.

The post-Protestant era is in large part the product of the flood-tide of immigration which poured into the United States during the

*Dr. Winthrop S. Hudson is Professor of the History of Christianity in Colgate Rochester Divinity School and author of *The Great Tradition of the American Churches.*

last two decades of the nineteenth century and the first decade and a half of the twentieth century. Major Jewish communities came into existence in a number of cities, and the adherents of the several national Churches of Eastern Orthodoxy formed significant clusters in some of the industrial centers. The more important shift in the population balance, however, was the result of the tremendous influx of Roman Catholic immigrants. At the time of the first census in 1790, Roman Catholics constituted less than one per cent of the population, some 30,000 out of 3,900,000. During the middle decades of the nineteenth century Roman Catholics began arriving in large numbers from Ireland and Germany, and toward the close of the century the Roman Catholic population was vastly augmented by the great tide of immigration from Central and Southern Europe. By 1906 Roman Catholics constituted approximately seventeen per cent of the population. Due to problems of adjustment in a new land, including the isolation from the general culture life imposed upon many of them by the language barrier, the influence of these new Americans was not to begin to be fully exerted until after World War I. From 1920 until the middle of the century, Roman Catholicism became an increasingly important factor in the life of the nation, and Protestantism was confronted by the difficult problem of adjusting itself to a status of coexistence with another major religious tradition.

The shift from a Protestant to a post-Protestant era in America, however, is not to be explained solely in numerical terms. The Protestant Churches still claim almost twice as many members as does the Roman Catholic Church. Furthermore, the projection of a United States Census Bureau study in 1957 indicates that two-thirds of all Americans think of themselves as Protestants, whereas only one-fourth think of themselves as Roman Catholics. There are few informed observers, however, who would regard these figures as an accurate indication of the actual balance of influence being exerted by the two religious traditions. Before the turn of the century the death of Phillips Brooks plunged the whole nation into mourning, but it has recently been noted by a discerning interpreter of the contemporary scene that today "it is inconceivable that the death of any national Protestant leader or political figure other than the President himself would command the massive 'interfaith' attention which accompanied the death of Samuel Cardinal Stritch in 1958." Illustrations of this type could be multiplied, and they serve to document the fact that there has been a more marked realignment of religious forces in the United States than the statistics suggest.

One of the factors contributing to the relative decline — in proportion to its numerical strength — of Protestant influence has been the fact that Roman Catholic strength has been centered in the cities, whereas the great stronghold of Protestantism has been among the farms and villages of the countryside. Since the cities have become the real power-centers of twentieth-century America, these differing strongholds of the two traditions spell out in part the difference of impact they have been able to exert. It is the concentration of strength in a few key cities which also explains to a considerable degree why the influence of the Jewish community is far out of proportion to its numbers. The relative weakness of contemporary Protestantism, however, is not to be understood solely in terms of its dependence upon a dwindling farm and village civilization. It is due quite as much to internal factors as it is to external circumstance, and these inner factors are the product of Protestantism's historical development in the United States.

For a variety of reasons Protestants did not find it easy to adjust to the necessities of a pluralistic society. They had possessed a near monopoly for so long that it came to them as something of a shock to discover that they were henceforth to live in a highly competitive situation in which many of the things which they had taken for granted would be sharply challenged. This discovery alone was to be sufficiently demoralizing, but were there other factors which made it difficult for American Protestants to respond vigorously to the demands of a pluralistic society.

For one thing, Protestantism had become complacent. In a very real sense, it had become a victim of its own success. Throughout the nineteenth century the Protestant Churches had been on the march, seeking to win men and women to the Christian faith, to penetrate the institutions of society with Christian principles, and to keep abreast of the retreating frontier. They had succeeded remarkably well and had brought into being a society and a culture that was recognizably Christian. By the end of the century the final frontier areas had been "churched," and the American people seemed to be settling down to a stable church-going existence defined in Protestant terms. There were, to be sure, non-Protestant enclaves in the cities, but given time it was assumed that these would be assimilated. Thus, at this critical juncture, the Protestant Churches — pleased with the past and confident of the future — tended to relax and become complacent. A mood of complacency was scarcely appropriate for the situation in which they were to find themselves as they moved forward into the new century and it heightened the sense of shock they were to experience when they discovered just how inappropriate it was. But there was a deeper malady than mere complacency which rendered American Protestantism at this particular moment in its history ill-prepared to cope with the realities implicit in a pluralistic society.

The deeper malady was the theological erosion which had taken place during the course of the nineteenth century. As has been suggested, a pluralistic society is a highly competitive society — a society in which various traditions are locked in debate. In such a situation presuppositions must be clearly defined and their implications carefully articulated if a particular religious grouping is to survive and make its influence felt. This means that the adherents of the several traditions must be knowledgeable and informed. If they are to participate effectively in the discussion and debate, they must be able to give both an account of and a reasoned defense for their faith, and they must be able to spell out its implications with clarity and persuasiveness. It was precisely at this point that American Protestantism had become weak.

The theological erosion that had taken place was the product of several factors. It was in part the result of the absence of any sharp challenge to the Protestant understanding of the Christian faith, for in this situation fundamental assumptions tend to be taken for granted. Consequently the Protestant community had become increasingly composed of adherents whose religious affiliation was more largely determined by accident of birth and persistence of custom than by conscious conviction. It was also in part the product of the attrition to which every religious movement is subject. There is always an alternation between periods of spiritual quickening and vitality and periods of decline and lethargy. Any great surge of religious life and spiritual renewal is always followed by a gradual diminution of zeal and a fading of the earlier imperatives. But there were other features of nineteenth-century Protestant life which accentuated and hastened this process.

Nineteenth-century Protestantism in America was the heir of the great tide of evangelical religion, stemming from the Great Awakening, which contributed the aggressive missionary spirit that gave to nineteenth-century Protestant Action its dynamic thrust. While the restless energy released by evangelicalism succeeded in placing a Christian stamp on American culture, evangelicalism itself was not an unmixed blessing. Doctrinal definitions tended to be neglected in the stress that was placed upon "heart religion" and the "conversion experience." The demands of the Christian life, to be sure, continued to be spelled out in terms of an earlier theological understanding, and so long as this theological structure persisted a formative influence was exerted upon society. But since the appeal of evangelicalism was directed more to the emotions than to the intellect, the tendency was for the inherited capital to be lost.

The theological erosion was also accelerated by the particular technique — revivalism — which evangelicalism developed as a means of winning men and women to Christian obedience. The revivalist faced at least two temptations. First, he was tempted to reduce the ambiguities of human life and the complexities of the Christian faith to simple alternatives so that he could issue a clear-cut call for decision. Second, he was tempted to stress results and to justify whatever tended to produce them. As a result of these two pressures, the tendency of the revivalist was to oversimplify the issues at stake, and the ultimate consequence as the century moved toward its close was to contribute to those forces which were rendering the faith of American Protestantism increasingly devoid of content. It should be acknowledged that the temptations implicit in revivalism were resisted with varying degrees of success by the greater revivalists, for they were men acutely sensitive to the hazards and uncertainties of the road to salvation. But often this sensitivity was lacking.

A third contributing factor to the theological erosion was the technique developed to make it possible for Protestants, in spite of the divisions which existed among them, to cooperate for the furtherance of common concerns. They marshalled their strength by organizing what has been called Protestant Action — a wide variety of voluntary societies designed to achieve specific objectives. By means of these societies and for the specific purposes they were designed to serve, the differences which divided Protestants could be by-passed. It is not surprising, as a result of this pattern of activity, that there should have been a growing conviction that the things which united them were more important than the things which separated them. Actually the differences were not too important when viewed in the light of their agreements, for they operated from a common theological base. The major groups participating in the voluntary societies stood largely within the Reformed tradition as it had been modified and reshaped by evangelicalism. Thus their differences were limited to questions of polity and did not involve fundamental theological disagreement. By the close of the century, however, the tendency was to push for a broader cooperation which extended beyond the hitherto limited theological base, and this in turn served progressively to reduce the necessary and important components of the faith to fewer and fewer essentials.

There was a fourth influence which contributed to the theological erosion. The new intellectual currents of the latter decades of the nineteenth century are familiar enough, having been repeatedly analyzed in detail. New scientific discoveries and hypotheses, most notably Darwin's theory as to the origin of the species, posed new problems of Biblical interpretation and tended to undermine accepted notions of Biblical authority. New methods of textual and historical study raised similar questions and created further uncertainties. The psychology of religion came into its own as a respectable academic discipline, and its analysis of the conversion experience tended to push to one side any emphasis upon the grace of God and the role of the Holy Spirit and centered attention instead on the significance of individual decision and commitment. Sociological studies were not initially so disturbing but they were distracting, for they emphasized how to get things done by manipulating the external environment. These sociological studies, dealing with the everyday aspects of life at first hand, were intensely absorbing, and in the end they were to be of crucial significance in interpreting the faith as a social phenomenon and the church as a social agency.

As has been intimated, American Protestants at this particular moment were ill-prepared to cope with this headlong rush into a new intellectual world. Their whole religious outlook had been shaped by the basic anti-intellectualism of evangelicalism. Impelled by the necessity to restate the Christian faith in terms that would be intellectually defensible and convincing, there was a strong tendency to forget that the Christian faith had any claim of its own to truth. Having been schooled to regard the subtleties of theological discussion with distaste, they were not equipped to do much more than appropriate uncritically the conclusions of supposedly objective scholarship. The theologians in the seminaries strove manfully to do more than that, as is amply evidenced in the repeated editions of their systematic theologies, but the demoralizing fact was that the whole apparatus of what remained of the inherited doctrinal structure seemed suddenly archaic and out-of-date. More and more they came to depend, for their basic affirmations, upon what was described as the unfolding revelation of God to be found in the scientific study of man, society, and the natural world. Thus the real theologians were no longer to be found in the theological schools. The men who served as arbiters of Christian truth and made plain the mind of God were the autonomous scholars in the universities who stood outside the faith in terms of their intellectual inquiries.

As a result of its several surrenders and the blunting of its theological particularities, Protestantism during the early decades of the twentieth century was in no position to meet either the challenge of the world or the challenge of other religious traditions with a sharp challenge of its own. It had largely lost the indispensable leverage of an independent theological perspective which formerly had enabled it to exert a creative and effective influence in society. There was, to be sure, the continuing influence of habit and custom, but this was much more conservative than creative. What was to become the most characteristic response to the competitive situation presented by a pluralistic society was the growing conviction among many Protestants that one religion is as good as another, that it is impertinent to raise divisive issues, that it doesn't make much difference what one believes so long as he is sincere, and that men of differing faiths by their different routes are all headed for the same place and striving for the same ends. This mood — "religion in general" it has been called — has penetrated Roman Catholicism and Judaism as well as Protestantism, and to the extent that it has penetrated these communities their influence has been emasculated. But, because of the theological erosion to which it had been subjected and because of the absence of social factors tending to create a group consciousness and solidarity, Protestanism has suffered most from this pervasive climate of opinion.

This picture of American Protestanism may be unduly bleak. There were, of course, survivals among Protestants of earlier theological structures, although the survival of anything resembling classical Protestantism was isolated and meagre. But, on the whole, one finds little reason to question the validity of Whitehead's judgment of Protestantism in 1932: "Its dogmas no longer dominate; its divisions no longer interest; its institutions no longer direct the patterns of life" (*Adventures of Ideas*, p. 205). On the other hand, at the very time Whitehead pronounced this verdict, there were signs of renewal.

While there were only isolated voices calling for a theological recovery during that decade, a theological revival became increasingly evident in Protestant theological seminaries during the 1940's. During the years that have followed a growing segment of the clergy have been caught up in the theological renaissance. It is not yet clear, however, whether Protestantism is to recover its full vigor. To do so, its theological structure must be further clarified, the new theological interest must penetrate the laity, and Protestant church life must undergo reform and reconstruction in terms of its fundamental understanding of the Christian faith.

FRANCIS X. CURRAN, S.J.*

III. The Religious Revival and
Organized Religion

In these days of semantic confusion "religion" is a much-abused word. It is applied to, or adopted by, groups and individuals who are fundamentally non-religious or even anti-religious. To many churchmen, the great enemy of religion is stigmatized by another abused word, "secularism." If it means the exclusion of God from human thinking and human living, then secularism is indeed the enemy of religion. Yet today we have that monstrous chimera, the religious secularist.[1] An individual or society which denies the existence of a divine being or which transmits the question of God as pointless is not, in any sense acceptable to a Catholic, religious. The Catholic cannot but feel uneasy when professed theists speak of a weak and fallible God perfecting Himself through human history; yet to these men religion still connotes God. He draws the line before those who profess that contradiction in terms, a theology of humanism. "Religion" is meaningless unless it is defined in terms of God.

And to the Catholic the word "religion" necessarily implies the Church. For to him religion is intelligible chiefly in terms of the Church. He knows that religion is something quite personal, grasped interiorly. But he knows also that, as a social being, he seeks expression of his intimate belief and experience in community. Every community is personal in its essence; it rises from personal relationships; it satisfies personal needs. The Church is such a community, a sacra-

*Rev. Francis X. Curran, S.J., is Professor of History at Loyola Seminary, Shrub Oak, N.Y., and a contributor to history periodicals. He is the author of *Major Trends in American Church History* (1941), *The Church and the Schools* (1954).

1. This anomaly is described in Herbert W. Schneider, *Religion in 20th Century America* (Cambridge, Mass., 1952), 143.

mental one — the *communio sanctorum;* indeed it is more than a community, it is an organism, the *corpus Christi mysticum.* These aspects of the Church as the communion of saints, as the mystical Body of Christ, are above and beyond the scope of human criticism. Not so the Church as the visible Kingdom of God, the society of the faithful existing beside other societies, the religious organization of men moulding and being moulded by the culture in which it lives. When the Catholic considers religion, automatically he thinks in terms of the Church.

When he considers the revival of religion, he considers it in relation to the Church. Just as "religion" is a term wider than the Church, so the revival of religion need not necessarily be gauged with reference to the Church. Religious revival implies a conversion, a turning to God. An immediate consequence of that turning to God would be a greater impact of religion on human life. To weigh these qualitative aspects of the revival is a difficult if not impossible task. Consequently many would gauge the revival by a more manageable quantitative aspect. Revival implies conversion. Has the revival brought converts to the churches and the synagogues?

That America is now experiencing a revival of religion is a truism. Religion is more respected, more discussed, more popular than it has been for a generation.[2] Certainly if we define a revival as renewed interest in religion after a period of indifference or decline, we are in the midst of a revival. It is a common assumption that the revival connotes a great popular movement into the churches and the synagogues. That is why, as proof positive of the revival, we are presented with figures — for example, the impressive totals of the attendance at the campaigns of Dr. Billy Graham, and even more impressive statistics of church membership. These figures may be indicative of a trend; they are certainly far from conclusive. Indeed, the statistics of church membership would tend to indicate, if these figures can be used to prove anything, that there is no revival of religion.

Our concept of religious revival is largely derived from Protestant experience and stems from the first major revival in America, the Great Awakening. This, I believe, is a fair description of that concept: After a time of decline in religion, when men's faith grows cold and large numbers fall away from the churches, comes a period of renewal. Faith is rekindled and sweeps across the nation like a prairie

2. This revival is well documented in Will Herberg, *Protestant, Catholic, Jew* (Garden City, N.Y., 1955), 58 ff.

fire. Great multitudes of men are converted to Christ, and the churches harvest a huge ingathering of souls.

While we do not have church statistics for eighteenth-century America, the extant evidence does indicate that the Great Awakening markedly increased the membership of the churches in the thirteen British colonies. At the turn of the nineteenth century, the new United States experienced a second wave of revivalism, known as the Second Great Awakening, and yet another which reached its peak about the fourth decade of the century. Obviously these revivals appreciably affected church membership, for by mid-century the Evangelical churches most closely identified with revivalism — notably the Methodist and the Baptist — had emerged as the largest Protestant denominations in the United States.

But while the concept of the religious revival has not changed, it appears that the later movements to which the term has been applied no longer fit the accepted description. Major revivals recur about once a generation — an interesting fact for which I know no adequate explanation. Minor revivals, affecting a town or small locality, can occur at any time. Indeed, many evangelical churches annually schedule revival weeks, and invite professional evangelists to conduct them. Since the Civil War the preaching of the revivals has lost much of its color. Early evangelists, spouting fire and brimstone, dealt chiefly in raw emotions; later practitioners were less likely to scare the sinner into heaven by scaring the devil out of him. One by-product of the early major revivals was the reaffirmation of the idea of the supernatural within Protestantism, which by the passage of time was being leached out of the churches. During the present revival the dependence of weak man on the transcendent God is once more preached in the churches. But this development is attributable more to the teachings of the theologians than the preachings of the evangelists.

During the past century, American Protestantism has experienced three notable waves of revivalism, the first identified with Dwight Moody after the Civil War, the second with Billy Sunday during the First World War, and the third with Billy Graham today. The fact that these revivals occurred during or after great wars does not imply that they were simply fits of repentance after the shedding of fraternal blood, nor the felt need to call upon God for the peace which man could not preserve. These elements may enter an explanation of the revivals; they are not, in themselves, an adequate answer. It is, howver, more than a coincidence that the revivals of religion occurred in periods when society was in flux, when readjustments in the intellectual, economic, and political orders were in progress, when men, disoriented, sought stability, reassurance, a firm foundation where they might rest. In such circumstances, it is the Protestant tradition to turn to the old-time religion.

A remarkable point is that these latest revivals have thrown up and have been characterized, symbolized, personified, by individual evangelists. Moody, Sunday, Graham are not better preachers, greater masters of mass psychology, more inspired prophets than scores of other professional evangelists whose names are forgotten. Their fortune is that they appeared when they did. And the consequence is that they have been moulded by their auditors into surrogates for God, who embody their listeners' hopes, realize their dreams, abolish their fears.

Have these latest revivals converted appreciable numbers of souls to God? If so, the rolls of the churches would give evidence of the fact, and a large share of the credit should be assigned to the preaching of Moody, Sunday, and Graham. Certainly the campaigns of these evangelists aimed to bring men into the churches. Local ministers and church groups supported them with that chief purpose in mind. The campaign teams carefully counted and released to the press the daily total of "converts." We know that their audiences were enormous. How many millions Moody addressed we can only surmise; without the aid of loud speakers Billy Sunday, it is estimated, was heard by 100,000,000 people; and unquestionably Billy Graham, with the aid of radio and television, has spoken to even more.[3] All three men climaxed their careers with campaigns in the modern Babylon. In 1876 Moody's preaching in New York drew 1,500,000 listeners;[4] in 1917, Sunday's tabernacle held a similar number;[5] the 1957 summer's attendance is a matter of debate, but certainly the figure is close to 2,000,000. (We may note, by the way, that while 56,000 "decisions

---

3. Gamaliel Bradford, *D. L. Moody* (New York, 1927), 16, cites an estimate that 100,000,000 people heard Moody; the same estimate for Sunday is found by William G. McLoughlin, *Billy Sunday Was His Real Name* (Chicago, 1955), 293; the estimate in Stanley High, *Billy Graham* (New York, 1956), 2, is a modest 20,000,000 up to the end of 1955.

4. Jerald C. Brauer, *Protestanism in America* (Philadelphia, 1953), 204.

5. McLoughlin, *op. cit.*, xxviii.

for Christ" were made in Madison Square Garden,[6] 98,000 hit Sunday's sawdust trail.[7])

How many of these tremendous numbers joined the churches? A million converts have been claimed for Moody; an equal number for Sunday; no one yet knows the total for Graham.[8] But the claims for Moody and Sunday are very questionable. These evangelists were called in to conduct campaigns by local churches which hoped that they could achieve what the churches could not — reach the unchurched. We do know that Moody and Sunday largely failed, that they preached salvation to the "saved," that they converted only too many church members. Undoubtedly the local congregations in the towns where these evangelists campaigned reflected their presence in an increase in membership. Only too often this increase was followed by a falling off. We have enough historical perspective to say that the evangelical careers of Moody and Sunday did not materially increase the membership of the Protestant churches. Unquestionably Moody and Sunday did good, as Dr. Graham does good; the saved too need salvation preached to them. Possibly the effects of Billy Graham's preaching will be different from that of his great predecessors. It is too early to judge.

To turn to the evidence of church membership statistics: no one need be reminded how unreliable these figures are, least of all the editor of the best compilation, the annual *Yearbook of American Churches,* which publishes the official estimates or censuses of the various churches. Sometimes the editor must wince, for at times the statistics are a bit on the incredible side. While paging through the *Yearbook* recently I was shocked to discover my profound ignorance of even the name of a major Protestant denomination, one of only fifteen churches with membership of more than a million. My only consolation is that all the writings on the American church that I have seen have been as uninformed as I about this obviously well-known Christ Unity Science Church, Incorporated. Nor was this church content to submit an estimate in round numbers of its mem-

6. *Time,* November 11, 1957, prints the revised and presumably final figures of the New York meeting: an attendance of 2,145,000 and 60,577 "decisions for Christ."

7. McLoughlin, *op. cit.,* 103.

8. For Moody, Bradford, *op. cit.,* 16, Brauer, *op. cit.,* 204; for Sunday, McLoughlin, *op. cit.,* 293; in High, *op. cit.,* 2, the number claimed for Graham is the usual 1,000,000.

bership; obviously it took a careful census, for its figures are complete to the last digit — 1,581,286.[9] Church headquarters are in Texas.

According to the *Yearbook,* the proportion of church members to the total population of the United States has increased steadily for the past several generations — from 18% in 1870 to 36% in 1900 to 57% in 1950 to 62% today.[10] Assuming the approximate accuracy of these estimates, a purist in language might insist that either there has been no revival or the revival has lasted for almost a century. For the word "revival" necessarily implies a preceding period of neglect or decline; and the figures just cited obviously indicate that there was no period of decline. But we will transmit this quibble. Just when the present revival began it would be difficult to determine; certainly it was after 1940. We may then be able to gauge the extent of the revival in some measure by contrasting statistics of church membership in 1940 with the most recent figures. For though the figures are not accurate, they do reflect official opinion within the churches as to growth of membership.

Certainly the statistics seem proof positive of a major revival in religion. In 1940, the churches and synagogues counted 64,500,000 members, 49% of the American people. The latest issue of the *Yearbook* shows that organized religion claims 103,000,000 adherents, 62% of the total population. An increase of almost 40,000,000 in less than two decades is certainly not a negligible growth.

Interesting facts emerge if we try to judge which of the three American religions has reaped the greatest proportionate harvest of souls in these fruitful years. We discover at once that these statistics tell us nothing of the impact of the revival on Judaism. For the number of Jews reported is not a census of synagogue membership, but rather an estimate of all Jews, religious and irreligious, in the United States. From these figures we cannot argue to a revival in Judaism.

The membership of the Catholic Church increased, according to the *Yearbook,* from 21,200,000 in 1940 to 34,500,000 today, — a growth of 13,000,000, a proportionate increase of about 62%. Can we determine how much of this growth was due to natural increase and how much to conversions? The *Official Catholic Directory,* the

9. Benson Y. Landis (ed.), *Yearbook of American Churches 1958* (New York, 1957), 260.
10. These and subsequent figures cited from the *Yearbook* will be found in tables on pages 286-289.

source of the *Yearbook's* Catholic statistics, does provide us with statistics on conversions — statistics, by the way, much more reliable than those on church membership. Since 1940, about 1,750,000 converts have joined the Catholic Church.[11] This is an impressive number — if we ignore the fact that it is only slightly more than 1% of the total American population. In the past year a record 140,000 Americans converted to Catholicism. If, in a year of revival, less than one-tenth of 1% of the people of the United States become Catholics, it can scarcely be said that the revival is a major factor in the growth of the Catholic Church. Certainly we are not being swamped by the inrush of eager multitudes.

Nor does an appeal to the revival seem necessary in order to explain the converts to the Church. Statistics on conversion, first gathered thirty years ago, indicate that there has been a steady growth in the numbers of converts rather than a sudden rush to join the Church. In the latter years of the Twenties, converts averaged about 35,000 a year; in the present decade the yearly average has mounted to about 125,000. This increase can be fairly adequately explained by the lessening of anti-Catholic prejudice and the greater presence and prestige of the Church. Summarily, there is no indication that the present revival of religion has had any important effect on the growth of the membership of the Catholic Church.

Can the statistics of church membership at least be used to demonstrate a revival within Protestantism? At first glance there seems no question of the fact. Protestant church membership, according to the *Yearbook,* has increased from 37,800,000 in 1940 to over 60,000,000 today — a growth of 22,000,000. Proportionately, however, this Protestant growth of 60% is very close to the Catholic increase of 62%. The Catholic growth can be broken down into two categories: an increase of about 54% by natural means, about 8% by conversions. Would similar proportions obtain in the Protestant Church? If so, the number of converts to Protestantism since 1940 would total about 3,000,000. But the situation of the two faiths is scarcely comparable. Many Protestant churches count their membership on a different basis than does the Catholic Church. The standards of admission into most Protestant churches are much lower than the requirements of the Catholic Church. It is highly probable, then, that the number of converts to Protestantism appreciably exceeds 3,000,000. If the num-

11. This is a conservative figure. The numbers reported in the *Directory* in the issues from 1941 through 1957 add up to 1,852,418.

ber greatly exceeds that estimate, the Protestant churches can indeed claim that the revival of religion has appreciably affected their membership. But that claim would also be an admission that the churches are failing to hold the children of their present membership.

Briefly: from the statistics usually given we cannot say that there has been a revival in Judaism; we can say that the revival has not notably affected the growth of the Catholic Church; and on the effect of the revival on Protestant Church membership we can only render the Scottish verdict of "not proven."

In discussing the revival of religion, one inevitably turns to suburbia. Indeed how can you discuss America without discussing suburbia? It took a hundred years after 1820 for 30,000,000 immigrants to enter the United States; in the dozen years since the Second World War a comparable number of Americans have entered suburbia. The old rural-urban dichotomy is outmoded; a third term has already been added. This mass migration out of the cities is reshaping the whole of American society — and not least the religions of America.

Suburbia is hailed as a chief center of the religious revival. Here it is that hundreds of churches and synagogues are constructed annually; here it is that daily new congregations are formed; here it is that the new householder joins a religious group almost as soon as he signs his mortgage.

Organized religion is booming in suburbia. Is this boom due to the revival of religion? Or can it be adequately explained by other factors? It appears to me that there are many factors operative in the suburbs which, apart from the question of a revival, would create an atmosphere favorable to the growth of organized religion.

It is a truism that cities are inimical to the practice of religion. Among the causes adduced to explain the fact are the anonymity of the city dweller, his lack of roots, his lack of traditions. These deterrents are modified, if not removed, in suburbia. Indeed the new suburbanites are consciously putting down roots. And these suburbanites are of that milieu whence the churches and synagogues have long drawn their major strength. They are middle class; most have completed high school; many have attended college; they are parents of young children. To a young couple the birth of a first child can be a somewhat shattering experience. The birth or, later, the education of the child may influence the parents to turn to the church or the synagogue. Completely apart from a revival, one would expect these young couples to join a local church or synagogue. That religion is popular, that their peer group are largely church members, may influence a young couple to join a church; but these factors are certainly not the only, or even the major elements in their decision.

Certainly these factors have little or no influence on young Catholic couples. The Catholic Church has grown tremendously in suburbia — probably the most important development within the Church in the present generation. The revival of religion has had nothing to do with this growth. It is simply that millions of practicing Catholics have moved from the cities to the suburbs. A few dormant Catholics may have, in their new homes, resumed the practice of their religion; a few converts may have joined the suburban parish. But the burgeoning strength of Catholicism in suburbia is due solely to the fact that Catholics have moved from one place to another.

The situation in Judaism, however, is markedly different. During the twenties and thirties practically a whole generation of Jews abandoned the practice of religion.[12] Now these people and their children are, in impressive numbers, joining the suburban synagogues. Judaism in suburbia is experiencing a revival. But a good many Jews are asking whether this revival can be called religious. Recently the Synagogue Council of America discussed allegations that the revival of Judaism is more sociological than religious, that the Jews in suburbia were turning to the synagogue more for identification in the community than for the worship of Yahweh.[13] And the Rabbinical Council of America heard a report that a very large segment of Jews — up to 90% — are joining the synagogues for social and secular reasons rather than from genuine religious motivation.[14] If these allegations are true — and certainly they are soberly considered in Jewish circles — then the revival in Judaism is one of synagogue membership, not a revival of religion.

Can the religious revival among suburban Christians be explained, as the revival in Judaism, by the urge to conform, the need to be identified with a group, the desire to achieve status? This question has not, as far as my knowledge goes, been adequately explored. It would not apply to suburban Catholics, who were already practicing their religion when they arrived in suburbia. Whether it would apply to

12. This is most bluntly stated in Nathan Glazer, *American Judaism* (Chicago, 1957), 85.
13. *New York Times,* March 26, 1957.
14. *New York Times,* June 28, 1957.

suburban Protestants I do not know. If it does, then we are moving in an area of paradox — a revival of religion which does not affect organized religion; a growth of organized religion which is not religious; finally a revival of religion which is not a revival and scarcely religious.

The flight to suburbia has had consequences for the cities. The urban areas are no longer the strongholds they once were of Judaism and Catholicism. The rush to the suburbs has not left the cities empty. Vacant spaces are soon filled; in the exceptional case of New York, mostly by Puerto Ricans; in most cities, chiefly by migrants from the rural South. This inrush of newcomers is sounding the knell of the Little Italies, the Jewish ghettoes. With the old dying off, the young moving out, and strangers moving in, the old national enclaves are in process of dissolution. It is already obvious that many national parishes of the Catholic Church are in their last years of usefulness. Within a generation it will be the rare rabbi who will address his congregation in Yiddish, the exceptional priest who will preach in a foreign tongue.

The interesting point is that urban neighborhoods once heavily Catholic or heavily Jewish are now populated by people of Protestant background. Is it possible that Protestantism has a second chance in the cities? that it can regain the dominant position it once held in the urban areas? Several generations ago, the Protestant churches, faced by the challenge of non-Protestant immigrants swarming into the cities, answered that challenge by evading it, by abandoning the slums, by moving uptown with their constituency. The consequences were that Protestantism lost the great cities, that Judaism and Catholicism emerged from the slums to become accepted American faiths.

The presence in the cities of these newcomers from the South presents a challenge — not to Judaism, which is not a missionary religion — but to the Christian churches. This time the churches will not answer the problem by walking away from it; but thus far they have not fully faced up to it. Neither Christian church is making a major effort to recruit and organize the new urbanites. Each church, it is true, has its special problem. The migrants come from a culture colored by Protestantism and they have not escaped a deep-seated anti-Catholicism. That this difficulty is not insurmountable is indicated by the experience of the Catholic churches in Harlem. Deserted by white Catholics, for years practically empty on Sunday, they were kept open and are again filled, this time by Negro converts. In the same area the East Harlem Protestant parish has had a notable measure of success. Whether this is an indication that Protestantism will solve its peculiar problem remains to be seen. To the present day the major churches, identified with the middle and upper classes, have not been able to recruit a large following among the lower classes. If the great denominations do not shatter this caste barrier, Protestantism will lose its opportunity to re-emerge as a dominant religious element in the great urban centers.

Protestantism will, of course, share the cities with the other two great faiths. For generations Judaism and Catholicism in America have been identified as urban and as foreign. But suburbia now bears witness that they are decreasingly urban and no longer foreign. The grandchildren of the immigrants are in suburbia in their hundreds of thousands, in their millions. If the chief cause of religious bigotry is lack of knowledge of one another, the suburbs, mixing together Protestant, Catholic, and Jew, should do much to eliminate it. Judaism and Catholicism are and will largely remain urban. But is it possible that we are witnessing in these faiths a shift to the suburbs, if not of numerical strength, at least of leadership?

Certainly this seems true of the Catholic Church. For the suburbs present the Church with its major problems and its major hope. The problems are to put roofs over the multiplying congregations, priests before the altars, teachers at the blackboards, desks before the pupils.

But the problems are worth facing and solving. For the suburban parishes are filled with young people, ambitious, flexible, intelligent, educated — the best products of our nation, wholly American. And wholly Catholic; these young couples do not have greater faith than their parents, but they do have a greater knowledge of their faith. For them a theology of the laity is developing, a literature on the lay apostolate, an investigation of lay spirituality. They are taking into their own hands, and quite properly, more of the work of the Church. They are developing new and remodelling old organizations of the laity. They manifest a religious vitality, an enduring zeal, a profound faith that augurs better for the Catholic Church in America than any temporary revival of religion.

SECTION II

Catholicism in America

R. L. Bruckberger, o.p.*

IV. The American Catholics
as a Minority

My title defines perfectly the limits which I shall observe and the general outline which I shall follow.

As a matter of fact there are two meanings of the word "minority." The first meaning which comes to mind, a material one, designates *a small number* within a given group, by comparison with and in opposition to a larger number.

The second meaning is primarily a legal meaning, but takes us far beyond the legal domain. According to this second meaning, "minority" designates a restriction in the use of one's powers or of one's rights, as opposed to "majority," which implies a full use of one's powers and of one's rights. A sovereign is said to be a "minor" when he is still subject to a regent, and does not yet exercise his power of sovereignty. It is likewise said of a child that he is a minor when the law limits his power of voting, of entering into a contract, and even of disposing of his property. Minority is, therefore, a limitation of one's rights, of one's power or of one's responsibility. Minority can further be used in opposition to "maturity." The application of this last meaning to the situation of the Catholics in America can enlighten us a great deal.

It is a fact that the American Catholics are a minority in their country, that they represent the smaller number as compared to a larger number of non-Catholics. It would seem that this fact, evident

*Rev. Raymond Bruckberger, O.P., of the Dominican House of Studies in River Forest, Ill. Born in Muret, France in 1907, during the war he was Chaplain General of the Resistance. He is editor of *Le Cheval de Troie* and author of: *The Seven Miracles of Gubbio and the Eighth,* (1948); *The Golden Goat* (1952); *One Sky to Share* (1952); *Mary Magdalene* (1953).

in itself, does not call for much comment, and yet, I believe it must be analyzed a little more closely.

First of all, this "small number" is quite a considerable number: officially 33 or 35 millions in a nation with a population of 170 millions. There is reason to believe that this number is somewhat below the real figure. A recent survey showed that 29 per cent of the children born in this country are baptized in the Catholic Church. If this percentage is applied to adults, we find that the number of Catholics should be between 45 and 50 millions. You will object that all the children baptized as Catholics do not persevere, but on the other hand neither do we count in all the adults who are converted. It seems to me that when one belongs to a social group which numbers from 45 to 50 million members, one should not have the feeling of being all alone and lost. After all, France, which is considered a Catholic nation, does not have any more Catholics than the United States. Spain has less. Italy has less. Ireland has less. And these are facts.

What is the origin of this Catholic minority? At the time when America gained her independence, the Catholics were a paltry minority. Fifty years later they were already more numerous, but still quite a small minority. The principal cause of the present number of Catholics in this country was the mass immigration during the nineteenth century. Since then immigration has ceased to be an appreciable source of any increase in numbers. The American Catholics now have at their disposal two important means of increasing their number: births and conversions. It is noteworthy that they count much more on births than on conversions. It is certainly easier to produce a child than to convert a nation.

The significance of a minority status is determined also by the nature of the majority which is opposed to it. It is not enough to say that the majority in the United States is not Catholic; we must also know what it is. For example: in Algeria, the people of European origin, for the most part Catholics, are faced with a Moslem majority. This majority not only is not even Christian, it is radically hostile to Christianity, practically beyond the reach of conversion, impenetrable beings indeed. This Moslem majority is a solid, compact, religiously homogeneous bloc, with which the Catholics have really very little in common. The French government today understands that, in order to maintain a certain equilibrium between these two groups and to protect the rights of the minority, the number of this minority must be increased by births and immigration. Undoubtedly there is no other way, but still this is, in a certain measure, an admission of weakness. The ideal solution would be to merge gradually the two communities, the European and the Moslem.

In the United States, the situation is totally different. The majority does not constitute a single religious group, compact, homogeneous, and impenetrable. The majority is not anti-Christian, but quite the contrary. All the elements of this majority have many things in common with the Catholics; they do not form a single bloc opposed to Catholicism. They are not beyond the reach of conversion. There is a multitude of churches and their opposition to Catholicism is infinitely less than that of the Moslem world. In fact, most often, the non-Catholic Americans have from a religious point of view no strict orthodoxy; they hardly know what to think, and are often very curious to know what we think.

My opinion is that this situation is exceptionally favorable to Catholics. However, it happens that American Catholics do not seem to understand how favorable it is for them and they react to the non-Catholic majority of their country as if it were hostile, homogeneous, and beyond conversion. To increase their number, now that the flow of immigration has just about dried up, they hardly count on anything but births, just like the European minority in relation to the Moslems in Algeria. They are playing a losing game from the start, and usually they do not even seem to entertain the idea that they might possibly convert the nation as a whole. This, too, is an admission of weakness. In this respect they remain a minority and seem to be determined to remain so.

Is there a religious majority in the United States? The *Catholic Digest* has published some interesting surveys on this point. It is obvious that the vast majority of Americans, almost all of them, believe in God and in the principal mysteries of Christianity, including the divinity of Christ. In this respect they are not at all different from Catholics. Outside of that, the strictly religious convictions of the non-Catholics are as vague, inconsistent and different as they can be. Besides, there is not a single Protestant sect with as many members as the Catholic Church. The Catholics form numerically the largest religious group in the United States and even if they do form an absolute minority, relatively speaking they are in the majority. That, too, is a fact and a very important one.

Their strength is not only in their numbers. They have a precise and well-knit doctrine, a discipline and a centralized hierarchy, a tradition of theology and of Christian philosophy; they know what to think and in matters of action they know better than the others what is good and what is bad — or at least they should know. Personally, I think that in America at the present moment Catholics enjoy the advantages of a minority without its disadvantages. They still do not have the disadvantages of a majority, but they do have its advantages. I shall explain what I mean.

I am a Frenchman. I come from a country where, for centuries, the Catholics have been and still are in the majority. For a long time this majority profited enormously from the situation. Up to the French Revolution, the Catholic Church in France was loaded with privileges. It was the richest body in the nation. It was the only teaching body of the nation. It was politically associated with the State and was the only religion recognized by it. All this was justified historically by the services formerly rendered the nation by the Church. The day came when people forgot the services and saw only the privileges, which appeared exorbitant. The French Revolution did as much against the Catholic Church as against the Monarchy.

Since the Revolution, the situation of the Catholics in France has completely changed. They are still the majority in the nation. But the Catholic Church is looked upon with suspicion by the poor, because formerly it was rich. It is an object of suspicion to the University, because formerly it held a monopoly in teaching. It is also an object of suspicion to the State, because formerly it more or less controlled the State. The French Catholics have all the disadvantages of a majority without its advantages. If it so happens that a French Catholic has an important position in the University or in the Government, he is always afraid of being suspected of partiality and so in order to wipe out this suspicion, will do less for the Church than a freethinker would. Although a majority in their own land, the French Catholics have reached the point where most of them are afraid to admit that they are Catholics. As soon as they do admit it, people fear them and hate them. Therefore, they do not have the advantages of the majority that they really are. Neither do they have the advantages of being a minority. Their position in the history of the nation has been so large, their former privileges so great, that people even now are unwilling to grant them the common rights of man. Historically speaking there is no more unfavorable position to be in than to have been a privileged class and to have been stripped of one's privileges. Knowing full well what would happen, I would beg American Cath-

olics never to desire any privileges. Even if they should one day become the majority in their land, which I hope with all my heart, I
would beg of them always to be satisfied with that which is the right
of all and never to use their number and their strength to obtain from
the national community advantages which the other citizens do not
have.

There are many reasons for a minority wishing someday to be a
majority. Of all these reasons, the most sordid, the less legitimate on
the religious level is the desire for political power. In a democracy
the majority has the power. It is possible that many American Catholics wish political power. I am warning them. For centuries in France,
the Catholic Church has had political power. The present miserable
situation of the Catholic Church in France comes in a great part from
this fact.

Candidly speaking, I consider it very childish for American Catholics to complain of never having had a Catholic President. They are
fortunate. A President, even if he is Catholic, is only a man. He is
exposed to many errors and arouses many hostilities. If he were Catholic, people would not fail to say that all his errors come from the
fact that he is a Catholic. What a great blessing it is that American
Catholics have never had to exercise political power. After all they
cannot be reproached with having signed the Yalta Pact or having
dropped the atomic bomb on open cities. Likewise, it might be interesting for the White House to have an ambassador at the Vatican.
But how can that be of interest to American Catholics, who from another source are perfectly united to the Pope through the hierarchy?

I hope that American Catholics will always keep the art of enjoying the privileges of a political minority. I still wish it if they become
the actual majority — especially if they do.

The word "minority" has a second meaning. Being a minor has
a legal side to it, that is when the law prevents someone from exercising his rights. Such is the case of children. Such is now the case for
French Catholics, as Catholics. In France a priest, just because he is
a priest, cannot even take the examination which would make it possible for him to teach in the French universities. This is monstrous,
but that is the way it is.

From a legal point of view, the Church in America is in a position
infinitely better than in France. It enjoys full freedom. At any rate

it is in a much better position than some other American minorities, such as the Negroes or the Indians.

But the second meaning of the word "minority" implies more than a legal status. From the psychological and sociological point of view it can be considered as the designation of a system of complexes: inferiority or superiority complexes, persecution or terrorism complexes, etc. . . .

Observing the French Catholics, I find in them an inferiority complex and a debility complex, both of which come from old age. They are shot through with the feeling that they are not equal to the situation, that they run aground, that they can do nothing. That creates a kind of fatalism or else a childish credulity: by gaining some time, everything will work out. But nothing ever works itself out just by the passing of time. But even now French Catholics are sometimes afraid of their present isolation in a nation which, in ages past, they not only dominated but even created. And so in order to feel at home in their own country, they make concessions and try to get themselves accepted at any price.

On the intellectual level, the situation of the Catholics is still in a certain sense easier in France than it is in America. Not a single one of the great men of the United States was a Catholic. The great men of France in the past have been Catholic. Even today writers such as Claudel and Bernanos have enhanced French literature, and everyone found that rather normal. Chateaubriand was Catholic; Pascal was Catholic; Guillaume de Machault was Catholic; Villon was Catholic — without mentioning Jeanne d'Arc and Saint Louis. And all Frenchmen have come to consider these persons as some of their greatest. American Catholics feel very keenly this impossibility of counting any of their great national heroes among their own.

There is a very bad way of being a minority, and that is to let yourself be influenced by the majority and thus leaving yourself wide open to its harmful infiltration. In this way a minority loses its identity up to a certain point, by adopting the ideas, the tastes, and the social judgments of those around them. The upshot of the whole affair would be that the American Catholic would find all his tastes, his reactions and his ideas on moral issues colored by the people around him and thus he would be more like an American Baptist or Presbyterian than, let us say, a Mexican or Italian Catholic. Such a situation would be extremely serious, for it would compromise the catholic,

that is the universal character of the Church. I wonder if this danger
does not exist among American Catholics when it comes to Puritanism.

What is Puritanism? A French Jacobin, Saint-Just gave the most
perfect definition of it that I know: "Either virtue or a reign of terror." This was also the attitude of Josue in the Old Testament: the
ideal being less to convert sinners than to exterminate them. Sin must
be repressed by all possible means of force and of civil and social legislation. One must force people to be virtuous. Virtue and sin are
identified with human law.

Now Puritanism is something which decidedly is not Catholic.
Jews can be Puritans: the entire Old Testament is dominated by a
fierce conception of legal purity. Protestants can be Puritans: Luther
and Calvin were, to be sure. Nothing is more fundamentally opposed
to Catholicism than Puritanism. But the Puritan influence is very
deep in America. Many non-Catholics suffer from it and would like
to free themselves from it. Now, you would think that they should
be able to count on the Catholics in this endeavor. But such is not the
case and one often has the impression that American Catholics are
more Puritan than anybody else and that they are very close to setting themselves up as the champions of Puritanism. In short, many
non-Catholics in America fear that some day or other American Catholics will adopt Saint-Just's program: "Either virtue or a reign of
terror."

Nothing in the world is more opposed to Puritanism than Catholicism. In my opinion, Protestantism is characterized by a concern for
purging Christianity of everything which does not belong to it. In its
contact with pagan civilizations, Catholicism has always taken care
to respect in each of them everything which was not incompatible with
Christianity. It seems quite obvious to me that Catholics have a better idea of Christian civilization than Protestants do, an idea that is
broader and more diversified and consequently in the final analysis
more liberal. If after visiting the United States you go to Mexico, you
cannot help being struck by the way Catholics have respected the customs and traditions of the Indians. It is easy to say that these people
are more pagan than Christian. As far as I am concerned, I believe
that they are through and through Catholic Christians.

Montesquieu, who visited Rome several times, wrote his impressions of it. After a thousand years of papal government, it would indeed be difficult to maintain that Rome was not a Catholic city at
the time of Montesquieu. And Montesquieu was an impartial observer,

whose testimony it would be hard to reject. Here then is what he wrote about Rome in the 18th century: "When I see Rome, I am always surprised that Christian priests have succeeded in creating the most delightful city in the world. . . . As for the government," he adds, "it is as mild as it can be." The liberalism of old Catholic societies has many disadvantages. In Rome it surprised Montesquieu; it scandalizes others. It puts up with many reprehensible things, which, moreover, it does not seek to justify. To put up with many things of which one does not approve is sometimes the greatest charity — and that is what the Puritans do not understand, because they do not understand love. This tolerance does not stand in the way of saintliness. Even in Montesquieu's time, Rome had more saints than the whole of Puritan America. But the point is that saintliness cannot be imposed and if Rome has had so many saints, it is because she has never made saintliness a matter of law. Law never makes saints; only God's love can do that.

It is, in my opinion, an extremely serious matter that American Catholics allow themselves to be won over so easily by Puritanism instead of combatting it. They are the only ones who, by their doctrinal and moral tradition, can effectively combat Puritanism and perhaps rid America of it. But they have to begin by not letting themselves be contaminated by it. The whole world, with the possible exception of South America, is now dominated by Puritanism and this is a terrible danger. Even Communism is essentially Puritan: it does not even have the same concept of virtue as we do, but it has an idea of virtue peculiar to itself, and intends to impose it by a reign of terror. Another instance of the same thing was the enthusiasm whipped up by McCarthy among certain American Catholics: "Either virtue or a reign of terror."

The important point is that America stands in an ever-increasing need of Catholics and Catholicism. Not only to combat Communism, but even to understand itself and, eventually, to correct itself. What greater evil is there in this country, for example, than the segregation of the races, a thing which is basically Puritan? And what about that other form of segregation, a more general and a more profound one, the segregation between men and women, a thing which is so striking in America.

The Catholics in America are few in number but they ought to be grown up enough to face all the problems of their own country and besides they are expected to have enough wisdom and love to help solve these problems. The traditional teachings of the universal Church and the no less universal experience of the Church give them a big advantage over everybody else, an advantage of superior wisdom, which they are expected to place at the service of their country. But they have to be saturated with it themselves to begin with.

I would have them remember one thing in particular more than anything else and that is: the only thing to do to win forgiveness for being right is to go and perform as many services as possible. Being a minority, they have only one possible course of action open to them — excellence in every department.

RT. REV. MSGR. EDWARD E. SWANSTROM*

V. The Newer Catholic Immigration

One of the factors which goes a long way to explain significant aspects of Catholicism in America is that the Church as a whole is a product of the newer immigration — at least compared with the predominantly Protestant and Puritan strain which informed our early American culture. There were, of course, Catholic settlements in Maryland, Florida, Texas, Arizona and California from very early days, but these groups did not seem to enter the main stream of American civilization as it exists of itself and as the world views it.

I have been asked to discuss the newer Catholic immigration, and I therefore assume that I am to deal with the migration movement that has occurred since World War II. It is precisely this newest Catholic migration movement with which I have been associated since the formation, in 1943, of Catholic Relief Services - N.C.W.C. as the agency of American Catholics for relief abroad and for the resettlement of foreign refugees.

First of all, a word on the dimensions of the newer Catholic immigration is in order. During the past twenty-five years, roughly, the period since World War II, I would estimate that about 2,000,000 immigrants have arrived in the United States under the regular quotas or through special legislation. Our annual quota is 165,000 but since it is heavily weighted in favor of Northwest Europeans, only about 90,000 visas are used each year. The various emergency laws allowed about 700,000 more to come in. I would estimate that about 45 per

*Msgr. Edward E. Swanstrom has a diploma from the New York School of Social Work, 1933, and Doctorate of Philosophy from Fordham University, 1938. He was the Assistant Director of the Catholic Relief Services of the N.C.W.C. from 1943 to 1947 and has been the Director since 1947. He is the author of *Waterfront Labor Problems* (1938), and *Pilgrims of the Night* (1950).

cent of all who came in were Catholic — in other words, close to a
million. Since World War II, our agency has been instrumental in
helping to resettle in the United States more than two hundred and
ten thousand Catholics belonging to more than a score of nationalities.
In the years immediately preceding our entry into this field — in fact
through most of the thirties — the Catholic Committee for Refugees
had been lending immigration assistance to the victims of Nazism. Our
emphasis was on Catholics because there were religious agencies of
other persuasions working in the field, such as the W.C.C., the Lutherans, and HIAS. It has been found that the dispossessed refugee himself preferred to be aided by the agency of his own faith. Do I need
to mention that our relief programs in forty countries have always been
carried out on the basis of need alone without reference to race, creed
or other factors?

The people we have assisted have been resettled in every state of
the Union. The groups comprised in this total give us a rather vivid
picture of the waves of refugees that surged over Western Europe during and in the wake of World War II. There were, first, the groups
from the D.P. camps representing the various national strains of Eastern Europe, Poles, Ukrainians, Czechs, Slovaks, Hungarians, Rumani-
ans, Croats, Slovenes and of course the refugees from the three Baltic
nations rather more northward.

Following the D.P.'s came the ethnic German expellees whose
homes had been expropriated. These were the Volksdeutsch enclaves
from Eastern Europe and the Reichsdeutsch who were expelled from
areas incorporated into Poland. Refugees of Italian origin from Vene-
zia Giulia were admitted to the United States along with a certain
number of regular immigrants from Italy. As the Iron Curtain became
a clearer demarcation line between East and West more and more
escapees took the risk of fleeing from what was the dark side over to
the bright side. These escapees included Poles, Yugoslavs, Czechs and,
of course, the Germans who have been fleeing from the Soviet Zone
of Germany by way of Berlin at the rate of about a quarter of a million every year. Perhaps the swiftest movement of people across the
Iron Curtain was that of one hundred seventy-five thousand Hungarians, who in a few months' time inundated Austria and were then given
haven elsewhere in the free world.

A part of each of these waves has been brought to America through
Catholic Relief Services - N.C.W.C. It is as though every wave of
refugees in Europe breaks on our shores, and this is as it should be.

At intervals, since December 22, 1945, the laws affecting the admission of immigrants to the United States have been modified to conform in some small degree with the changing need. The strength of each wave of refugees, as it broke on the shores of America since 1945, naturally corresponds with the provisions of the law as then in force. In passing, I might mention that the four laws under which the two hundred ten thousand Catholic immigrants have entered the United States were: the Presidential Directive of December 22, 1945, allowing for the entry of a special group of refugees and orphans; the D.P. Act of 1948 which opened the doors to certain numbers of displaced persons with the proviso that the quotas of the country of origin would be mortgaged; the Refugee Relief Act of 1953; and finally, the Presidential Proclamation allowing for the entry of Hungarian refugees on what has been termed a "parole basis." In all, these four pieces of legislation enabled about 700,000 to come to the United States. It is estimated that about 50 per cent were Catholics. The 200,000 or so we helped, therefore, represented a pretty good cross section of them.

Though I may be too close to the "topic," and though it may indicate some temerity on my part at this stage of the situation, I should like to advert to certain qualities in the newer Catholic immigration which did not seem to be so strongly present in the older groups. First of all, the earlier Catholic migrants were what we might call "willing pioneers" on the American scene. They had fled famine in the country of origin as did one of my grandfathers, or they had been glad to leave behind some limit on their freedom or initiative, such as the stratification of European society, or long-term impressment into military service. The newer Catholic migration consisted, in larger part, of people who had lived settled existences, and who had achieved status in their communities. When they arrived in America, they were in a sense "unwilling pioneers." They were unwilling, for example, to accept the unskilled jobs which earlier waves of immigrants had accepted without question. Because of their history of slave labor, of persecution and of expulsion which many of them had suffered, they were greatly fearful of being exploited, and sometimes cried exploitation where none existed.

Earlier migrations were not what we would call *"assisted migrations"* in the same sense that the newer Catholic immigration has had to be according to the provisions of American law. While the earlier immigrant "made do" in any environment in which he found himself, the newer immigrant — having been assisted in his passage and having been assured home and job on arrival through sponsorship by an individual American or by an American agency — could afford to be much more critical. When he had special skills, or had been uprooted from a situation in which he had had his own workshop or business, he seemed to expect that he would be aided by some kind of financing or loan to start up in the same field in this country. Though other agencies, notably the American Jewish Joint Distribution Committee, have had splendid experience in this field, Catholic Relief Services - N.C.W.C. was not financially able to assist in this manner.

Given the class structure which has obtained in Europe even to the present day, it was inevitable that immigrants to America during the Open Door Policy should be siphoned off from the peasant and laboring classes who shared least in the economic and cultural riches of the countries concerned. One of the results of this was that the new immigrant showed himself often rather ashamed of his cultural and linguistic differences, and was over-eager to shed them so that he could become at least one hundred per cent American. Some over-compensated by becoming Americans of even more than one hundred per cent — a trait that has shown itself in an excessively protective spirit with relation to everything American. This was brought out by Dr. Herberg in his paper.

The newer Catholic immigration is marked, in a very special way, by a clearer pride of heritage and language. Not only are the post-World War II immigrants anxious to preserve their own language and culture in addition to learning the American language and adapting to American culture, but they make many efforts to acquaint Americans with the riches of their background. Many new cultural associations and foundations attest to this fact. Naturally the educational level of the newer immigration is generally higher because, aside from any other factor, educational standards have risen throughout Europe since the great waves of Catholic migration in the nineteenth and twentieth centuries. However, in the newer migration, we can count a large number of professional people, including university professors.

It was a most interesting experiment for Catholic Relief Services - N.C.W.C. to cooperate with the Catholic Commission on International and Cultural Affairs in the preparation of a documented report on the number of professors in the D. P. camps in Europe up to 1949. To this end, we commissioned the late Father Gerald Walsh, S.J., and the Reverend Edward Rooney, S.J., to visit the camps and list the data on the Catholic D.P.'s of professional caliber. As professors could be admitted as non-quota immigrants if posts were available to them in American universities, many were brought into Catholic and non-

Catholic colleges over a period of five years. Some of these have made very real contributions to American Catholic intellectual life, and I can point to several books written in English by gifted men placed through our agency. As we all know, the great Catholic migration movements of earlier years boasted an infinitesimal percentage of people of professorial caliber — unless we include in this category the grass roots teacher who was known in one country of emigration as the "hedge-schoolmaster."

For many reasons the laity has played a more limited and perhaps subservient role in the life of the Church in America than has the laity in certain countries of Western Europe. The newer immigration has brought into the Catholic Church of the United States some lay Catholics who have a more questioning and venturesome spirit in the development of theology and related matters. Another aspect of the newer immigration that has had some impact in our communities is that many people who list themselves as members of the Church are not as religiously observant as the members of the community who arrived in earlier migration movements. This has shown itself to be true with regard to the intelligentsia, and with regard to those who suffered a certain demoralization either by living under anti-Catholic regimes or by existing over long periods in a camp atmosphere. The tolerant attitude of the European male toward church-going is often a shock to our parishioners here. In general, I would say that the American example in this regard has been a very salutary one.

I would like to point out a specific result of the newer Catholic immigration which has occurred to us who are very close to the whole resettlement activity. In order to find homes and jobs for the various waves of refugees whom I mentioned earlier, it was necessary to set up an organizational pattern within the United States. Eventually one hundred twenty-seven priests were named as resettlement directors throughout the dioceses of the United States. These priests were already engaged in other tasks, including functions in the Catholic social welfare agencies of the various dioceses.

In addition to their regular duties, these priests — often known as the D.D.'s — Diocesan Directors of Resettlement, had to marshall the facts to interpret to our Catholic people the need for offering homes and job opportunities to the new arrivals. When the refugees had arrived, the priests had to work with the local organizations on the difficult process of integration and assimilation. The total effect of this nation-wide Catholic effort on behalf of the refugees and in the matter of collecting funds for the program of Catholic Relief Services -

N.C.W.C. generally, has been a corporate act of charity on the part of the American Catholic Church that is without parallel in its history.

Never before, I believe, was the motley crowd that we American Catholics are, welded into such unity. This unity, I believe, could only be approached (I will not say achieved) on the basis of charity. In the furtherance of a total program for the post-war Catholic migration, a National Catholic Resettlement Council was formed. It brought together groupings of Catholics along ethnic lines including Polish Immigration Committee, American Relief for Poland, American Committee for Italian Migration, Ukrainian Catholic Committee, United Lithuanian Relief Fund, National Alliance of Czech Catholics, Slovak Catholic Federation, Croatian Refugee Committee, various organizations of ethnic Germans and several other groupings of Catholics who had bonds with refugee and emigrating groups in Europe.

It was amazing to see how the nationalisms which had often rent these groups in their home countries faded away after a series of meetings in which the common problem and the common misery were discussed. Italian spokesmen would recommend that Italian problems be put aside temporarily so that Polish refugees who had suffered so long and so dreadfully could be given first attention. Farmers of German stock in our Middle Western states offered places to refugee Poles with farm experience after the various ethnic committees had made the problem known. In the next wave of refugees, farmers of Polish origin accepted German expellees to work with them.

As long as the problem was presented in human terms and with supernatural motives, American Catholics rose in a marvelous way to the challenge offered to them by history. Naturally the legitimate nationalistic aims of the new waves of refugees have not been blotted out by the fact that they have come to the United States. The earlier Catholic immigrants brought over their irredentisms and planted them firmly on our shores. I do not need to mention the struggle that was waged from here against the occupation, and later against the partition, of Ireland. The newer groups have brought their irredentisms and will fulfill a purpose in explaining these continuing problems, and in keeping alive the moral questions involved in the occupation of Poland, for example, or the partition of Germany.

The newer Catholic migration served to light up some aspects of Catholicism in America. One aspect that surprised us all was that it was the American Catholics of the second or third generation in this country, Catholics without any special ties with the refugees, who came forward with the greatest number of offers of homes and job opportunities. The ones who came forward were generally not well-to-do people who wanted gardeners or maids, but ordinary people who would offer a floor of their two-story home as a temporary shelter for some displaced family. Such Americans would go to great lengths to find jobs in factories and workshops for the displaced men. It is probable that this charitable effort could be traced in part to a greater sense of security on the part of those who had been here the longest. The groups who had the strongest ties with Eastern Europe were often loathe to do more than plead the cause of their fellow ethnics. It is possible that they felt too insecure to play the host in receiving the newer refugees. There was also, of course, the question of different cultural levels in the same ethnic group.

Another aspect of Catholic life that has been brought into clarity by the newer Catholic immigration is the importance of the great system of parish schools as a bridge in integrating whole families into the American way of life. Families who were disaffected at first by the type of job offered the breadwinners, and by the type of shelter that they had to accept, became more integrated happier members of the community when their children attended the well-run parochial school where religious Sisters paid special attention to the language needs of the newcomers. We ourselves began to realize that we had built better than we knew when we saw the effect of the Catholic grammar school as the focal point of community integration, not only with regard to the refugees but with regard also to the ever-mobile American families who move in and out of parishes.

The resettlement in new communities of these refugees from war, slave labor, mass expulsion, redrawing of boundaries, has brought to our American Catholic communities new concepts of international life and the international responsibility of the individual Catholic. Refugees are asked to speak at parish communion breakfasts, at meetings of parish groups of women, at the meetings on various levels of the affiliates of the National Council of Catholic Women. Experiences of deportation into Siberia, of mass expulsions of slave labor, are recounted for our ordinary, settled parishioners far removed from the often precarious life of their ancestors. The many new arrivals who mourn lost causes enlarge the horizons of the Catholics of our country. Their tales raise many questions regarding morality in the international sphere, regarding the reasons for which World War II was originally fought, regarding the validity of peace treaties which flout norms of justice.

The newer Catholic immigration has served to open up to American Catholics the whole field of past, present and future immigration policy. The reasons for the restrictive policy along national origins lines is being analyzed. It was this policy which discriminated against people of Southern and Eastern European origin while it allowed easier entry for those of Northern and Western European origin. The necessity to make future immigration legislation a more flexible and more charitable instrument of American policy has been rather widely discussed.

The challenge brought to us of the Church in America by the newer Catholic immigration is certainly not over. This challenge is basically one of morality and charity. In seeking a solution for such problems, it is not sufficient to appeal to our people merely on the basis of enlightened self-interest.

Most of the refugees we have helped bring to this country have known, in some form or other, the terror or the fear of Soviet despotism. The Soviet system, as we know, has placed its reliance on the so-called scientific view of man and of society. The most startling evidence of Soviet achievement in science is, of course, the rocket now [October, 1957] circling the earth as the first man-made satellite. When the Moscow radio reads off Sputnik's timetable indicating the cities over which it passes on its global run, the Soviets are in effect saying, "We believe in science, and what we believe we practice. We have invaded space through the applied knowledge of man." I am sure you were as affected as I was when I read that Moscow added the following to its radio broadcast of the list of cities over which Sputnik would fly: "It will pass over Little Rock at 0636, Moscow Time, on Friday, October 11."

Moscow used this means to highlight its own achievements in the field in which it has put its belief while pointing down to the fact that we in the United States, who state our beliefs throughout the world on the dignity and inviolability of the individual, were in some instances failing spectacularly to implement them. Sputnik, on its global circling, streaks past many encampments of refugees around the world. The newer Catholic immigrants, despite any difficulties in the total resettlement program, serve as a reminder that the Catholic Americans have a continuing responsibility to include many more of the world's dispossessed in their community of charity, and to cooperate with and sometimes lead other Americans in this whole field.

JEROME G. KERWIN*

VI. The Catholic Scholars in the Secular University

Several years ago while I was teaching at Dartmouth College, a non-Catholic colleague of mine asked if he might accompany me to Mass one Sunday. I told him that I should be happy to have him come along. After the Mass was over I awaited the usual questions regarding the meaning of all that went on. I was fully prepared to give him a compressed explanation of the history of the liturgy, the theology of the Mass, and all that my not too extensive knowledge could afford. Came the first question: "I am curious about the money that one offers at the door as one enters — does one give according to his estimate of his sinfulness?" Allowing myself a few minutes to recover from this unique question, I replied that, were that the case, all who attended adjudged themselves equally and amazingly good, for each gave fifteen cents.

I cite this incident as indicative of the lack of knowledge existing among many of the educated on what Catholics do and why they do it. In all charity one must admit that the Mass to most strangers must appear quite incomprehensible. Nor do people working in disciplines far-removed from religion give much thought to the manner in which people worship — even to the worship of their own co-religionists if they have any. This incident it must be remembered took place over thirty years ago when the Church in this country was far removed in every way from the secular colleges. The situation today is somewhat different. There are more Catholic students and faculty members in

*Jerome G. Kerwin is Professor of Political Science at the University of Chicago. He was Chairman of the University of Chicago Institute of Sociology and Religious Studies from 1944 to 1953, and is Chairman of the Walgreen Foundation. He is the author of *Schools and City Government* (1938) and *The Great Tradition* (1947).

57

the American university world, particularly on the secular campuses. It is not possible to indicate with any degree of accuracy the number. Unquestionably a comparison of the figures of today with the figures of thirty years ago would be interesting.

As far as I can determine the number of Catholics on the faculties of the secular universities is increasing, rather slowly to be sure. In my own University the numbers show a higher increase in the Biological Sciences (particularly medicine) than in the other fields. In the Physical Sciences and in the Humanities an increase may be noted. In the Social Sciences the rate of growth is slow but noticeable. I have no reason to doubt that this represents the national picture. In the Social Sciences and the Humanities dealing as they do with the affairs, the thinking, and the history of men, Catholics are still suspect in many quarters. It is unhappily true that frequently scholars in these fields believe that Catholics have all their ideas and opinions formed for them by that mysterious force called the hierarchy. In recent years, however, I have noticed a marked increase in the number of Catholic graduate students who give very impressive performances. I am very hopeful that they will affect greatly much of the adverse thinking about the objectivity of Catholic scholars. It is in no wise fulsome praise to say that Notre Dame has sent us some of the best we have.

In relation to his vocation, in relation to his colleagues, and in relation to his own Catholic community, the Catholic scholar, whether graduate student or member of the faculty, occupies a unique place. I agree with Father Weigel that the Catholic scholar should not look upon himself as a kind of self-appointed missionary to the non-Catholic world. He should center his attention on his field. This, however, is not to say that he should go furtively about avoiding every Catholic occasion and every Catholic contact for fear that he will get himself classified. I have known people of that kind and I have no respect for them. By the self-appointed missionary I mean that type of Catholic who wears ostentatiously the badge of his Faith for all to see, or who goes out of his way to seek dialectical combat in religious controversy. He may say the right thing but at the wrong time, but more frequently the wrong thing at the wrong time. In a true sense a Catholic is always a missionary; that is his vocation. Not so many years ago his functions on the secular campuses were many. A Catholic found few if any Catholic colleagues and any recognition of a special apostolate at the secular colleges and universities was withheld by the Church authorities. In this situation the Catholic had to act as a kind of lay chaplain attending to both spiritual and material needs of the Catholic students and representing the Church as an unofficial ambassador in an overwhelming non-Catholic environment. How many have been the ambassadorial tasks I have been asked to perform in years past! Had I gone to the late Cardinal Mundelein with all the requests and missions given to me by various groups and persons I should have become a permanent lobbyist at the Chancery Office. Ironically enough I never had the privilege of meeting the late Cardinal and the late Cardinal did not like the University of Chicago. This I feel most certain is not the proper role for the Catholic scholar. Fortunately most of the duties of an earlier day do not now fall upon the Catholic teacher at a secular school, especially with regard to the spiritual guidance of students, an activity now taken over by Newman Club chaplains. At the present time, therefore, the Catholic scholar is free to pursue his vocation with the single-minded intention of grasping the truth in his field and broadening the horizons of knowledge.

Yet there is scarcely any field that does not touch at some point upon Catholic dogma, policy, or general Catholic concerns. Is there any field, I may ask, that does not touch upon religion in its broader sense? The physical and biological scientists meet these matters at several points; and, I believe, the humanist and the social scientists meet them at many more. The scholar, of course, knows that he must pursue truth rigorously within the boundaries of his discipline, but there are areas where boundaries overlap. It is both natural and becoming that the Catholic scholar will show a special interest in those areas impinging upon his faith, particularly where contradiction seems to exist. I am even prepared to say that an obligation rests upon the Catholic scholar to resolve these difficulties insofar as he can for his own benefit and for the benefit of society. The social scientist meets problems of this kind with considerable frequency — for the most part matters involving Church policy either past or present. These problems cover a wide field: church and state, race relations, international relations, taxation, education, capital and labor, population, and the customs and traditions of Catholic lands. These questions are so numerous and of such vital interest to any social scientist that the Catholic scholar becomes an information center for his non-Catholic colleagues.

From my own limited experience I can say that no week passes without some questions coming my way from colleagues seeking either information or dialectical battle on some matter of current interest in

which the Church is involved. A few days ago a colleague just back
from Italy (I sometimes wish that Nordic non-believers would stay
away from Latin lands) told me that in the small town in southern
Italy where he did his researches for a year that the local parish priest
charged very high fees for performing marriages for the very poor
peasants but no fee at all for funerals. Why? I assured my disturbed
colleague that this did not mean that the parish priest in question preferred to see his parishioners dead than married. And it is rather interesting how some custom of no great social significance for a project
will remain uppermost in a good researcher's mind such as the fact
that St. Anthony is the patron saint of animals. So it goes. Why may
not widows marry, they ask, or why may not Jesuits smoke — the usual
interpretation of two recent papal pronouncements. And, I might say,
that the controversy over the embattled Father Halton at Princeton
has kept me busy at the lunch hour for weeks. Not infrequently the
Catholic will find that in some discussions with his colleagues if he
disagrees with the statement of some prominent Catholic, wherein disagreement is both justifiable and permissible, he then becomes a fine
"liberal," and if he agrees, he may then fall under suspicion of being
a reactionary, ultra-montane apologist.

Let us look for a moment at the relation of the Catholic scholar
to his non-Catholic colleague more fully. The person attached in any
official way with a secular university will tell you that the university
is a community of scholars dedicated to the pursuit of truth in research
and teaching. As to the general purpose of any university we can all
accept this. When such a person talks about virtue he will say that
the university's concern is with the intellectual virtues and not the
moral virtues. But large numbers of scholars at such institutions will
insist upon the relativity of all truth and frequently in their official
teaching (though not in their daily living) will assume an attitude of
ethical neutrality. I simply state the fact without examining the un-
tenable nature of such a position or the amazing dogmatism that often
accompanies it. At the same time there is most often an admirable
observance of the natural virtues (particularly honesty) and of charity.
Even among the people at these universities who do not accept extreme
relativism, there exists the conviction that everything is open to questioning and examination. In other words *freedom*, many times under-
scored, is the general watchword. The faculties at the secular schools
are most sensitive to any invasions of this broad area of freedom. This
is not to say that there are no limits to this freedom and most scholars

feel the responsibility that goes with that freedom. But it is assumed that the responsibility is self-imposed. No honest person can fail to admire the sturdy defense of an untrammeled and objective search for the truth found in our secular schools. All administrators at our institutions of higher learning know the innumerable pressures brought to bear to curb this freedom, a situation known at all institutions and unfortunately some institutions yield in crucial crises in order not to offend the powerfully rich.

Keeping in mind, however, this strong sense of freedom, one may understand without approving the feeling that the Catholic is circumscribed in his scholarly activities by a multitude of musts and mustnots. Granted that the idea of a Catholic's subjection to authority is greatly exaggerated, the Catholic is regarded as bound by dogma (and the conception of that dogma is exaggerated) by the provisions of the Canon Law, by the Index of Forbidden Books (which creates more suspicion of us than almost anything else), by the directions of the Legion of Decency, and, unfortunately, by every statement of every Pope and every Bishop from the beginning of the Christian era. All of this makes it appear to the non-Catholic scholar as if his Catholic counterpart is confined and restricted at every turn of his life. When there comes forth from the pulpit a swinging condemnation of a current moving picture, I gird myself for the coming onslaught of my colleagues most of whom will forthwith go to view the picture and return to report that there was nothing to it to excite anyone. It is comforting at least to be aided by the experts in art or drama from time to time who will vouch for the fact that the condemned moving picture is bad art or bad drama. After many years of experience one will come to look with some amusement upon a situation wherein he will make a statement regarding a Catholic matter only to have it looked upon as a trick of propaganda while noting that if a non-Catholic colleague makes the same statement it is regarded as unbiased fact. The best evidence of this is the success of Messrs. Adler and Hutchins in the field of Thomistic philosophy among non-Catholic students.

It remains for the Catholic scholar to convince the secular world of scholars that he is capable of objective scholarship and is not just a propagandist — I find this to be particularly true in the field of the social sciences and the humanities. I am optimistic enough to believe that this attitude will change as the number of Catholic scholars increases. There may always remain a temptation, nay, even a necessity, for the Catholic scholar to place himself in the role of defender of the Faith as long as he meets with abysmal ignorance of things Catholic among his non-Catholic colleagues. It is, as we all know, possible for a good scholar to be an expert in his own field, employing the best techniques of scientific accuracy, and at the same time to be a chronic bigot in all questions of religion. Scientific thinking in one line is no guarantee of scientific thinking in all lines. As a Political Scientist I have had many occasions in which to meditate on this after talking politics with a natural scientist. It makes little difference if I am ignorant in the field of astro-physics, but it makes a great deal of difference if a prominent scholar lives in inexcusable darkness in matters affecting the common good. Nor can I feel especially happy about a great scholar's ignorance of the belief of one-third of his fellow citizens. So it may be quite essential from time to time for the Catholic scholar to run the risk of being classified as an unthinking apologist.

The relation of the Catholic scholar to his own co-religionists merits more consideration than I am at present able to devote to it. Here let me say, however, that he goes through periods of contrasting and conflicting emotions from hope to despair, from accomplishment to frustration, and from a sense of belonging to a sense of isolation. My confreres in the secular schools assert, rightly I believe, that daily they occupy a position on the front line of defense of the Church — even if they are never called upon to handle concerns of the Church in their disciplines. They complain that among their brethren there is too little appreciation of this important fact. They resent having their position made more difficult by well-publicized statements in high and low places in the Church — statements that are either unnecessary or have worn rather thin. Here I refer only to statements affecting the universities. Frequent references — often exaggerated — to our communistic, godless, pagan, immoral secular universities, may be made with fervent sincerity, but they create neither respect for the Church nor for its adherents at the secular schools. For over thirty years I have listened to charges of this nature and it is with great regret that I recognize the source of them in an unreasoned opposition to our great centers of scholarship. Most often these statements are made for the purpose of defending our own institutions. We have good colleges and universities and they need no such negative defense. I do not appreciate a person's tearing down a neighbor's house in order to build one of his own. Too much emphasis of this kind misleads some Catholic parents who are looking more for a reform school for their sons and daughters than an educational institution. They look to the Catholic institution of higher learning not only to give their students a firm foundation in the Faith, but also to do that which is not the function of an institution to do, to reform the behavior of inmates rather than to make intelligent and responsible young citizens. The effect on some Catholic students, who elect for some reason or other to go to the secular college or university, is often disastrous when they find that at least in the sphere in which they are working the charges are greatly exaggerated or even untrue.

The Catholic member of a secular school faculty experiences a feeling of disgust and resentment at charges such as I refer to aimed at the secular university and generally this feeling descends to the Catholic members of the student body. I have already acknowledged that there are non-believing members of the faculties at the secular schools, but let us remember that these universities present a cross-section view of American life and that no matter how deplorable it may be that these scholars are godless they are most often competent men in their fields. I may wish that Professor X were a devoutly religious man, but I must bow to his discovery of truth whatever his personal religious convictions may be. I may regret the late Professor Einstein's fuzzy ideas on the nature of God, but I must confess his scholarly contributions to the field of the natural sciences. To the non-Catholic scholar Catholic attacks on the secular universities appear as assaults on the whole field of objective scholarship and on freedom of opinion and research. They affect adversely, if sometimes remotely, the reputation and work of the Catholic scholars.

Catholic scholarship cannot advance very far in many lines isolated from the whole field of American scholarship. In every way possible it is incumbent upon us to promote effective scholarship among all scholars in the manifold fields of research and education, for this obviously means the promotion of the truth. The aim should be a fraternal cooperation of our schools with the schools of the secular world. We must expect to find in the secular schools wide varieties of personal opinion, great divergences from our fundamental beliefs, but God confers abilities and scholarly gifts in mysterious ways, so that even from the mouths of unbelievers we frequently hear the truth. Catholics should not wait for the time when all scholars will have performed their Easter duties before dealing with them or directing others to learn from them. Let us not forget how our forebearers of the twelfth century flocked to the Islamic universities of Toledo and Cordova to absorb the learning that made the accomplishments of the thirteenth century so memorable.

At the meeting of the Federation of Newman Clubs held in New York in September, 1957, the eminent Catholic historian, Professor Carlton J. Hayes, made these remarks regarding Catholics and the secular institutions of higher learning: "But isn't there bigotry and intolerance at our non-Catholic colleges and universities? Isn't there prejudice which militates against the advancement of a Catholic in them? Yes, there is, occasionally and exceptionally. I would emphasize the *occasionally* and the *exceptionally*. The more that the Catholics penetrate into a secular institution, and the better they acquit themselves in it, the less, if any, is the discrimination and prejudice against them. They seldom encounter anything that can properly be described as bigotry; much oftener it is ignorance of, or indifference toward religion and religious values. And this can and will be lessened in measure as the Newman movement expands and carries on its work intelligently, with understanding and, above all, with charity.

"Of one thing, I am quite sure, and it should be stressed. It is that the great majority of professors in the secular universities, regardless of their religious belief or lack of it, possess and cherish an ideal of honesty and sincerity in the scholar's search for truth, whether in laboratory or library, and in exposition of its findings. It is the same ideal which the Catholic scholar should possess and pursue, an ideal whose attainment requires an open-mindedness and charitable attitude toward the work of other scholars.

"May I suggest that bigotry and intolerance are sometimes evidenced on the part of Catholic educators who are blind to the honesty and tolerance of non-Catholic colleges and universities and who see in them only seats of 'godlessness' and of a peculiarly evil 'secularism.' Indirectly, and I fear, ignorantly, such educators would quarantine Catholics not only against great seats of learning, but against learning itself, against a full intellectual life. Their attitude, however innocently or zealously assumed, must bear a considerable responsibility for the prejudices that still exist against Catholics in the United States. It can only serve, I submit, to narrow and limit the mission of the Church. For the restrictions and rigidities of 'ghetto Catholicism' are quite impossible to anyone who aspires to a position of influence in contemporary society and thought."

I am often impressed by the attitude of European Catholics towards the secular schools of this country. They come to the University of

Chicago in fairly large numbers — priests and laymen. I am always interested in learning about their attitude towards my own institution which has so frequently been characterized as the devil's workshop by many of my fellow Catholics. They tell you that they are interested in the work of one of our famed scholars in economics, anthropology, or physics, or some other field and how they are anxious to work with him. Accustomed as these people are to a great variety of points of view at their own universities (for the most part state-controlled) they have come to think of diversity of belief as irrelevant to their own pursuit of knowledge. Not long ago a French priest tried to register as a student under our Theological Faculty because of one man on that faculty who was a specialist in pastoral sociology. To his amazement he had to be informed that this was not done in the Catholic world of America.

I have good reason for believing that a Catholic scholar's prestige among his colleagues is enhanced by the amount of recognition he receives from his co-religionists on the college and university levels. The honor conferred does not go unnoticed. Yet I have seen too many Catholic scholars go unrecognized while too many prospective donors receive the scholarly rewards. Have American Catholic schools fully recognized the productive scholarship of Jacques Maritain? One of my own Catholic colleagues, just retired from the distinguished professorship of pharmacology, has gone unrewarded and unsung after many years of productive labor. I wonder if there are not many more of this kind whom we do not even pause to think about. Maybe this is not a factor of the greatest importance to the good scholar himself who under any circumstances will pursue his work regardless of honorific awards, but the failure to recognize achievement of this nature does not speak well for some of our Catholic schools.

Finally one may note another field in which recognition of the Catholic scholar in the secular university could profitably be noted. In these days when grants from foundations seem abundant, the uninformed may think the necessity for further outlays unnecessary. The number, nevertheless, of worthwhile projects that might well be financed by Catholic donors at both Catholic and secular universities is increasingly great. But the habit and spirit of giving for research have not infected our Catholic people. We fall far behind our Jewish brethren in this respect. A few years ago a colleague of mine was looking for twenty-five thousand dollars to finance a careful translation and study of Maimonides. It was proposed that a meeting of wealthy Jewish businessmen be called together at the Standard Club in Chicago for the purpose of raising the necessary funds. I was invited to speak on the subject of the relation of St. Thomas to Maimonides. But before the meeting was even held the money was raised. I once proposed a modest five thousand dollar project to a couple of Catholic businessmen only to be met by that kind of look that seems to say: "We don't know what you are talking about but if we did we don't think it is worth five thousand dollars." Maybe the fault was in my method of communication or maybe in the project or maybe in both. Generosity along these lines, however, affords a fair measure of a people's intellectual interest. I often wonder if there would be Catholic funds forthcoming for a translation and annotated edition of all the works of St. Thomas? Or would money be readily obtained for a study of how well the faith of Catholic students stands up at the secular colleges and universities? We have too many wild guesses on this question at the present time. My conviction at the moment is, and I should like to be in error on the point, that by and large Catholics do not appreciate the value of research, except, perhaps in what Americans call the practical. In universities the standing and reputation of a member of the faculty depend not only on his ability to do research but on his ability to secure the necessary resources for it.

We Catholics are faced with the necessity of doing a great deal of hard, serious thinking about the whole problem of higher education. The number of Catholic teachers and students is increasing at the secular schools and will continue to increase in the immediate years to come. As self-sacrificing as we may be we cannot maintain the substantial number of institutions which the increasing number of Catholic students requires. Not in the quantity of our institutions will our problems be solved but in the quality. Considering the competition in resources and personnel which face the small private college or university — secular or religious-affiliated — we cannot think of a multiplication of our schools. On the Junior College level, perhaps, but on the higher level of education, no. With the secular institutions absorbing more and more of our Catholic students, what are we to do? Some method of accommodation is essential. Are we to be bold in our approach? Are we to continue to think of our Catholic young manhood and womanhood as too weak to face the type of diversity of thinking, occasionally antagonistic, found at the secular schools? Or must we find better ways than we now have of aiding them to face opposition with intelligence? In addition to the present Newman Club set-up, should we seriously consider the possibility of establishing Catholic colleges or houses of study on the secular campuses? The future of the education of Catholic youth in this country bristles with problems which we must not neglect. A people who against great odds have built up the Church in this country with its vast institutions, its vast services, and its vast spirit of enterprise can they not meet these problems courageously if called upon to do so?

I have traversed a large field and perhaps I have struck too many pessimistic notes. My purpose has been to present the situation of the Catholic scholar in the American secular university. Despite these problems I should have you take counsel of your hopes and not your fears. But I would not have you smug. If we feel that there are too few Catholic scholars in the Catholic school and in the secular school as well, it must be remembered that some Protestants do a great deal of worrying about the absence of the devout practicing Protestant in the scholarly field. In fact there are men of all faiths who deplore the absence of what they call "the religiously affiliated" person among all scholars. Recent attention to this situation, while not within the scope of this paper, merits the serious consideration of the university world. With regard to the Catholic situation it is with satisfaction that one notes the increase of graduate students, of teachers on the staffs of the secular colleges and universities, and a similar increase in communication between Catholic and non-Catholic scholars in the learned societies. While the whole picture leaves much to be desired, there are hopeful signs that the Catholic scholar will in the future have a position of respect in the world of secular scholars. After all, it is not alone the problem of Catholic scholarship in America that should concern us, but the promotion of all scholarship, the discovery of truth in all fields of human interest for the spiritual and material benefit of all mankind.

Some Unsolved Problems

AARON I. ABELL*

VII.   The Catholic Factor in the Social Justice Movement

Viewed as a minority group relatively poor, unprivileged and insecure, Catholics have immensely benefited from the social justice movement of the last seventy-five years — from its attempt to eliminate abject poverty and pauperism and attendant evils, from its crusade against monopoly and irresponsible wealth, from its campaign to humanize and to democratize industry, and, in later years, from its insistence that government guarantee economic security to all citizens. But the Catholic Church was no idle bystander; she was not content to be a passive recipient of its material advantages without making her own contribution to the enrichment of the movement. Besides urging changes in the economic and social order, the Church at all times took care to guard faith and morals against error centering in extreme environmentalist theories of social causation, notably the socialist philosophy.

As the transition to urban industrialism got under way, the reforming elements in American society — Christian, humanitarian and democratic — were quick to see that while wealth rapidly increased, poverty, even pauperism, increased even more rapidly. The resulting industrial conflict — continuous and chronic after 1885 — was the call to action. Believing with Washington Gladden that labor discontent stemmed "from that false political economy which teaches that between employer and employed there are no moral relations,"[1] the

---

*Professor Aaron I. Abell is Professor of History in the University of Notre Dame and author of *The Urban Impact on American Protestantism, 1865-1900.*

1. "A Plain Talk With Employers," *Christian Union,* July 3, 1885; for Gladden's elaboration of this thesis, see his *Applied Christianity* (Boston, 1886); *Tools and the Man: Property and Industry Under the Christian Law* (Boston, 1893), esp. Chapter II, "Economics and Christian Ethics"; and his *Recollections* (New York, 1909), pp. 294-315.

reformers countered with a concept of social justice — the notion that society is a moral organism, the parts of which should co-operate and engage in a mutual sharing of advantages and burdens. Not personal effort or merit but personal needs as related to the common good was the criterion of the new justice.[2] Apart from the agrarian and labor agitations, the crusade for social justice was carried forward by the more progressive clergy and by the products of the new scholarship and the new education — professors, social scientists, and college women. Not content merely to put right what social conditions had put wrong, these architects of the new charity set out to put right the social conditions themselves.[3] As object lessons in democracy and social justice, these reformers had established by World War I well over four hundred social settlements in cities distributed through two-thirds of the states of the Union. "Such simplicity, joined with comfort, is sought in them," wrote Vida D. Scudder of the College Settlements Association, "as would be possible to all men under a normal distribution of wealth."[4] Moreover, "the influence which emanated from these social centres has been the leaven of social reform in our cities," concluded William Jewett Tucker, Dartmouth College President and himself a pioneer in the movement.[5] Enthusiasts for justice in work and wages — the newer charity as it was sometimes called — the urban reformers supported the trade union movement, lobbied with no little success for protective labor legislation and championed the progressive political movement — the New Nationalism of Theodore Roosevelt or the New Freedom of Woodrow Wilson, and later the New Deal of FDR.

In this broad social movement Catholics have been continuously

2. Frank Chapman Sharp, "The Criterion by Distributive Justice," *American Journal of Sociology*, II (September, 1896), 264-73; Harry Allen Overstreet, "The Changing Conception of Property," *International Journal of Ethics*, XXV (January, 1915), 165-78; same author, "Philosophy and the New Justice," *ibid.*, (April, 1915), 277-91. The conception of social justice is explored at length by Westel Woodbary Willoughby, *Social Justice* (New York, 1900), from the viewpoint of T. H. Green and the English School of Idealists, and by Thomas Nixon Carver, *Essays in Social Justice* (Cambridge, Mass., 1915), from a neo-Malthusian angle.

3. William Jewett Tucker, "The Gospel of Wealth," *Andover Review*, XV (June, 1891), 631-45; same author, "The Work of Andover House in Boston," in W. T. Elsing and others, *The Poor in Great Cities* (New York, 1895), pp. 177-94.

4. Quoted in A. I. Abell, *The Urban Impact on American Protestantism, 1865-1900* (Cambridge, Mass., 1943), p. 84.

5. "The Progress of the Social Conscience," *Atlantic Monthly*, CXVI (September, 1915), 291.

involved. Catholic social thought and the general social justice movement have mutually influenced and reinforced each other. In no other
field of endeavor have the relations between Catholics and the American public been happier or more fruitful. On the assumption (it was
hardly a conviction) that the rising labor movement of the late nineteenth century aimed to resist oppression and injustice and was not
inherently socialistic in tendency, American Catholics quite generally
endorsed it. Bristling controversy marked the process of accommodation between the two groups, as over the threat of the Holy See, at
Quebec's insistence, to condemn the Knights of Labor, and the attempt of Father Edward McGlynn and his friends to mobilize Catholics behind land socialization. These controversies called forth a rich
and extensive, often explosive and sometimes revealing social literature.
Thus Cardinal Gibbons' memorial in behalf of the Knights of Labor,
intended only for Roman eyes, was a frank and candid document
which showed that a large majority of the American hierarchy looked
upon the aspirations of the working people with understanding and
sympathy.[6] The ideology of the Americanization drive as worked out
by the lay congresses of 1889 and 1893, included a thorough and comprehensive discussion of the social question.[7] Moreover, endless commentary accompanied the shift in papal emphasis from the benevo-
lence-resignation concept to that of social justice.

In *Rerum Novarum,* Leo XIII defended the institution of private
property, along with inheritance, and did not reject the wage system.
But he insisted that the worker receive a socially necessary reward,
namely wages sufficient to maintain himself and his family in reasonable and frugal comfort. To this end, he urged the further formation
of workmen's associations and a measure of state help — in the words
of Bishop Keane "wisely limited and carefully guarded but evidently
necessary legislative intervention. . . ."[8] In their anxiety to check
"foolish and costly" strikes and to silence the rent confiscators, many
American Catholics, perhaps a majority, called for state intervention

6. Henry J. Browne, *The Catholic Church and the Knights of Labor* (Washington, D. C., 1949); John Tracy Ellis, *The Life of James Cardinal Gibbons,
Archbishop of Baltimore, 1834-1921* (Milwaukee, 1952), I, 486-546.

7. For the Americanist controversy broadly and critically interpreted, see
Thomas T. McAvoy, C.S.C., *The Great Crisis in American Catholic History,
1895-1900* (Chicago, 1957).

8. "The Catholic Church and Economics," *Quarterly Journal of Economics,*
VI (October, 1891), 44; see also his "The Encyclical 'Rerum Novarum',"
American Catholic Quarterly Review, XVI (July, 1891), 595-611, a masterly
analysis.

in industry, not merely for factory legislation and protective labor laws, but also for the settlement of major industrial disputes by judicial or quasi-judicial process. With few exceptions, Catholic publicists urged reformers and statesmen to include legally enforced arbitration in their plans for allaying social discontent and industrial strife during the depression of 1893-1897 and the phenomenal business consolidation which ensued with the return of prosperity. In the discussions regarding the Homestead strike of 1892 and every major industrial disturbance for two decades thereafter, Catholic reformers almost uniformly endorsed compulsory arbitration, however widely they differed on other solutions.[9]

The "Catholic Mugwump," John Brisben Walker, editor of the *Cosmopolitan* magazine and one of the earliest of the "muckrakers," laid down a program which enjoyed wide support. When the Carnegie interests at Homestead employed armed Pinkertons against the Amalgamated Iron and Steel Workers, Walker branded the action an assault on the people's liberties. "For if one man may hire 300 poor devils ready to shoot down their brothers in misery, there is no reason," he thought, "why he may not hire 10,000." The inequality which encouraged arbitrary displays of industrial power, Walker would lessen through high income taxes, public ownership of railways, telegraphs and telephones; heavy taxation of land and other properties held for speculative purposes; and a currency system, self-regulated by means of postal saving banks. "Finally, let it be a recognized principle," he wrote, "that when men employ many laborers their business ceases to be a purely private affair, but concerns the State, and that disputes between proprietor and workmen must be submitted, not to the brute force of many Pinkerton mercenaries, but to arbitration." [10]

Some Catholic advocates of compulsory arbitration wished mainly to suppress lawless labor; others looked to the third party in employer-employee disputes, namely that of "the public and the public interests." Mostly, they expected compulsory arbitration to secure higher wages and better working conditions for the laboring population. Even though compulsion was not adopted, its agitation in social justice circles popularized the living wage principle. One of the militant advocates of compulsory arbitration was the Reverend John A. Ryan, a

9. A. I. Abell, "American Catholic Reaction to Industrial Conflict: The Arbitral Process, 1885-1900," *Catholic Historical Review*, XLI (January, 1956), 385-407.

10. " 'The Homestead' Object Lesson," *Cosmopolitan* XIII (September, 1892), 572.

Minnesota Populist, whose book in 1906, *A Living Wage,* became the
Uncle Tom's Cabin of the minimum wage movement. Ryan believed
that a compulsory arbitration law for all quasi-public industries of a
monopolistic character, along with "indirect methods" such as eight-
hour day and child labor legislation, public housing, old-age pensions
and progressive income and inheritance taxes, would pave the way for
the realization of the living wage idea in all sectors of the economy
in the not-too-distant future.[11]

For a time Catholics feared that reform would be submerged by
the onward sweep of socialism.[12] The slight progress during the new
century's first decade of the reform forces working through the old
parties against entrenched plutocracy discouraged many seekers of social justice, some of whom found an alternative in the newly organized
Socialist party, a compound of radical laborites, middle-class intellectuals, and Marxian revolutionists. With the aid of priests Thomas Mc-
Grady and Thomas J. Hagerty, an unknown number of Catholic laymen, and the Protestant Christian Socialist Fellowship, the Socialist
party of America brought unremitting pressure on Catholic workmen
to affiliate with the Socialist movement, contending that it was neutral on the religious question and promising an improvement of their
material interests — "more of the product of their hands, shorter hours
and better working conditions, *here and now.*"[13] As the movement
penetrated the labor unions and the electorate, few informed Catholics
doubted its irreligious tendency. Bishop James E. Quigley of Buffalo
(later Archbishop of Chicago) voiced their sentiments. Alarmed at the
impact of Socialist propaganda on Catholic trade unionists in his jurisdiction, he branded this "recent importation from Continental Europe" as an agitation marked "by unbelief, hostility to religion and
hatred of the Catholic Church."[14]

Some Catholic leaders, chiefly German-American, were sure that
trade unions were becoming "hot-beds of anarchy and socialism" and

11. John A. Ryan, *Social Doctrine in Action: A Personal History* (New
York, 1941); Patrick W. Gearty, *The Economic Thought of Monsignor John
A. Ryan* (Washington, D. C., 1953).

12. A. I. Abell, "The Reception of Leo XIII's Labor Encyclical in America,
1891-1919," *Review of Politics,* VII (October, 1945), 464-95.

13. Fred D. Warren, *The Catholic Church and Socialism* (Girard, Kansas,
1914), p. 7.

14. "Social Democracy: Bishop Quigley Strongly Condemns It," *Northwestern Chronicle,* March 8, 1902; "For a Catholic Social Movement," *The Review*
(St. Louis), IX (November 11, 1902), 167-169; W. Thurston Brown, "Socialism and the Church," *Wilshire's Magazine,* No. 46 (May 1902), 37-47.

suggested that Catholics withdraw and form separate unions of their own. For a time at least, Sebastian Messmer, the Milwaukee Archbishop, was of this opinion.[15] Archbishop John Ireland, on the other hand, continued to favor the expansion of trade unionism, provided only moral suasion, not violence, was brought to bear on prospective recruits. Beyond this, he saw little need for change in the nation's economy. He feared that the campaign for municipal ownership of public utilities, if successful, must plunge the country into socialism. "Let all be on guard," he warned in 1906. "Common ownership in one direction leads readily to common ownership in another — all the more so," he added, "when the purpose really held in mind is to grasp wealth without much personal effort, to despoil others to make up for one's own deficiencies."[16] A prelate of neo-Puritan sympathies, Ireland thought it sufficed if Catholics practiced thrift, sobriety, and the other economic virtues. Not a few Catholics in the Ireland tradition, though not the Archbishop himself, were wont to declaim against child labor, minimum wage and similar legislation as slavish paternalism only a step short of outright socialism.[17]

On this point, evolutionary Socialists and conservative Catholics were in agreement: that successive pieces of social legislation would lead eventually to socialism. But progressive Catholics contended that social reforms worked to opposite effect, that by weeding out abuses and injustices they strengthened the existing system and undermined the socialist appeal. Mere denunciation availed little; arguing against socialism without presenting a substitute program served to spread, not kill, the infection. In *Rerum Novarum,* as sociologist Father William Kerby of the Catholic University pointed out, Leo XIII had devoted "to the outline of a plan of reform" incomparably more "thought and space" than he had "given to the condemnation of socialism."[18]

15. Thomas McGrady, *The Clerical Capitalist* (New York, 1901); "On the Necessity of Catholic Labor Unions," *The Review,* IX (February 13, 1902), 81-83; "Catholic Labor Unions," *ibid.,* (November 21, 1902), 330-31; "Labor Unions Once More," *ibid.,* (July 10, 1902), 417-20; "Points of View," *The New Century,* June 18, 1904.

16. "The Social Unrest as Archbishop Ireland Sees It," *The Independent,* December 13, 1906.

17. R. C. Gleaner, "From the Catholic Viewpoint," *Catholic Columbian Record,* September 2, 1910; Edward Maginnis, "The Outlook: Signs of the Socialistic State," *The Catholic Standard and Times,* December 27, 1913; "Individualism and Collectivism: The State and Legislation," *The Live Issue,* January 10, 1914.

18. William J. Kerby, "Socialism," *The Dolphin,* V (February, 1904), 141.

Recognizing the wisdom of this attitude, the American Federation of Catholic Societies gradually abandoned its defensive policy as it grew from humble beginnings in 1901 to three million members in 1912 affiliated through 60 colleges and universities and 24 societies of nationwide scope. On labor-management relations it accepted the policies of the National Civic Federation and threw its support behind the living wage movement, the abolition of child labor, and other forms of protective legislation.

One of the affiliated societies, the Central Verein, resolved to specialize in social justice, establishing in 1908 a Central Bureau for the Promotion of Social Education and a German-English magazine, *Central-Blatt and Social Justice,* exclusively devoted to social advancement. Besides social education, the Bureau stressed trade unionism as the best instrument through which to secure progressive labor legislation. Well-adapted to its clientele, which was fairly educated and largely Americanized, the Verein's policy was scarcely applicable to the New Immigrants, the millions of Catholics from Southern and Central Europe with a high percentage of low-paid labor, illiteracy and spiritual destitution. Mainly for the benefit of these immigrants, better-circumstanced Catholics streamlined the Church's charity, organizing nearly a hundred social settlements by World War I as well as multiplying various other forms of the new social service. Lay women, through hundreds of clubs, leagues or guilds, some of which were national in scope, were mainly responsible for these efforts at social betterment. In the National Conference of Catholic Charities, formed in 1910, these women were to find a much-needed agency for the extension and perfection of their work. Alongside its promotion of remedial and preventive charity, the Conference resolved to be "the attorney for the poor in modern society. . . unto the days when social justice may secure to them their rights." [19]

The maturing Catholic social movement brought to the fore its full quota of energetic leaders. As the older men and women passed from the scene or slowed their pace, new ones appeared. Not least significant were Father (later Bishop) Edwin V. O'Hara and Caroline Gleason, of the Catholic Women's League of Portland, Ore., and the State's Industrial Welfare Commission, one of the great testing grounds of radical Progressivism. Patrick H. Callahan, paint manufacturer of Louisville, reorganized his plant on profit-sharing lines, and as Chair-

19. Frederic Siedenburg, S. J., "Federation of Catholic Societies," *Catholic World,* CXI (July, 1920), 441.

man of the Knights of Columbus Commission on Religious Prejudice discovered that Catholic participation in community projects was the best way to counteract misunderstanding and bigotry. Social settlement workers included Grace O'Brien, Marion F. Gurney, Josephine Brownson, Mary J. Workman and Margaret Tucker, this last a pupil of Father Peter E. Dietz whose social service training school developed into a Catholic Labor College, the first in the English-speaking world. A union labor enthusiast, Dietz after 1910 associated Catholic trade union leaders into a Militia of Christ which aimed by counteracting socialism in the unions to enlarge the labor movement in the Catholic segment of the population. As secretary of the Social Service Commission which he helped to set up in the American Federation of Catholic Societies, Dietz gained the ear of a large audience.[20] In debates and controversies with Socialists and conservative Catholics, Ryan and other academicians injected plans for industrial democracy into the concept of social justice.[21]

For a time, during World War I period, these men and women enjoyed a field day: with other progressives they expected post-war reconstruction to usher in a new age of social justice. To some extent the hierarchy itself shared this view, creating in August, 1917, the National Catholic War Council whose Administrative Committee of Bishops directed and supervised a far-reaching program of social service along with civic education for immigrants. With future industrial reform in mind, the Committee issued in February, 1919, the Bishops' Program of Social Reconstruction which urged, among other things, social insurance; a federal child labor law; legal protection of labor's right to organize; progressive taxation; government competition with monopolies if necessary to insure effective control; worker participation in management; and co-operative productive societies and co-partnership arrangements in order to enable the majority of wage earners to "become owners, or at least in part, of the instruments of production."[22] Almost immediately, this program was pronounced "socialistic" by the National Civic Federation, a strong battalion in the gathering army of post-war reaction against further reform. Instead of the anticipated advance, the reform impulse lost its force and frenzied reaction gripped the country in the course of which the re-

20. Mary Harrita Fox, *Peter E. Dietz, Labor Priest* (Notre Dame, 1953).
21. See Morris Hillquit and John A. Ryan, *Socialism, Promise or Menace?* (New York, 1914).
22. Aaron Abell, "The Catholic Church and Social Problems in the World War I Era," *Mid-America,* XXX (July, 1948) esp. 148-151.

cent gains of union labor were wiped out and the whole structure of pre-war social legislation imperiled. The clumsy preparations of Bolshevist zealots for a communist revolution in America frightened many people who lent a ready ear to the clever propaganda of business and other conservative groups that all reformers were Bolsheviks in disguise or the naive and witless abetters of violent revolution. It was this mood of reaction and fear that forced Father Dietz to close his Cincinnati labor school even though it had demonstrated its capacity to promote social peace in the community.

The hierarchy was less easily intimidated. Undeterred by the clamor raised by Ralph Easley, the Civic Federation's leader, and his Catholic associate, Condé B. Pallen, the bishops went forward with their organizational plans, setting up late in 1919 the National Catholic Welfare Council (Conference after 1922), comprising five departments, one of which — and the strongest — was the Department of Social Action. With Bishop Peter J. Muldoon as chairman and Ryan as director, assisted by John A. Lapp and Father R. A. McGowan, the Department fearlessly, if cautiously, applied the Church's social teachings to the current situation, insisting at the crest of the "Red scare" that the reduction of wages and the drive against labor unions violated social justice.[23] When with the revival of business after 1922 hysteria gave way to smug satisfaction in the social field, the Department repeatedly warned that economic conditions were unsound "so long as productivity was high and the income of the masses, including that of the farmers, low." In addition to the usual means of communication, such as books, pamphlets, lectures and study clubs, the Social Action Department developed "a traveling school of social thought" in the Catholic Conference on Industrial Problems, formed in 1922, whose many national and regional meetings freely discussed the findings of experts on all controversial economic questions and presented hundreds of thousands of people with an opportunity to learn, often for the first time, of Catholic social doctrine and its relevance to present-day issues.

These Conferences were more widely attended by wage-earners and educators than by businessmen. As Callahan reported, Catholic em-

---

23. Thomas T. McAvoy, C.S.C., "The Catholic Church in the United States," in Waldemar Gurian and M. A. Fitzsimons, editors, *The Catholic Church in World Affairs* (Notre Dame, 1954), pp. 358-76; John Tracy Ellis, *American Catholicism* (Chicago, 1956), pp. 138-43. For opposition to the Conference, see Arthur Preuss' statements in *Fortnightly Review*, XXXIII (June 15, 1926, August 15, 1926), 259-61, 267, and 355-57.

ployers, himself and a few others excepted, did not take kindly to the three "Programmes" — *Rerum Novarum,* the Bishops' Program of Social Reconstruction, and the Bishops' Pastoral of the same year. These Catholics did not believe that the Holy Father could possibly know anything about digging subways or getting honest work from "Wops" and "Hunkies." [24] More and more, in fact, as the 1920's got under way, Catholics as a group severed, so to speak, their erstwhile alliance with the militant progressives now coming to be known as liberals. To many Catholics it now seemed that reform merely placed additional powers in the State to be used against the interests of the Church. Mainly responsible for this attitude were the attempts of the Ku Klux Klan in state after state to illegalize parochial schools and other Catholic institutions. Initiated by the voters, the Oregon law to this effect was disallowed by the United States Supreme Court. This experience turned most Catholics against legislative and constitutional change. When Congress in 1924 submitted a Child Labor Amendment to the States for ratification, the opposition to the proposal took on a "Catholic cast," in the words of ex-Congressman Edward Keating, joint author of the first of the two Federal child labor laws declared unconstitutional by the Supreme Court.[25] To no avail, Catholic liberals — Callahan, Haas, McCabe, Ryan, Keating and Montana's Senator Walsh — demonstrated that the proposed amendment gave Congress jurisdiction over the labor, not the education, of youngsters under eighteen years of age and that the manufacturers, who inspired the crusade against the amendment, were a voting minority and therefore powerless to reciprocate effective aid to the Church in an hour of need.[26]

A more liberal spirit prevailed in the charities or social services. As a matter of fact, the earlier widespread disapproval of the professional social worker largely disappeared during the 1920's as various religious orders of women shifted to the new charity and many priests and nuns prepared themselves for teaching or administrative careers in applied sociology. The steadily increasing number of diocesan so-

24. P. H. Callahan, "The Catholic Industrial Conference," *Fortnightly Review,* XXXII (August 15, 1925), 333-35.

25. "Child Labor Criticism," *Fortnightly Review,* XXXII (February 15, 1925), 65-68.

26. P. H. Callahan, "The Child Labor Question: Real vs. False Issues," *Fortnightly Review,* XXXII (March 1, 1925), 166-69; "The Child Labor Amendment: An Editorial," *The Salesianum,* XX (January, 1925), 53, 61; "The Child Labor Amendment Again," *ibid.,* (April, 1925), 29-36.

cial service bureaus made it easier for the Church to participate in community fund drives as well as to extend its influence over foreign-born peoples, many of whom it had been unable to reach during the immigrant invasion of pre-war years. With immigration now virtu-ally ended by federal law, the Church at last had a chance in its parish-extension work to make performance approach aspiration.[27] Inasmuch as immigration could be no longer a source of the Church's growth, far-seeing Catholic leaders urged that the necessary steps be taken to expand Catholicism in the rural areas. The countryside, it was argued, provided the better environment for the nourishment and exercise of the Christian life, and by its higher birth rate would com-pensate the Church for its inevitable decline in cities which without rural accessions were unable to reproduce themselves. These views were personified by Edwin V. O'Hara who after a brilliant career in the field of labor legislation secured in 1921 the establishment of a Rural Life Bureau in the National Catholic Welfare Conference, ex-perimented successfully with church extension in an Oregon rural parish, and in 1923 launched the National Catholic Rural Life Con-ference. Besides serving to "de-urbanize" Catholic attitudes, the rural crusade has many victories to its credit in the way of church extension and social betterment.[28]

The rural movement might well have become the Church's pri-mary social interest had economic conditions remained normal and stable. But world-wide depression during the 1930's, entailing unem-ployment and indescribable misery for millions of human beings, fo-cused attention on the industrial system, the causes of its breakdown, and the search for reform and stabilization. Now, for the first time in American history, the promotion of social justice gained priority position in public policy. The steps taken to implement the policy followed Catholic prescriptions in the sense that eleven of the twelve major proposals in the Bishops' Program of Social Reconstruction were enacted into law. This does not mean that Catholic social plan-ners created the New Deal, only that they anticipated more accurately perhaps than other major groups the course it was to take — or had to take as a serious effort to achieve reform under the capitalist sys-tem. Catholic social theory was of course brought to bear on imme-

27. A. I. Abell, "The Catholic Church and the American Social Question," in Gurian and Fitzsimons, editors, *The Catholic Church in World Affairs*, 396.
28. Raymond Philip Witte, S. M., *Twenty-Five Years of Crusading. A His-tory of the National Catholic Rural Life Conference* (Des Moines, 1948).

diate issues involving the New Deal. On the patristic argument that the poor in their need had a rightful claim to the superfluous goods of the rich were based some of the more powerful pleas for a generous Federal policy toward unemployment relief.[29] As for the New Deal plans to achieve recovery and reform, these were discussed from the vantage point of an enlarging concept of social justice.

In a special sense, the reigning pontiff, Pius XI, proved a source of inspiration and guidance. Anxious to bring doctrinal precision as well as more energy into all forms of Catholic action, this erstwhile librarian and mountain climber constantly extolled the ideal of social justice, making the concept a focal point of his social teachings.[30] This was apparent in his notable pronouncement on reconstructing the social order, an encyclical issued in May, 1931, on the fortieth anniversary of *Rerum Novarum*. In *Quadragesimo Anno,* as the encyclical was generally called, the Pope declared that workingmen were in justice entitled to wages of "ample sufficiency." He recommended that where possible co-partnerships be introduced so that wage earners might become "sharers in some sort in the ownership or the management or the profits." [31] In the event that industrial depression undermined the ability of businessmen to pay living wages, the situation should be corrected through the joint action of employers and employees, aided by the public authority. Similarly, the causes of unemployment, one of which was "a scale of wages too low, no less than a scale excessively high," should be removed. In these ways Pius XI lent his sanction to the movement for economic planning which in this country was being popularized by some segments of labor and business and by numerous intellectuals of whom Stuart Chase and Charles A. Beard were the most vocal.[32]

In order the better to promote social justice and its great objective, namely, the common good, Pius XI urged that the direction of economic life be assigned to vocational groups, one for each trade, pro-

29. "Editorial Comment," *Catholic World* CXXXIII (May, 1931), 225-34.
30. John A. Ryan, "The Concept of Social Justice," *Catholic Charities Review,* XVIII (December, 1934), 313-15.
31. "Quadragesimo Anno," in Appendix, Joseph Husslein, *The Christian Social Manifesto* (Bruce Publishing Co., Milwaukee, 1931), pp. 284-323.
32. John A. Ryan, "The New Things in the New Encyclical," *The Ecclesiastical Review,* LXXXXV (July, 1931), 7-8; A. I. Abell, "Labor Legislation in the United States: The Background and Growth of the Newer Trends," *Review of Politics,* X (January, 1948), 51; L. L. Lorwin, "The American Front," *The Survey,* LXVII (March 1, 1932), 569-71; *idem,* "The Encyclicals of Leo XIII and Pius XI," *Current History,* XXXIV (July, 1931), 486-87.

fession, or industry, in which employers and employees should "join force to produce goods and give service." These groups ought to be "in a true sense autonomous," that is, self-governing bodies, with power to set prices, determine wage scales, and in general to control and regulate industrial conditions. The State would assist, not dominate the process, imposing restraints only when necessary to adjust unresolved differences or to safeguard the interest of consumers and the public generally. Bringing employers and employees into the same organization would put an end to class conflict and bind men together "not according to the position they occupy in the labor market, but according to the diverse functions which they exercise in society." The Pope strongly endorsed "unions" of a "private character," that is, trade unions, employer associations and the like. He counseled these "free associations" which had produced so many "salutary fruits" to "prepare the way and do their part toward the realization of those still more ideal guilds or occupational groups which we have previously mentioned." [33]

In America as elsewhere vast numbers viewed *Quadragesimo Anno* as the social justice norm and sought out ways to attain its realization. Not a few insisted that the unionization of workers must precede, and as the Pope suggested "prepare the way" for the establishment of a modernized guild system. An uncompromising champion of this viewpoint was Monsgr. Francis G. Haas, dean of the newly established School of Social Science at the Catholic University of America. Lashing out against "a narrow and selfish open shop individualism,"[34] in his opinion the basic cause of the Great Depression, Haas in common with many students of the industrial situation predicted, in 1931, that "the permanent recovery of industrial society is impossible unless wage earners are frankly accorded the right to organize and bargain collectively for wages and working conditions. Union organization, intelligently led," he said, "is the only effective method of securing an adequate share of the national wealth for workers and their families."[35] Had eighty per cent rather than ten per cent of organizable workers been in independent unions by 1929, the country would have been spared the horrors of widespread poverty and unemployment. Rightly,

---

33. *Quadragesimo Anno, loc. cit.,* pp. 304-06.

34. "Freedom Through Organization," *Salesianum,* XXVIII (October, 1933), 9.

35. "Catholic Doctrine and Industrial Practice," *Proceedings, Seventeenth National Conference of Catholic Charities,* 1931, 248; reprinted in *Salesianum,* XXVII (January, 1932), 1-9.

the Pope, in proposing integrated occupations with the government acting as mediator between and over the component parts, demanded more than labor unions as they existed in the United States. But his plan "assumes that workers are almost, if not entirely, unionized." Haas believed that "we are wasting our time and our energy if in promoting the Catholic industrial program, we neglect, or what is worse, try to dodge this important fact." Only by helping workers to form free unions, "can we hope ultimately," he opined, "to make the social program of the Holy Father a reality." [36]

A different approach was taken by the "radio priest," Charles E. Coughlin of Royal Oak, Michigan, whose eloquent microphonic oratory was principally concerned after 1930 with the social justice issue.[37] Father Coughlin possessed an "uncanny ability to make himself the articulate voice for the manifold and deep discontents of the age." [38] Unrivalled in his power to expose abuses, he unsparingly attacked by name the alleged instigators and beneficiaries of injustice and fraud. His dealing in personalities, along with his partisan political and legislative commitments, made him a highly controversial figure. Indirectly, however, he publicized Catholic social teachings more widely than any contemporary, not only on radio, but on the public platform and after 1934 through the propaganda of the Union for Social Justice and its weekly journal, *Social Justice*.[39]

Coughlin did not envisage social justice as the function or product of integrated occupations.[40] He wrongly restricted the vocational group plan or the guild system to labor unions and relied on compulsory arbitration to secure peace and justice in the industrial field. He suggested that organized labor — which he strongly favored — be placed under the protective tutelage of the Department of Labor.[41] If this indicated a Fascist approach, as many of his enemies and critics al-

36. "Competition and Social Justice," *The Salesianum*, XXX (October, 1935), 17-24.

37. Ruth Mugglebee, *Father Coughlin of the Shrine of the Little Flower* (Boston, 1933), pp. 156-321.

38. Wilfred Parsons, S. J., "Father Coughlin and Social Justice," *America*, LIII (May 18, 1935), 129-131.

39. "Father Coughlin: Whither?," *The Guildsman*, III (January, 1935), 9; *ibid.*, V (October, 1936), 10-11.

40. "The Coughlin Controversy," *ibid.*, III (July, 1935), 10; "Provocatives," *ibid.*, IV (May, 1936), 12; "Father Coughlin's Recent Program," *ibid.*, V (November, 1936), 2-4.

41. Charles E. Coughlin, *Eight Lectures on Labor, Capital and Justice* (Royal Oak, Mich., 1934), pp. 115-32; Wilfred Parsons, *op. cit.*

leged, the tendency owed less to Mussolini or Hitler than to the tradition represented by the late nineteenth century Single-Taxers and Populists. Like these earlier reformers Father Coughlin did not believe that the heart of the trouble lay primarily in conflict between employers and employees but rather in profound disturbances, chiefly of a financial and monetary character. In his view public ownership was the only cure of these maladies. "I believe in nationalizing those public necessities which by their very nature are too important to be held in the control of private individuals. By these I mean," he enumerated, "banking, credit and currency, power, light, oil and natural gas and our God-given natural resources." He stressed the nationalization of banking and currency with a view to keeping prices on an even keel and liquidating "unbearable and unpayable debts." [42]

On a platform mainly of monetary reform, this "shepherd of the air" gained a wide following during the early 1930's, but for various reasons was unable to hold it intact. In behalf of labor, he demanded that every worker be guaranteed a minimum annual wage of $1,800. This tended to alienate small employers and other middle class backers, many of whom made considerably less than this sum. Moreover, the clergy shunned their confrere either out of envy or distrust, or because he did not invite or welcome their cooperation. They may well have concluded that the priest's movement was more personal and political than religious in character. They were repelled by his ambition to be a "religious Walter Winchell" and to put "the universal credo into Christianity." Aiming "to extend American ideals," the Union for Social Justice lacked a definitely Christian basis and gradually drifted into the Anti-Semitic camp.

These objections did not apply to the Catholic Worker movement headed by Dorothy Day, journalist, radical, and social worker who portrayed her conversion as a pilgrimage from Union Square to Rome.[43] Aroused by the taunts of the Communists that Catholics had no love for the poor, she resolved late in 1932 to devise ways to personalize Catholic sympathy for the harassed victims of depression, especially the homeless and unemployed worker. Early the next year, with the help of Peter Maurin, a French-born itinerant social philosopher, she opened in lower New York a house of hospitality which combined the functions of soup kitchen, a discussion club, and a re-

42. *Ibid.;* "The Coughlin Sixteen Points," *The Guildsman,* III (April, 1935), 10-11.
43. *From Union Square to Rome* (Silver Spring, Maryland, 1938).

form center. Similar houses — thirty of them by 1940 — were established in cities from coast to coast.[44] A monthly paper, *The Catholic Worker,* also begun in the spring of 1933, pinpointed Catholic social doctrine and attained within a short time a circulation well in excess of a hundred thousand. Its phenomenal success inspired similar ventures elsewhere in the field of Catholic social journalism.

Like the Communists, the Catholic Workers engaged in tireless indoctrination of the poor, the "ambassadors of God." The better to influence them, Miss Day and her co-workers practiced voluntary poverty, combined manual and intellectual labor, and performed works of mercy in a highly personalized manner. Their zeal and self-sacrificing spirit recalled, in fact continued in more intense form, the work of the early college social settlements. Like these precursors, the Catholic Workers actively supported the labor movement. While they did not deny that social legislation was needed, they stressed "personal responsibility before state responsibility." [45] More to their liking, therefore, was their participation in strikes and union organizational activities which afforded them excellent opportunities to counteract Communist influences and to expound the Christian philosophy of labor. From the outset the Catholic Workers furnished a sense of direction to Catholics anxious to crusade for social justice. "Sometimes," as Jesuit Albert Muntsch wrote, "neither clergy nor laity know exactly what to do in order to follow out the so-called 'Catholic Program'." *The Catholic Worker* "tells what to do and how to do it," he observed. "It comes down to the level of the people." [46]

The Catholic Workers did not, of course, exhaust Catholic organization in the social field. Thus some Catholics of education and substance — scholars, publicists and men of affairs generally — mobilized to bring influence on the business community, heretofore impervious to Catholic social teachings. Under the auspices of the National Catholic Converts' League, scores of the "best known leaders in finance and industry, many non-Catholics as well as Catholics" met in New York City early in 1932 "with Catholic economists and teachers of ethics." The main speakers, John Moody, the noted business statistician, and the Apostolic delegate, the Most Reverend Pietro Fumasoni-Biondi,

44. Dorothy Day, *House of Hospitality* (London, 1939), V-XXXVI, pp. 257-75; Will Woods, "And Hospitality Do Not Forget," *Social Justice Review,* XXXIII (September, 1940), 152-53.
45. Dorothy Day, *House of Hospitality,* p. 60.
46. "A Promising Journalistic Venture," *The Guildsman,* III (April, 1935), 6-7.

attributed the current social chaos to the divorce in practice between
business and ethics. Announcement was made at this meeting that
steps were being taken by the Calvert Associates, publishers of *The
Commonweal,* to form a nation-wide League of Social Justice for
the study and application of the economic teachings of Pope Pius XI.[47]
The guiding light in this endeavor was Michael O'Shaughnessy, oil
executive and industrial publicist.[48] "Several Catholic laymen, businessmen of substantial means," he reported later in the year to
America, the Jesuit weekly, "have reached the conclusion that the social, financial and industrial dislocation that has overwhelmed the
world demands that we conform our human relations to our spiritual
ideals, that the value and security of all property and the material
happiness of all the people of the United States depends on the attainment in this country of social justice as propounded by our Holy
Father, Pope Pius XI, in his inspired Encyclical, *Quadragesimo
Anno.*"[49]

No success was possible, he stressed, without "Divine assistance,"
so "overwhelmingly great" were the obstacles to be overcome. For this
reason the League-a-forming would exact of each member a pledge
to attend Holy Mass daily and receive Holy Communion weekly, so
far as possible, "and to do everything in his power — in his family and
religious life and in his social and business contacts — to promote the
principles of social justice as defined by our Holy Father."[50] Under
the new technological conditions men's greed, as O'Shaughnessy pa-
tiently and graphically explained, induced an endless production of
goods and services without providing the consuming masses with sufficient income to satisfy even their basic needs.[51] The redistribution
of wealth, the special responsibility of the privileged few, called for a
curb in the desire for excessive gain. All too many, having lost faith
in their ability to curb their greed and to be fair to one another in
the conduct of the world's business, "seek laws to force them to do
what they can only do for themselves." Citizens devoid of moral re-

47. "A League of Social Justice," *The Commonweal, XV* (January 27,
1932), 337-38.
48. O'Shaughnessy refers briefly to his business career in "An Open Letter,"
Social Justice Bulletin, IV (August, 1941) 2-3.
49. Letter to the editor of *America.* "Communications: Praying for Social
Justice," *America* XLVII (September 24, 1932), 602.
50. *Ibid.*
51. "How Strong is the World's Industrial Arch?," *America,* XLVI (January 30, 1932), 400-401.

sponsibility would not obey laws, be they ever so reasonable and necessary.[52]

The remedy lay in human beings "practicing self-restraint and doing to others as they would be done by." It was easier to change human nature "to the extent of making men fair and honest in business than it is to force them to be so by law." The duty of Catholic laymen, leaders in finance and industry, was to use their brains and resources to curb avarice and "to establish Christian principles in the conduct of the world's business. If a baker's dozen of outstanding Catholic industrial and financial leaders could be induced to organize and finance such a movement," he confidently asserted, "they might easily be the lump that would leaven the whole mass and do the country a service of inestimable value."[53] Great numbers need not at once join the Catholic League for Social Justice. Only thirty-one leading colonial citizens in The Declaration of Independence, he reminded the hesitant, "defied the most powerful monarch on earth and made possible the United States of America." A comparatively few Catholics, similarly dedicated, "can start a movement to bring the blessings of social justice to all the people of our country."[54]

O'Shaughnessy did not fail to correlate the attitudes of his group with the movement for economic planning which was popular with liberal intellectuals, trade unionists, and progressive businessmen during the early 1930's. He elaborated a plan of his own in a carefully written pamphlet, *Men or Money?* published in the summer of 1932.[55] Prudently omitting mention of *Quadragesimo Anno,* he set out to show how the central idea in that encyclical could "be applied to American economic life."[56] Believing that State Capitalism, as well as Communism, meant slavery to government, O'Shaughnessy called for the reform of the Capitalistic social order. "The profits urge, prostituted by greed, must be controlled," he argued, by forcing industry to cooperate and not compete destructively in the conduct of the nation's business. Industry, through legalized monopolies, must be forced to conduct its affairs in the interests of the various units which constitute it and in the interest of labor and the public with a minimum of Fed-

52. "Greed Is the Witch," *The Commonweal,* XV (November 4, 1931), 9-11.
53. *Ibid.*
54. "Communications: Praying for Social Justice," *loc. cit.*
55. "The O'Shaughnessy Plan," *Commonweal,* XV (April 20, 1932), 673-74.
56. Aloysius J. Hogan, S. J., "The Catholic Church and the Social Order," *Proceedings,* National Conference of Catholic Charities, 1933, p. 52.

eral Government supervision." He warned that the corporations could
not be destroyed without destroying the country. "But they must be
controlled in a manner to preserve," he insisted, "as great a degree of
individualism to the citizen as is consistent with the changed conditions of our national life."[57] O'Shaughnessy proposed that trade associations be formed in all major industries for the purpose of insuring
equal partition of available work among workers entitled to work in
the industry; to maintain production on a profitable basis; to fix maxi-
mum and minimum prices; to keep employed in each industry the
average number of employees engaged in the industry over the period
of the preceding ten years at wages large enough to support decently
their families; and to set aside reserve funds to provide for fair and
stabilized wages for workers and owners, based on the operations of
the industry in the preceding decade.

In O'Shaughnessy's plan the trade associations would be controlled
by nine directors, three each from and by management, labor, and
the consuming public. The plan also provided for a Federal agency
with power to settle disputes and to veto decisions, chiefly price-fixing
ones, the veto to be subject to Court review.[58] O'Shaughnessy's proposals were circulated among people of influence, including every
Cabinet member of the incoming Roosevelt Administration.

Meanwhile, the Catholic League for Social Justice gained mo-
mentum, having been publicly approved by Cardinal Hayes of New
York on the Feast of Christ the King in October, 1932.[59] In the
course of the following year 65 bishops in the United States, along
with several in Canada and Mexico, extended similar sanction.[60] Although the League had "no formal organization, officers, initiation fees
or dues," it enjoyed active support in twenty-four dioceses of the
United States (about one-fourth of the total) in the way of Diocesan
Recorders, who circulated membership pledges, and organization committees which sponsored study clubs and discussion groups. Impelled,

57. *Men or Money?* (New York, 1932), pp. 20-21.
58. *Ibid.*, pp. 26-27.
59. "In Retrospect," *The Social Justice Bulletin*, I (September, 1937), 2-3.
60. "Here's Your Resolution," *Columbia*, XII (January, 1933), 17; "A
League for Social Justice," *America* XLVIII (March 18, 1933), 565-66; "The
Crusade for Social Justice," *ibid.*, XLIX (May 27, 1933), 170-71; "New Social Justice Bulletin," *ibid.*, (September 30, 1933), 605; "Report for the Year
1933," *Social Justice Bulletin*, I (December, 1933), 1-2.

as he claimed "by an uncontrollable urge to do something for God and my country in the most serious crisis in our history," O'Shaughnessy edited and published, largely at his own expense, *The Social Justice Bulletin,* a monthly review of current events in their relation to the social justice crusade.[61]

Not unexpectedly, enrollment in the League was small, not more than ten thousand. Yet, indirectly, through the press and various Catholic organizations, it seems to have exerted a persuasive influence.[62] In the Archdiocese of Chicago, for example, the Holy Name Society, at the suggestion of Bishop Bernard J. Sheil, director of the highly successful Catholic Youth Organization, urged its members to sign the League's pledge, while the National Council of Catholic Men endorsed "as worthy of universal support the object of the Catholic League for Social Justice and will cooperate in advocating adoption of its simple but most efficacious requirement." [63]

The League was to find its strongest echo in the National Catholic Alumni Federation which from its formation in the mid-1920's displayed a growing interest in social questions. Through its regional and national meetings the Federation in the early 1930's worked out "a definite and specific program" which in the interests of economic stability called for a better ordering of industrial relations, to be secured by trade associations in partnership with labor and government. "This is a far cry indeed," one commentator thought, "from the negative protests against Marxian socialism and the all too feeble pleas for greater justice to labor which characterized Catholic action just prior to the war." [64]

As Catholic leaders mobilized for social justice, they were in a

---

61. *Ibid.* (November, 1933), 1-2. *The Social Justice Bulletin* was published monthly at New Canaan, Connecticut, from January, 1933 until June, 1934 (in mimeographed form from January to August, 1933; from June, 1934, until November, 1943, the journal appeared about four times a year at irregular intervals.)

62. John Corbett, S. J., "The Crusade for Social Justice," *Social Justice Bulletin,* I (November, 1938), 2-3; "Youth and Social Justice," *ibid.,* II (May, 1939), 2-4.

63. *Social Justice Bulletin,* I (December, 1933), 2; see also "Significant Activities," *ibid.,* (February, 1934), 2.

64. "National Catholic Alumni Federation," *Catholic World,* CXXXVI (December, 1932), 367; Richard Dana Skinner, "Social Justice — a Program," *The Commonweal,* XVIII (July 28, 1933), 320-22; "Radical Catholic Action," *The Christian Front,* II (April, 1937), 51.

position to evaluate the New Deal recovery and reform measures. Few denied that the New Deal's grandiose plan, The National Industrial Recovery Act, resembled, superficially at least, the vocational group system outlined in the Pope's recent encyclical.[65] Through industrial codes — 731 in all — the Act sought "to induce and maintain united action of labor and management under adequate governmental sanction and supervision." By relaxing the anti-trust laws, the code authorities, manned by business leaders, were empowered to check overproduction and ruinously low prices, the result, it was held, of excessive and unfair competition, low wages, long hours and child labor. The codes, therefore, provided for a minimum wage from twelve to fifteen dollars a week, reduced the work-week to forty hours and abolished child labor. These features were designed to stimulate re-employment, increase purchasing power and improve working conditions.

The Act expressly affirmed labor's right to self-organization, declaring in Section 7 (a) that "no employee and no one seeking employment shall be required as a condition of employment to join any company union, or to refrain from joining, organizing, or assisting a labor organization of his own choosing." This provision, along with its other guarantees, led O'Shaughnessy to write that the NIRA ended "industrial slavery" in the United States and aimed to establish a nation-wide "partnership status" between employers and employees for "the orderly conduct of industry." [66] Actually, labor had no direct voice in the new arrangement, not being represented in the code authorities at policy-determining levels. Labor's exclusion was deplored by virtually all Catholic social leaders.[67] The more optimistic, including John A. Ryan, now a Monsignor, hoped for a speedy correction

65. "Recovery or State Socialism," *America* XLIX (July 22, 1933), 362-63; F. J. Eble, "Bankrupt Economic Individualism," *The Guildsman,* II (October, 1933), 4-7; "Which Way, Leader Roosevelt?," *ibid.,* I (March, 1933), 11-12; "Betraying the True Alternative," *ibid.,* III (November, 1934), 5-6.

66. "The NIRA," *Social Justice Bulletin,* I (September, 1933), 3-4.

67. R. A. McGowan, "Testing the NRA by Catholic Teaching — III," *Catholic Action,* XVI (January, 1934), 11-12, 31; "Is the NRA 'Ideal'?," *America,* L (December 23, 1933), 266; "Employers and the Government," *ibid.,* (March 10, 1934), 533-34; "New or Old Deal?," *ibid.,* (March 24, 1934), 584; "Labor Revolts," *ibid.,* LI (July 28, 1934), 361-62; Clarence J. Enzler, "The NRA and the Future," *Columbia,* XIII (October, 1933), 12-13, 15, 20; "Dictating Industrial Recovery," *The Guildsman,* I (July, 1933), 8-10; "When Labor Is Bought and Sold," *ibid.,* (August, 1933), 11-12; "A Critique of the NRA," *ibid.,* II (February, 1934), 10; "Organization and Organic Structure," *ibid.,* III (October, 1934), 3-5; "The Exit of the NRA," *ibid.,* (June, 1935), 5-6.

of the defect. In that event the code authorities, he wrote, "would become substantially the same as the occupational groups recommended by Pope Pius XI." [68]

Some feared that the new legislation unduly magnified the powers of government. Pius XI's encyclical "does not contemplate the extent of intervention on the part of the State that is now in evidence," argued the Central Verein. [69] The Verein's sociological representative, Frederick P. Kenkel, doubted if anything was to be gained by "the exchange of Individualistic Capitalism for a planned economy politically controlled by a central government — i.e., State Socialism." [70] Speaking mainly for small businessmen and farming families, Kenkel wished government to be divorced from corporate enterprise rather than used, as the economic planners desired, to incorporate labor and agriculture into the monopoly structure. In his view low wages, even low farm prices, would be in the public interest provided relief was afforded the people from high tariffs, unfair taxes, intolerable debts, and the excessive prices exacted, often for inferior wares, by trustified industries. [71] The Kenkel group favored anti-monopoly measures designed to reverse the trend toward business concentration. In an anti-monopoly and minimal government context, Christian forces could the more successfully combat the profit-making craze, the root of the prevalent social disorganization. The New Deal recovery and social security measures, on the other hand, by providing temporary relief, tended to perpetuate the existing system and to divert attention from the pressing task of building up Christian attitudes towards industry and property.

The Catholic planners admitted that the insatiable desire for gain endangered the success of the New Deal program. The New Deal Administration had exercised its vast powers "wisely and justly . . . in the interests of all the people," O'Shaughnessy claimed, "but human

68. "Shall the NRA Be Scrapped?," *Proceedings,* National Conference of Catholic Charities, 1934, 57.
69. "Resolutions of the CV Convention," *The Guildsman,* I (September, 1933), 14-15.
70. Quoted in "Views on the Recovery Act," *ibid.,* (August, 1933), 14-15.
71. "The Farmer and Economic Planning," *Proceedings,* National Conference of Catholic Charities, 1932, pp. 200-204; "The Irrepressible Agrarian Conflict," *Central-Blatt and Social Justice,* XXIII (March, 1932), 412-13; "What the Farmer Needs Most," *ibid.,* XXIX (June, 1936), 84. See also "On the Eve of State Branch Conventions," *ibid.,* XXV (April, 1932), 22; "Catholic Farmers State Their Position Towards Farm Problems," *ibid.,* XXVI (June, 1933), 99.

greed and selfishness are intervening to nullify its efforts." [72]   After
interviewing representative persons in many parts of the country —
corporation managers, labor leaders, workers, farmers and consumers,
he concluded that "all were considering this program from a standpoint of personal self-interest." [73]   No person or group seemed willing
to make sacrifices for the common good. Most at fault were the business leaders who thwarted the efforts of the government to restore
the purchasing power of workers and farmers and unjustly passed on
the costs of recovery to the consuming public. O'Shaughnessy regretfully noted that the leaders of both capital and labor sought domination, not partnership. By herding workers into company unions employers aimed to defeat the effectiveness of the collective bargaining
principle on which the Recovery Act was based. Equally wrong was
the attempt of an "over-lordship of labor organizers" to represent all
workers rather than to encourage their organization, as the law intended, on a nation-wide scale, industry by industry. He recalled that
the Act conferred privileges of organization on both corporations and
workers "to enable them to cooperate, as a partnership, each upon
terms of full equality, to serve consumers efficiently and justly, to sta-
bilize property values and to promote social security." [74]

The crux of the difficulty, as O'Shaughnessy lamented, was that
too few realized that recovery was impossible without reform. He
warned the privileged classes not to block the "social revolution," lest
they "force the Government to collect, through excessive taxes, the
larger part of capital required to finance all industry, agriculture and
commerce." [75]   Monsignor Ryan also believed that should the NIRA
fail, the people in all probability "will turn to government operation
of the essential industries." [76]   Sharing this belief and fear, most thinking Catholics urged that the National Recovery Administration be retained and perfected. When the Supreme Court invalidated the
measure in the spring of 1935, 131 distinguished leaders of Catholic
thought and action affixed their signatures to *Organized Social Justice,*
a pamphlet published by the NCWC's Social Action Department urging an amendment to the Federal Constitution which would empower

72. "The AAA and the NRA," "Revolution and the New Deal," *Social Justice Bulletin,* I (October, 1933), 3-4.
73. "Public Opinion and the 'New Deal'," *ibid.,* (November, 1933) 3-4.
74. "Section VII (a)," *ibid.,* (September, 1933), 4.
75. "Public Opinion and the 'New Deal'," *loc. cit.*
76. "Shall the NRA Be Scrapped?," *loc. cit.,* 62.

Congress to re-establish the NRA along genuine vocational group lines.[77]
The project largely of Monsignor John J. Burke, *Organized Social
Justice* was pronounced by John A. Ryan "the most fundamental, the
most comprehensive and the most progressive publication that has
come from a Catholic body since the appearance of the Bishops' Program of Social Reconstruction." [78]

Partly as a result of observing the NRA experiment, a coterie of
Catholic leaders denied that partnership in industry involved a substantial increase in union membership. Brilliantly representative of
this viewpoint was Aloysius J. Muench, successively professor of sociology in St. Francis Seminary, its rector, Bishop of Fargo, N. D., and
Papal Nuncio to West Germany. Not solidarity, but intense conflict,
he pointed out, had marked, and continued to mark the relations between capital and labor in this country. In their attempt to wrest from
plutocratic capitalism the right to a living wage, the right to collective
bargaining, shorter hours, and better working conditions, the trade
and industrial unions had become aggressively militant organizations.[79]
Precisely for this reason, "they do not appear to offer the right approach," he felt, "to a cordial and harmonious understanding between
capital and labor, and therefore to the corporate reconstruction of the
social order according to the ideas of Pope Pius XI." In like manner,
capital, fearing domination by organized labor, was "wary of a corporate reorganization of business in which both the employers and employees own and manage on a basis of mutuality." Overtures from
labor to this effect were viewed with suspicion and distrust by most
employers.[80]

Muench did not think the situation a hopeless one — far from it.
A foundation on which to build a corporative industrial order had
been laid, he believed, by the "few ideally constructed employee representation plans." Just as some independent unions were radical or
venal, so also some company unions were in the workers' interest. He

77. John A. Ryan, "Organized Social Justice," *The Commonweal,* XXIII
(December 13, 1935), 175-76; "Catholic Plan for Organized Social Justice,"
Catholic World, CXLII (January, 1936), 488-90.
78. John A. Ryan, "Monsignor Burke and Social Justice," *Catholic Action,*
XVIII (December 15, 1936), 19-20.
79. "Self-Government in Industry," *The Salesianum,* XXIX (April, 1934),
33-40; "Strikes and Recognition of Unions," *ibid.,* (July, 1934), 1-7; "Labor's
Struggle for Collective Bargaining," *ibid.,* (October, 1934), 8-15.
80. "A New Alignment of Capital and Labor," *ibid.,* XXX (January, 1935),
1-5.

listed the William S. Filene Sons Company, Dutchess Bleacheries, the Boston Consolidated Gas Company, and Callahan's Louisville Paint and Varnish Company as firms which had made a tender of business fellowship to their employees. The Philadelphia Rapid Transit Company and the Columbia Conserve Company permitted employees, he poined out, "to acquire common stock, own it as a group, vote it as a block, elect their representatives to the Board of Directors, and, if desired, ultimately to obtain control." The better employee representation plans had given employees a degree of control and ownership not ordinarily obtainable through the collective bargaining process. While organized labor should maintain its defensive power, it should also withdraw its opposition to the good employee representation plans and join with well-disposed industrialists to extend them over as wide a field as possible. Otherwise, the idea of the corporative reconstruction of the economic order "will never be achieved." [81]

Little heed was paid Muench's suggestions. After the passage of the National Labor Relations Act (the Wagner Act) and the formation of the Committee on Industrial Organizations (the CIO), both in 1935, the attention of mass-production workers centered on unionism the rapid progress of which entailed no end of violence and bitterness. If the vocational group plan provided the truly sane and just solution, neither side was in a mood to accept it. Discussing the subject with John L. Lewis, Bishop R. E. Lucey complained that industrial unionism did not "go far enough. The Holy Father wants the workers to join the employers in the management of industries." "I realize that," Lewis replied. "I have read the encyclicals and I use them, too, but I don't dare advocate workers' sharing in management just now. It would mean a great furore and I would surely be put down as a Communist." [82] The failure of the guild idea to catch on encouraged many Catholics, no doubt, to seek alternative solutions, notably consumers' cooperation along the lines of the Rochdale system. Editor Edward Koch, uncompromising guildsman, regretfully reported in 1936 that the Catholic people were "predominantly devoted to the Cooperative and Coughlin programs." [83]

The success of co-operatives among Catholics, mainly fisher-folk,

81. *Ibid.,* 5-9.
82. "Labor in the Recession," *The Commonweal,* XXVIII (May 6, 1938), 47.
83. "Promote the New Order!," *The Guildsman,* IV (September, 1936), 9.

in Antigonish, Nova Scotia, and in lesser degree in St. Mary's County, Maryland, was widly publicized.[84] About fifty thousand Catholics participated in parish credit unions, some two hundred in number.[85] The movement derived its strongest support from the Central Verein whose conventions and publications, particularly the *Central-Blatt and Social Justice,* were increasingly preoccupied with the study of the subject in all its aspects. Kenkel's opinion that "Cooperators are the guildsmen of the 20th century," was shared by many without as well as within the Central Verein. Kenkel believed that if consumers' cooperation became widespread in the American economy, it would serve as a "yardstick" against monopoly, and help to rehabilitate the concept of "the just price." His position was thus a medial one. He would not, on the one hand, subordinate cooperation to the guild or occupational group system,[86] or, on the other, attempt to bring the whole economy under consumer sway.[87]

The opinion of the more ardent guild advocates to the contrary, the enthusiasm with which many Catholics supported consumers' cooperation is best viewed as further indication of American Catholicism's social awakening. The increasing output of social literature also suggested a renaissance in Catholic social interest. In 1940 Kenkel alluded to the "tremendous" number of references contained in recently compiled Catholic social study lists "as compared with those of a quarter-century ago." He explained that American Catholics were "apparently attempting to make up for lost time and by a desperate burst of energy to acquire at least a talking knowledge of the social

84. Virgil Michel, O.S.B., *Christian Social Reconstruction* (Bruce Publishing Co.: Milwaukee, 1937); Edward Hugh Dineen, S. J., "Beyond the Cooperatives," *Columbia, XIX* (November, 1939), 6; same author, "The Limits of Cooperation," *ibid.,* (May, 1940), 6, 23; George Boyle, "Down to Earth," *ibid.,* (January, 1940), 6, 20; same author, "Co-Ops Are Concrete," *ibid.,* XX (December, 1940), 5, 23.

85. Gerald M. Schnepp, S. M., "Credit Unions," *The Christian Front,* II (July, August, 1937), 113-15.

86. "Merits of the Co-operative Movement," *The Guildsman,* I (November, 1932), 6-9, and similar comments in nearly every succeeding issue, I-IX (December, 1932) - September, 1941).

87. J. Elliott Ross, *Co-operative Plenty* (St. Louis: B. Herder Book Co., 1941), a distillation of the author's many magazine articles, including "Toward a Consumers' Economy," *Central-Blatt and Social Justice,* XXXII (June-November, 1939), 75-78, 113-14, 154-56, 190-92, 229-31.

88. "The Social Question to the Fore," *Central-Blatt and Social Justice,* XXXII (February, 1940), 348-49.

question." [88] Catholic leadership realized that the Church's safety and progress now rested in large part on social gains. What with unemployment continuing, the birth control movement making inroads on the Catholic population, and Communists infiltrating the new industrial unions, the Church's hold on her membership would be jeopardized unless a large measure of social justice could be speedily secured.[89] The clergy were more alive to this need than were the laity. Catholic employers denied — often openly — the Church's authority over economic matters while Catholic workingmen seemed indifferent to the Church's social teachings, now that the public authority had placed social justice high on its agenda of aims. A large segment of the clergy, on the other hand, yearned as never before for social knowledge and studied in Summer School Institutes and in the larger lay-clerical gatherings, notably the two national Social Action Conferences held in 1938 and 1939 at Milwaukee and Cleveland respectively.[90]

Socially competent priests sponsored a vast amount of worker education designed to prepare Catholics to play a more constructive role in the organized labor movement.[91] If greedy and unjust Catholic employers — and they were surprisingly numerous — made grist for the Marxian mill, the apathy and ineptitude of Catholics in unions frequently enabled a few disciplined Communists (or racketeers) to win office and dictate policy. Some priests were active in the Association of Catholic Trade Unionists, formed in 1937 under the aegis of the Catholic Worker group in New York. With chapters in several leading cities by 1940, ACTU helped Catholics to function effectively in union organizational drives and instructed them in the Christian teachings concerning labor and industrial relations.[92] ACTU followed the admonition in *Quadragesimo Anno* that "side by side with . . . trade unions there must always be associations which aim at giving

---

89. Louis Minsky, "Catholicism's Social Awakening," *Christian Century*, LIII (June 10, 1936), 837-38.

90. *Proceedings*, First National Catholic Social Action Conference (Milwaukee, 1938), esp. pp. 5-46, 366-401; for other comments, see "Marks of a Christian Social Order," *The Guildsman*, VI (June, 1938), 1-2; Charles J. Cooke, "Don't Quote Me," *The Christian Front* IV (June, 1939), 84; Wilfrid Parsons, S. J., "The Congress at Cleveland," *Columbia*, XIX (August, 1939), 2, 22.

91. Bp. Robert E. Lucey, "Are We Fair to the Church?," *Commonweal*, XXVIII (September 9, 16, 1938), 490-92, 521-523.

92. Norman McKenna, "Catholics and Labor Unions," *Columbia*, XVIII (May, 1939), 6, 24; Sebastian Erbacher, O.F.M., "The ACTU," *Christian Social Action*, V (December, 1940), 330-37; Joseph Oberle, C. SS. R., *The Association of Catholic Trade Unionists* (New York, 1941).

their members a thorough religious and moral training, that these in turn may impart to the labor unions to which they belong the upright spirit which should direct their entire conduct." Though ACTU was in no sense a Catholic clique in the labor movement, as Professor Philip Taft has shown,[93] the accusation that its influence, however effective and salutory, was divisive, prompted the Chicago chapter, the Catholic Labor Alliance, to open its membership to non-unionists and persons of all faiths who subscribe to the labor teachings of recent popes.

In order to perfect its work, ACTU added several labor schools to the three score or more opened by Catholics in the decade after 1935. The labor schools offered workers — and others too — systematic instruction in labor ethics, labor history, parliamentary practice and various phases of labor-management relations.[94] Their teaching and administrative personnel — professors, lawyers and industrial experts — was recruited from men and women in close touch with the Catholic Worker movement, the Catholic League for Social Justice, the National Conference of Catholic Charities and the various departments of the National Catholic Welfare Conference. Catholics trained in the labor schools entered effectively into the fight for honest, democratic unionism which has been a conspicuous phase of the labor movement in recent years.

The labor schools climaxed the effort which made Catholic social action "second to none" in the decades after World War I.[95] Earlier, in the late nineteenth century, the social justice ideal was associated with non-Catholic reformers — ministers, social workers and professional scholars. Gradually leadership (outside the political field) passed into Catholic hands as immigrants Americanized, as social experts — Ryans, Dietzses and Kenkels — appeared on the scene, and as the hierarchy itself assumed collective responsibility for social progress by setting up the National Catholic Welfare Conference. In the wake of the Great Depression the post-war Bishops' Program of Social Reconstruction was translated into public policy, excepting only the

93. "The Association of Catholic Trade Unionists," *Industrial and Labor Relations Review,* II (January, 1949), 210-18.

94. Raymond S. Clancy, "Detroit ALI," *Christian Social Action,* IV (December, 1939), 210-16; Linna E. Bresette, "Labor Schools Promote Catholic Teaching," *Catholic Action,* XXII (March, 1940), 8-9; William J. Smith, *The Catholic Labor School* (New York, 1941); John F. Cronin, *Catholic School Action* (Milwaukee, 1948), 229-35.

95. James Hastings Nichols, *Democracy and the Churches* (Philadelphia, 1951), pp. 131, 251.

proposals to modify or supplement the wage system through producers' cooperation and co-partnership. Although neither capital nor labor showed any real interest in industrial partnership, Catholic social thinkers continued to insist on its adoption, fortified as they were after 1931 with *Quadragesimo Anno* and its plan to invest the co-partnership principle with public authority. The vocational group plan was not adopted — in fact it was sharply criticized — but it provided an ideal in the light of which Catholics estimate the strength and shortcomings of all reform measures in the industrial field.

Raymond F. Cour, c.s.c.*

VIII. Catholics and Church-State Relations in America

Finley Peter Dunne's unforgettable character, Mr. Dooley, was once asked the question: "Are you a Roman Catholic?" His immediate and emphatic reply was: "No. Thank God, I am a Chicago Catholic." Surely by these words this transplanted fountain of Irish wisdom intended no offense to the Holy See or to the Eternal City or to the homeland of his imbibing and philosophizing acquaintances of Italian ancestry on Archey Road. He was merely expressing a preference for membership in the Catholic Church combined with the general spirit and mode of life of the great Midwestern metropolis on the banks of Lake Michigan.

States differ from one another not solely or even principally because of climate or geography or even governmental forms. They differ chiefly in the general spirit and characteristics of the people who compose them, the men and women whose ideals and aspirations beget and inform their social and political institutions. The joining of the words, Chicago and Catholic, or, more broadly, to fit the theme of the symposium, American and Catholic, introduces one of our social and political institutions — our system of relations between Church and State. What *is* the American system of Church - State relations which is the object of Mr. Dooley's preference? Would his views receive a sympathetic hearing from his fellow Catholic laymen, from the American hierarchy, and from the popes of this century? These are the questions which this paper will treat and in a modest way endeavor to answer.

Perhaps a key to the answer to the question, What is the American

* Father Raymond Cour, C.S.C., is Assistant Professor of Political Science in the University of Notre Dame.

99

system of Church-State relations? can be found in several sentences
of the *Zorach* v. *Clauson* decision of April, 1952. There Justice Doug-
las, speaking for a majority of the Supreme Court, said:

> We are a religious people whose institutions presuppose the exis-
> tence of a Supreme Being. . . . When the state encourages religious
> instruction . . . it follows the best of our traditions. For it then
> respects the religious nature of our people and accommodates the
> public service to their spiritual needs. . . . We cannot read into the
> Bill of Rights . . . a philosophy of hostility to religion.[1]

The emphasis in this text is on the people, the Americans responsible
for our political heritage, those who freely adopted and freely continued the institutions of this nation. It is possible to distinguish in a
study of this subject first, the text of the Constitution and laws, which
are religiously neutral, second, the practice of our government, which
is positively friendly to religion, and third, the spirit of the people who
adopted the Constitution and who control the practice of government.

In the political arrangement approved by the American people
what is the role of religion? The term, religion, appears in only two
places in the federal Constitution. Article VI of the original document
reads as follows: "No religious test shall ever be required as a quali-
fication to any office or public trust under the United States." The
First Amendment contains the familiar words: "Congress shall make
no law respecting an establishment of religion or prohibiting the free
exercise thereof." While no specific mention is made of religion or religious freedom in the Fourteenth Amendment, the Court has interpreted the "liberty" clause contained there as extending to state legislatures the same restrictions regarding establishment and religious freedom which the First Amendment imposed on Congress.[2] It was the
"liberty" clause of the Fourteenth Amendment that was at issue in
the three most important Church-State cases of the last decade, the
Everson,[3] the McCollum,[4] and the Zorach[5] cases.

But the term, constitution, has another and broader meaning. In
this wider sense the constitution of a nation embraces the entire body
of rules, both legal and customary, by which a people governs itself
and seeks its temporal welfare. Customs, traditions, attitudes — all

1. 343 U.S. 314 (1952)
2. 310 U.S. 296 (1940)
3. *Everson* v. *Board of Education*. 330 U.S. 1 (1947).
4. *Illinois ex. rel. McCollum* v. *Board of Education*. 333 U.S. 203 (1948).
5. *Zorach* v. *Clauson*. *Op. cit.*

factors in producing an accepted pattern of conduct in civic life — are
included here and have their influence. About twenty-five years ago,
Charles E. Merriam, the distinguished political scientist of the University of Chicago, published a small volume entitled *The Written Constitution and the Unwritten Attitude*. Among his observations are the
following:

> It is a common fallacy to believe that a written constitution is a
> bulwark of property and persons, of law and order, of fundamental
> justice. But those who thus rely upon the words of any constitution
> for such support are leaning upon a broken reed; and their sense of
> security is a false one.
>
> All words may be interpreted and the power of the Supreme Court
> does not depend upon the text of the Constitution but upon the
> general attitude of the people and their willingness to acquiesce in
> its decisions. If this should change radically the whole attitude of
> the Court would change, and all alleged guarantees with it.
>
> Imagine a Tammany President, a Tammany Senate made up of
> 96 sachems, a House of 435 braves, a Cabinet of ten Tammany men
> tried and true, a Supreme Court of nine Tammany adherents, and
> what would the Constitution be counted among friends?
>
> A party or group electing a Congress and a President could com-
> pletely control the courts and work its will through law and inter-
> pretation without legal checks.
>
> The true guaranty of liberty lies not in parchment barriers, but in
> the fact that there is a common understanding that government
> shall be in the hands of agents who are responsible to the people,
> and who may displace them or overthrow them as they will.[6]

This point is noted because it was through reference to the unwritten
constitution, or, the general spirit of the American people, that the
Supreme Court decided two famous cases involving Church-State relations, the Trinity Church case of 1892 and the Zorach case sixty
years later.

The best review of the teaching of the Court on our subject is to
be found in the first of these cases, *Church of the Holy Trinity* v.
U.S.[7] The case involved the interpretation of an immigration statute.
Trinity Church in New York City had contracted to bring a Rev. Mr.
Warren, a resident of England, to serve as its rector and the minister
of its congregation. The government sought to deport Mr. Warren

6. Charles E. Merriam, *The Written Constitution and the Unwritten Attitude* (New York, 1931), pp. 14-19.
7. 143 U.S. 457 (1892).

because the contract in question violated the Immigration Act of 1885 which prohibited "the immigration and migration of foreigners and aliens under contract or agreement to perform labor in the United States." The case was won by Trinity Church, the Court holding that, even though the wording of the statute was general enough to cover the contract under consideration, Congress did not intend such coverage. The case is significant for two reasons, the Court's review of our religious history, and its reason for holding that Congress did not intend to forbid this type of contract.

After considering the specific language of the statute in question, the Court stated:

> But beyond all these matters, no purpose of action against religion
> can be imputed to any legislation, state or national, because this
> is a religious nation. This is historically true. From the discovery
> of this continent to the present hour, there is a single voice making
> this affirmation.[8]

It then illustrated this point by historical references from the commission of Queen Isabella to Columbus to the 1870 Constitution of the State of Illinois, citing pertinent passages of many famous documents among which were the Mayflower Compact, the Fundamental Orders of Connecticut, the Charter of Privileges of the Province of Pennsylvania, and the Declaration of Independence. The Court particularly noted that "The constitution of every one of the forty-four States contains language which either directly or by clear implication recognizes a profound reverence for religion and an assumption that its influence in all human affairs is essential to the well-being of the community." It then observed:

> There is no dissonance in these declarations. There is a universal
> language pervading them all having one meaning: they affirm and
> reaffirm that this is a religious nation. These are not individual
> sayings, declarations of private persons; they are organic utterances;
> they speak the voice of the entire people. . . . because of the gen-
> eral recognition of this truth the question has seldom been pre-
> sented to the courts. . . .[9]

After this consideration of basic charters and constitutions, the Court continued its study of the question in another field.

8. *Ibid.*, 465.
9. *Ibid.*, 470.

If we pass . . . to a view of American life as expressed by its laws, its customs, and its society, we find everywhere a clear recognition of the same truth. Among other matters note the following: The form of oath universally prevailing, concluding with an appeal to the Almighty; the custom of opening sessions of all deliberative bodies and most conventions with prayer; the prefatory words of all wills, "In the name of God, amen;" the laws respecting the observance of the Sabbath, with the general cessation of all secular business, and the closing of courts, legislatures, and other similar public assemblies on that day; the churches and church organizations which abound in every city, town, and hamlet; the multitude of charitable organizations existing everywhere under Christian auspices; the gigantic missionary associations, with general support, and aiming to establish Christian missions in every quarter of the globe. These, and many other matters which might be noticed, add a volume of unofficial declarations to the mass of organic utterances that this is a Christian nation.[10]

In conclusion the Court asked:

In the face of all these, shall it be believed that a Congress of the United States intended to make it a misdemeanor for a church of this country to contract for the services of a Christian minister residing in another nation?

Suppose in the Congress that passed this act some member had offered a bill which in terms declared that, if any Roman Catholic church in this country would contract with Cardinal Manning to come to this country and enter into its service as pastor and priest; or any Episcopal church should enter a like contract with Canon Farrar; or any Baptist church should make similar arrangements with Rev. Mr. Spurgeon; or any Jewish synagogue with some eminent Rabbi, such contract would be adjudged unlawful and void, and the church making it subject to prosecution and punishment, can it be believed that it would have received a minute of approving thought or a single vote?

. . . the general language [of the 1885 statute] is broad enough to reach cases and acts which the whole history and life of the country affirm could not have been intentionally legislated against.[11]

In substance the Court declared: the members of Congress would not — and did not — seriously entertain for a single moment or support with a single vote a proposition so much at variance with the whole history and life of the American people. That this is a "religious na-

10. *Ibid.,* 471.
11. *Ibid.,* 472.

tion" was deduced not from any specific provision of the Constitution, the supreme law of the land, but from a consideration of the religious quality of our history and general way of life. For the highest of our courts to take official notice of this fact and to use it as the basis for its interpretation of the immigration statute is significant.

For the next fifty-five years this doctrine was not called into question. As the Trinity Church decision stated, because of the general recognition of the religious character of our people, seldom prior to 1892 had religious issues even been presented to the courts. It was not until February 1947 that the traditional stand of the Court was interrupted. In the Everson decision of that date, the Court upheld the practice of providing bus transportation for parochial school children on the grounds that this was a safety measure and involved no aid to religion. However, the majority opinion enunciated the "wall of separation" doctrine, asserting that Congress and state legislatures could not "pass laws which aid one religion [or] aid all religions," since the Constitution had erected between Church and State a wall which, in Justice Black's words, "must be kept high and impregnable."[12] The inclusion of the ban on aid to *all* religions was novel doctrine, a clear departure from our traditional friendliness to religion in general. One year later in the McCollum case, the Court, citing the wall of separation principle as its basis, declared unconstitutional the released time program of Champaign County, Illinois, where the Board of Education permitted ministers of various faiths to come to public schools and give religious instruction to those students who had written parental permission to receive such instruction.

While this decision involved only an application of the Everson ruling, it attracted much more attention. In the Everson case only one religious group, the Catholic, was affected and that in a beneficial way whereas in the McCollum case many religious groups were affected and that in a way adverse to their interests. The importance of the much publicized McCollum decision lies in its having alerted the country to the implications of the Everson doctrine.

The reaction to the McCollum case is informative. Technically, each Supreme Court decision stands alone, affecting only the matter presented for judgment. In practice, however, it settles all similar cases because, given consistency on the part of the Court, these will be decided in the same way. In this case the Supreme Court reversed

12. 330 U.S., 18.

the decision of the Illinois Supreme Court, which then ordered the discontinuance of the released time program in Champaign County. It was only there, however, that the Court's teaching was applied. Throughout the rest of Illinois — and throughout the rest of the country — ministers continued to give the invocation at public school commencement exercises, parochial basketball teams were permitted to hold their contests in city- or county-owned gymnasia, and interfaith groups were allowed the use of municipal auditoria for their meetings. Four years of this type of reaction to its decision could not have been lost on the Court.

In the spring of 1952, in the case, *Zorach* v. *Clauson,* the Court upheld as constitutional the released time program of the State of New York. The only significant difference between this program and that condemned in the McCollum case is that in Illinois the religious instruction was given in tax-supported buildings whereas in New York pupils left the schools to get instruction elsewhere. In approving the latter program the Court stated:

> The First Amendment within the scope of its coverage permits no exception; the prohibition is absolute. The First Amendment, however, does not say that in every and all respects there shall be a separation of Church and State. Rather, it studiously defines the manner, the specific ways, in which there shall be no concert or union or dependency one on the other. That is the common sense of the matter. Otherwise, the state and religion would be aliens to each other — hostile, suspicious, and even unfriendly.[13]

It then noted, as was stated above, that we are a religious people whose institutions presuppose the existence of a Supreme Being, that in encouraging religious instruction and cooperating with religious authorities by adjusting class schedules to sectarian needs the state follows the best of our traditions, and that a philosophy of hostility to religion cannot be read into the Bill of Rights.

There are two points of special significance in the Zorach decision. First, the majority opinion makes no mention of the "wall of separation" doctrine which was central in both the Everson and McCollum cases, and second, the basis of the decision is our religious tradition. Although the text of the Constitution is religiously neutral, in practice our government is friendly to religion in general but partial to no de-

13. 343 U.S. 312.

nomination. It is not neutral or irreligious. Its attitude is religious but non-sectarian.

The constitutional theory involved here is clear. The American people, exercising the basic sovereignty which it possesses, framed, ratified, and amended the federal Constitution, the supreme law of the land. Some powers it assigned to the central government, others to the states, still others to neither, the last class being reserved to the people themselves. Through the First and Fourteenth Amendments the people have denied to our governments the power to establish a religion and the power to restrict its free exercise. The objective of this double limitation is to guarantee freedom for religion, not its exile from public life. All other powers affecting the field of religion in national life the government will be free to use — at the bidding of the people. There is a traditional preference for expecting religious groups to work out their own welfare without assistance from the government. But that no isolation of religion was intended is evident from the fact that the Congress which introduced the First Amendment provided at government expense chaplains for the Senate and House of Representatives as well as for the armed forces. This action of Congress did not involve establishment nor did it restrict religion but it did touch the religious side of national life. The legislators who enacted this measure were acting as agents of the American people who chose in this way to employ governmental power and public funds for a specific religious end which met with their approval. Each of the Congresses since that date has made similar provision, simply as a matter of course. When we denied to our legislatures the power to establish or restrict religion, we did not withhold from them authority over other phases of the religious question. We simply required that any exercise of this authority be approved by the people.

The religious neutrality of the text of the Constitution, the legal silence on any positive role for religion in national life, and our traditional preference for self-help by the churches bring into prominence another feature of our system of Church-State relations — the role of the individual citizen. In the Trinity Church and Zorach cases the Court looked not to particular legal or constitutional provisions or former court decisions but the quality of the people forming our nation. The conclusions reached were based on the religious history of an entire people. But the law must deal with individual men and women living here and now.

In democratic societies such as ours the citizen occupies a key

position. He shares both the authority and the responsibility of directing the affairs of the state. He is the maker and modifier of governments, the formulator and repealer of public policy. What the constitution, written or unwritten, states will be what he wishes it to state.
What the government does will be what he approves or tolerates. In
a real sense he — not alone but in company with his civic equals — *is*
the State. Consequently, what the Church encounters in its dealings
with the State is not the temporal order in the sense of the government
but rather the citizen armed with all the institutions of popular rule.
In like manner, what the government encounters in the religious field
is not an ecclesiastical hierarchy or body of church officials but the
individual citizen who chooses to exercise, alone or in communion with
others, his government-protected freedom of worship.

In law the American is treated not as a believer in a particular
creed but simply as a citizen. For example, there are many Catholic
priests, Protestant ministers, and Jewish rabbis serving American congregations today whose education to the ministerial profession was
financed, in part, at least, through the GI Bill of Rights. These benefits were theirs not because of the religion of any of them but because
they had performed a civic service, coming to the defense of the country in time of war. They were rewarded as citizens — who then used
their civic benefits to attain religious ideals without any inquiry or objection from the government or the people at large.

Thus placed in a mediating position between Church and State,
the individual citizen has status in both societies, status entailing obligations as well as privileges. For assistance in his life as a citizen, he
looks to his church for the doctrinal instruction needed for perspective,
for moral guidance to conscientious conduct, and for spiritual motivation and strength. In aiding him, and millions like him, our churches
reach American society, the American state. To assist him in his life
as a church member, he has the civil supports of freedom of worship,
freedom of speech and of assembly, and the right of property needed
for religious purposes. In the protection of these rights for the individual citizen, and the millions of his religious-minded neighbors, the
American state affords protection for religious groups. Church and
State meet in him — and his fellows of religious persuasion — and it
is in him and through him that any interchange of influence or assistance will come. In the Scandinavian countries, the Lutheran is the
official religion, legally designated as such. In this country the American state and the Lutheran Church are joined in the persons of those

citizens professing Lutheranism. In England the Episcopal is the official religion through a provision of law. In America the state and the Episcopal Church are united through the individual men and women who are at once American citizens and Episcopalians. In some countries with large Catholic populations, the Catholic is the official religion in law. In the United States the Catholic Church and the state meet in those persons who, like Mr. Dooley, are both Catholic and American.

This relation exists on the non-governmental plane, the government itself being formally neutral, confining its action to the protection of basic civil rights. Whether an individual American chooses to exercise these rights and join a church is a private matter. The amount of time and effort which he or his church expends in religious pursuits is not a governmental concern although the value of religion in national life is recognized in many ways, as the Trinity Church case indicated. But public life covers more than the area of governmental activity. The government is an agent of the people chosen to perform certain functions in the temporal order. Alone it can do only a small portion of what is needed for the common good. In fact, the less that it is necessary for it to do, the better the society in question is. The greater the number, the scope, and the vitality of the sub-groups which compose society, the healthier and freer the state will be. It is in this non-governmental field of public life that religion's place is recognized in America and the churches' opportunities abound.

Like members of other religions, Catholics are taught that their faith is a value in itself, a personal good, something of incalculable worth to be treasured and lived to the fullest. They are also taught that their faith is a value for society, a social good, assisting men and women in various phases of domestic, economic, and civic life. Protestant and Jewish congregations have similar teachings. All share in our religious heritage, not only by using the freedoms that are part of that heritage, but by contributing to it whatever their sincere convictions dictate. Hampered by no governmental restrictions, each sect is free to progress according to the energy of its members and the appeal of its doctrine. In an atmosphere of mutual tolerance and even friendly cooperation by members of all denominations, religion has an opportunity to impregnate American public life, free to supply a religious basis for our concept of the citizen and his mission on earth, to bolster with spiritual sanctions the respect due to civil authority, and to teach citizens the obligation to base their civic conduct on accepted moral rules. These functions of our churches touch intimately American public life. As Peter Drucker put it, in our system there is "strictest separation between State and Church and closest interpenetration of religion and society." [14]

To what extent is the system just described in harmony with the views of the Catholic Church? If we consider the Catholic laity — the many Mr. Dooleys in our land — and their lengthy record of loyal and faithful service of the country in peace and war, we find a practical, if unspoken, approval. Their lives are clear testimony to their stand. Commander O'Shea's advice to his young son, "Be a good Catholic and you cannot fail to be a good American," and Justice Brennan's testimony before the Senate Judiciary Committee are typical expressions of their attitude. Although Catholics differ among themselves on economic, political, racial and other questions in much the same way as do their non-Catholic neighbors, in their views on Church and State there is remarkable agreement among them. Like their fellow citizens they are little given to theorizing about the subject but in their practical life, their day to day efforts to be conscientious citizens they encounter nothing to prompt them to reject any of the particulars of our Church-State arrangement. The suggestion that they are only "provisional patriots," less devoted than others to our national institutions is resented, as is the implication that their evident loyalty to country involves compromise with their religious convictions. The average Catholic layman would be both surprised and hurt by any inquiry suggesting a possible conflict between his religion and his country.

What of the American hierarchy? Our hierarchy and our Constitution began together; the first American bishop was consecrated in the same year in which George Washington took the presidential oath for the first time. Six years ago, Msgr. John Tracy Ellis published in *Harper's Magazine* a survey of statements by the leading Catholic bishops of America over the last century and a half. The conclusion of this article reads:

> When one considers that the position which I have been outlining has been held from 1784 when the future Archbishop Carroll was found publicizing his acceptance of the American pattern of Church-State relations, to 1948, when the late Archbishop McNicholas made unmistakably clear his wholehearted avowal of the separation of Church and State in this country — and that no variation from this theme has been heard from an American Cath-

14. Peter F. Drucker, "Organized Religion and the American Creed," *Review of Politics,* XVIII (July, 1956), 297.

olic bishop — this should constitute an argument entitled to respect.[15]

Reflecting as they do the thinking of the most important of the Church's leaders in this country from the earliest years of the Republic to our own day, the statements reveal an authentic tradition. In its annual statement for the year 1948 the bishops heartily endorsed this tradition and deplored the Court's reasoning in the McCollum case as novel doctrine. In an article in the *North American Review* in 1909 Cardinal Gibbons wrote:

> Other countries, other manners; we do not believe our system adapted to all conditions; we leave it to Church and State in other lands to solve their problems for their own best interests. For ourselves, we thank God we live in America, "in this happy country of ours," to quote Mr. (Theodore) Roosevelt, where "religion and liberty are natural allies."[16]

Now, nearly half a century later, the hierarchy would surely nod approval of the Cardinal's words. After quoting them in a speech a decade ago, Archbishop Cushing added: "So spoke in his day Cardinal Gibbons. So do we speak in our day."

If we look to the writings of those popes who have had an opportunity to become familiar with the American pattern of Church-State relations, we find in their statements, particularly those of Pope Leo XIII, Pope Pius XI, and Pope Pius XII, acceptance of our system as entailing no conflict with Catholic teaching. In his Encyclical to the United States[17] Pope Leo XIII specifically states this. For the past century and a half the principal concern of the papacy in this field has been the secularist state, a state which in its religious outlook is either noncommittal or hostile. The American political experience as described in the Trinity Church case has evinced from the beginning neither indifference nor hostility to religion but general friendliness. The liberal separatism of the Continent, often the object of papal censure, has no counterpart in the philosophy of our First Amendment.

Among the papal statements pertinent to our question are those related to the profession of religion by the state in the *Immortale Dei*,[18]

15. John Tracy Ellis, "Church and State: An American Catholic Tradition," *Harper's*, CCVII (November 1953), 67.
16. Cited in Ellis, *ibid.*, 65.
17. *Longinqua Oceani*, January 6, 1895.
18. November 1, 1885.

the teaching on religious tolerance in the Encyclical on *Human Liberty*[19] and in the *Ci Riesci* of Pope Pius XII,[20] and the teaching on democracy in the Christmas Message of 1944. Surely this last must be regarded as one of the most important statements of our generation on the subject of democracy. The points of similarity between its teaching and American political ideals are numerous and striking.

But apart from these general teachings, if sheer repetition counts for anything, the constantly recurring emphasis on Catholic Action and its role in civic life establishes the papal attitude. Since Pope Pius XI ascended the papal throne in 1922 there have been scores of pontifical instructions urging Catholics to take part in public life in a formal, organized way. Their assignment is spiritual, to implement the Church's mission in the world by instilling a Christian spirit in temporal institutions. The Holy See is aware that the mere inclusion of a clause in a constitution declaring the Catholic (or any other) the official religion of the state will not automatically assure civic virtue, teach the dignity of man, promote respect for civil authority, or guarantee the type of external order which men need for existence and proper development in this life. These objects will be realized, if at all, through the efforts of men of good will, Catholics and others, using their civil opportunities. The Church places the fate of her mission in the civil order today in the hands of groups of zealous laymen willing to labor generously for the welfare of Church and nation. While following strictly the papal directive to remain "outside and above party politics," Catholic Action is to work for the betterment of civil society through the conscientious use of civil liberties available to individuals and groups in their own countries. For Catholic Action the Church seeks from the modern state only freedom to exist and freedom to work for spiritual ends — freedom to speak, to teach, to assemble for religious purposes. As the studies of Father John Courtney Murray have repeatedly emphasized, all of these are part of the basic pattern of liberty for which the United States is well known.

In this paper the author has chosen to treat not any specific unresolved problems of Church-State relations in America but rather the general setting in which any such problems which may arise will be solved. The American people will meet these problems in its own way. It can leave their solution to the energy and resourcefulness of private groups on the non-governmental plane — its usual practice — or, if such seems wise, it can demand positive action by its government

19. *Libertas Prestantissimum*, June 20, 1888.
20. December 6, 1953.

through measures which stop short of establishment and restriction of religious freedom. There are historical precedents for each type of solution. Questions of bus transportation for school children, school lunch programs, free non-religious textbooks for sectarian schools, and even state or federal aid to religious institutions — these will be settled not through any reference to the theology or religious affiliation of the potential beneficiaries but through the response of the people to the civic needs of their communities. In the solution of these and other civic problems with religious implications, the persons and groups involved will be treated as members of the American state rather than as members of any American church. Our Constitution is a civil, not a theological, charter. Its provisions state what the people approve or tolerate. With proper regard for the self-imposed constitutional limitations on establishment and religious liberty, the American people will decide the manner in which common problems involving Church and State in this country will be settled.

In summary it can be said that the American system of Church-State relations is characterized by an atmosphere of mutual respect and friendly co-operation by people of all faiths. Although the text of the Constitution and laws is religiously neutral, the spirit of our political institutions and the practice of our governments reveal an attitude of positive friendliness to religion on a non-sectarian basis. All creeds benefit by this arrangement and through it make their individual contributions to our civil society. Far from being "separated" from American public life, religion actually supplies it with a secure foundation through its teaching on the dignity of the person and respect for authority and provides a code of conduct by which men regulate their dealings with one another in the civic order. Not specified in law, the role of religion is informal, its influence indirect. Its work is carried on through the private efforts, individual and collective, of religious-minded citizens using the fundamental civic freedoms of speech and assembly. Seeking from the government only the freedom to operate, and progressing according to the zeal of their members and the appeal of their doctrines, the churches of America, as Father Gustave Weigel put it, "are the conscience of our nation, and our government is the instrument of a nation with a conscience." [21] American Catholics, clerical and lay, are one with their fellow citizens in their support of this arrangement.

21. Gustave Weigel, S. J., "An Introduction to American Catholicism," in Louis J. Putz, C.S.C., Ed., *The Catholic Church, U.S.A.* (Chicago: Fides Press, 1956), p. 13.

JOSEPH H. FICHTER, S.J.*

IX. The Americanization of Catholicism

An analysis of the Americanization process of Catholics is made difficult because of the variety of definitions of the term and because of the variety of criteria employed to measure the process. The diversity of definition seems to stem from the fact that Americanization is a relative term. We are not easily able to determine exactly at what point the person or group has become "completely" Americanized; and there is no wide agreement on the particulars (patterns of thinking and acting) that may serve as norms of Americanism.

WHAT IS AMERICANIZATION?

From the historical point of view, and in sociological terminology, it appears that Americanization of Catholics has not been one but several social processes. We may say that the processes of socialization, accommodation and assimilation have all occurred more or less simultaneously. Socialization means that the society transmits its culture from one generation to the next, and from the native-born to the foreign-born immigrants. The individual "takes on" the customs of the society in which he lives. Accommodation is the process in which persons or groups interact in order to prevent, reduce, or eliminate conflict. It is a means of living peacefully, of co-existing with one another, which may eventually lead to positive cooperation. Assimilation, or acculturation, is a process through which persons or groups accept and perform one another's patterns of behavior so that the resultant pat-

---

* Father Joseph H. Fichter, S.J., is head of the Department of Sociology in Loyola University in New Orleans and author of *Dynamics of a City Church* (1951), *Social Relations in Urban Parish* (1954), and *Parochial School: A Sociological Study* (1958).

terns are different from either of the two from which they originated.[1]

What we call Americanization can be thought of as all of these processes and also their result, sociocultural integration. The immigrant group gradually takes on the behavior patterns and values of the host culture and develops social relations with the people in the new society. Even if all of the immigrants were fully absorbed into American society, complete integration will probably never occur, nor would it be desirable, in a pluralistic society like our own. In spite of a noticeable trend toward a relatively homogeneous sociocultural system, there is probably still more heterogeneity here than there is in any other large modern country.[2]

"Becoming an American" implies both conformity by the people who are being Americanized, and acceptance by the people who are already Americans. Besides this, the processes leading to Americanization are really a two-way street in the sense that the inductor and the inductee are both recipients and donors in the process. The general goal of the trend toward integration seems to be that each person and group should become "true American." Foreign observers often contend that this goal is impossible because various and conflicting loyalties interfere with a centralized loyalty to the country itself. Americans of all types, however, continue to maintain their allegiance to various groups: familial, political, economic, religious, and others. In this kind of society, in which authority is polyphasic and values are multiple, Americans find multiple allegiance not only possible but desirable.

CRITERIA OF AMERICANIZATION

To what extent are Catholics in this country "true Americans?" An essential preliminary question to this is the matter of criteria. How do we measure, and what norms can be used to measure, the degree to which Catholics have been Americanized? I should like to eliminate at once three commonly used approaches to this measurement: the amount of tension between Catholics and others, the status of Catholics in the social structure, and the treatment of Catholics as a subculture.

It seems that Americanization cannot be adequately measured by the amount of tension that exists between Catholics and non-Catholics.

1. For a further discussion of these processes see Joseph H. Fichter, *Sociology* (Chicago: University of Chicago Press, 1957), pp. 22-23, 228-230.
2. *Ibid.*, chap. 18, "Sociocultural Integration."

If tension means disagreement and conflict it can indicate a serious internal social problem among Americans.[3] But if it refers to nothing more than the ever-present clash of interests and values going on among segments of our population it is a typically American phenomenon. Tension is a normal property of an expanding dynamic and progressive society. If it is viewed negatively, it is part of the price we pay for living in this rational, secular, pragmatic culture. There has been tension in all parts of the society, between employers and employees, between laity and clergy within the Church, between religious and ethnic groups, between a half-dozen Southeastern states and the United States. Although the tense people call each other un-American and Communist, this does not prove lack of Americanism in any of them.

Nor can we measure the degree of Americanization by the relative class status of American Catholics. It is true that Catholics are rising higher into the upper middle classes; and also true that Catholics do not have proportional representation among the scholars and statesmen, the merchants and millionaires, of this country.[4] We could hardly suggest that only upper class people are Americans, or that the members of religious and ethnic groups must be evenly spread among the social strata before they can be called Americans. The River Bottom people of Yankee City, the mountaineers of the Piedmont region, like many of the rural immigrants to our big cities today, are old-line, lower-class Anglo-Saxon Americans. Negroes, many of whom in the lower class are treated like second-class citizens, may be given other titles, but they cannot realistically be called non-Americans.

Nor can we measure the degree of Americanization on the assumption that Catholics possess a sub-culture. If this norm is employed to show that certain aspects of Catholicism, for example, the family system,[5] are at odds with some aspects of other sub-systems, the best we can conclude is that Catholics are identifiable, like all other Americans, as members of a minority. Membership in a minority, or the practice

---

3. See John Kane, *Catholic-Protestant Conflicts in America* (Chicago: Regnery, 1955), who treats of the main issues over which there is tension.

4. *Ibid.*, chap. 5, "The Social Structure of American Catholics"; also *Catholicism in America*, a series of articles from *The Commonweal* (New York: Harcourt, Brace, 1954).

5. John Thomas introduces cautiously and tentatively the concept of the Catholic family as a cultural sub-system. See *The American Catholic Family* (Englewood Cliffs: Prentice-Hall, 1956), chap. 1, "Minority Survival in a Complex Society."

of certain behavior patterns of a sub-culture, does not mark one off as a low-grade, unassimilated type of American. If this were true, there would be no Americans in existence. Dorothy Thompson deplores the way "the concept of American minorities has crept into the American language. It must be stated here," says she, "there are no minorities in the United States. There are no national minorities, racial minorities, or religious minorities. The whole concept and basis of the United States precludes them." [6]

In rejecting these three criteria of Americanization I want to make the crucial point in this discussion. Becoming American does not mean dissolving all differences, losing identity, and melting into the general masses of the population. Catholics do not cease to be Catholics when they become Americans; they cease to be Irish, or German, or French, or Polish. There is an interesting similarity here between world-wide Catholicism and culture-wide Americanism. The Catholic Church embraces people of all nationalities who are Catholics despite their national and ethnic differences. The United States embraces people of all religions who are Americans despite their religious differences.

THE LOSS OF ETHNIC STATUS

This comparison is, of course, an over-simplification, but it helps to point up the central problem of Catholics in America. It is the question of whether today American Catholics are an ethnic or a religious minority. It is on this point that the argument hinges, and it is on this question that the greatest confusion seems to exist. A brief historical reflection will help us here.

It is probably sage to say that if America had not been invaded by large numbers of non-English immigrants, the Catholic Church would not have been so bitterly attacked as a foreign ideology. In the seventeenth and early eighteenth century the colonies were an English mission served by priests who were mainly English Jesuits. Intellectual and cultural life was unmistakably English. As Nuesse says, "Absence of marked cultural differences in all fields except religion set in bold

6. Dorothy Thompson, "America Demands a Single Loyalty," *Commentary,* March, 1950. Oscar Handlin answered this with an article, "America Recognized Diverse Loyalties," in which he said in part, "the national interest was never revealed as an ideal above and beyond all the individuals in the nation. It was rather discovered by realistic compromise achieved through free discussion and open exposition of all the diversities of opinion and interest involved."

relief the intense and persistent antagonism to the Catholic Church which was characteristic of American colonials." [7]

But this was a legacy from England, and a reflection of the religious conflicts going on there, at a time and among people, who thought that theology and religion were something worth fighting about. In 1784 John Carroll was appointed prefect-apostolic. "By the end of the eighteenth century, American Catholics had outlived the prejudices earlier directed against them. They then constituted a community that was small in size but well-established and secure in social position. Composed primarily of the native-born, the Church counted among its communicants some of the wealthiest merchants and planters in the country." [8] There were some French among them, some Germans in Pennsylvania, and toward the end of the century some Catholic Irish began to come in "imported chiefly as indentured servants and convicts."

For about thirty years of the nineteenth century the Church in America continued its adaptation and growth with the country. The native-born Catholics had social status and prestige; they were accepted like other Americans; they made converts among the Protestants. But immigrants were coming in large numbers, and by the middle of the 1830's the Irish priesthood was already prominent. "Soon thereafter, the full impact of the great migration transformed American Catholicism. Church membership became overwhelmingly Irish in composition, and Irish-Americans assumed some of the most distinguished places in the hierarchy in the United States. By the middle of the nineteenth century Catholicism in this country showed a pronounced Hibernian cast." [9]

What happened after that is well-known history. The important point here is that we have basically an ethnic problem rather than a religious problem. The development of the American Catholic church, and the absorption of immigrants into it through the Americanization process, was halted for decades by the sheer weight of numbers. The

7. C. J. Nuesse, "Social Thought among American Catholics in the Colonial Period," *The American Catholic Sociological Review*, VII (March, 1946), 43-52.

8. Oscar Handlin, *The Uprooted* (Boston: Little, Brown, 1952), p. 130. See his whole chap. 5, "Religion as a Way of Life."

9. *Ibid.*, pp. 131-132; see also Carl Wittke, *The Irish in America* (Baton Rouge: Louisiana State University Press, 1956), chap. 9, "The Irish and the Catholic Church."

Germans, Italians and Poles, like the Irish, were trying to transpose
to America the main features of their own native village Catholicism.
It was an impossible task that caused deep rifts within the Church,
and even defections from the Church, and it was not settled with the
temporary system of national parishes. The opposition that arose outside the Church is significantly termed the "nativist" movement; it was
anti-immigrant and anti-ethnic, rather than merely anti-religious.

In the beginning of his new book on Americanism, Father McAvoy
remarks that "to find a common denominator for this variegated
American Catholicism in the 1880's, outside of the essential dogmatic
and sacramental principles, is very difficult. . . . The government of
the American Catholics had been taken over almost completely by
the English-speaking Irish clergy, with a minority of German, French,
and other non-English bishops. If these Irish are considered as foreign in culture, the historian must see that to the American Protestants
of English descent Catholicism was a foreign organization of many
parts, and that, for the European ecclesiastical observer, to speak of
an American Catholicism was a misnomer. To complicate matters
further, the Irish clergymen insisted that they were fully American." [10]

It would be naive to suggest that the antagonism against the
Church in America was less anti-Catholic because it was primarily
anti-immigrant. Obviously the so-called "Protestant Crusade" attacked
Catholics and their Church, and it flared out in the nativist movement, in the American Protective Association, in the Al Smith campaign and the Ku Klux Klan,[11] but all of this was filtered through
the un-American and anti-ethnic strainer. Along this line, it appears
significant that the first Blanshard book against the Church in America
was followed up by an attack against the Catholic Church in Ireland.[12]
Preoccupation with the "foreign" aspect of American Catholics has
become so entangled with the religious aspect of Catholicism that they

10. Thomas T. McAvoy, *The Great Crisis in American Catholic History*
(Chicago: Regnery, 1957), p. 3. See the whole of chap. 1, "The Catholic Minority." For earlier and later periods see his "The Catholic Minority in the
United States, 1789-1821," *Historical Records and Studies of the U. S. Catholic
Historical Society*, XXXIX-XL (1952), 33-50; and "Bishop John Lancaster Spalding and the Catholic Minority, 1877-1908," *Review of Politics*, XII,
3-19.

11. See Ray Billington, *The Protestant Crusade* (New York: Macmillan,
1952, also H. J. Desmond, *The A. P. A. Movement: A Sketch* (Washington,
1912).

12. Paul Blanshard, *American Freedom and Catholic Power* (Boston: Beacon Press, 1949); also *The Irish and Catholic Power* (1953).

are hard to unravel. At last, however, it appears that contemporary objections to Catholicism by American intellectuals (as someone said, "anti-Catholicism is the anti-Semitism of the liberal") are moving out of the anti-immigrant focus.

ARE CATHOLICS STILL A MINORITY?

This change of focus has been noted in numerous recent studies. Marden remarks that "to any extent to which the Irish are now, or may be in the future, a minority, it will be as Catholics and not as Irish." [13] Warner and Srole found that in Yankee City, "The Irish group is now differentiated according to position in the city's class system. The growing identification with class level and the usual manifestations of extreme class distance have served to break up the Irish group's inner cohesion." [14] Terms like Codfish aristocracy, lace-curtain Irish, and shanty Irish, served to demonstrate these distinctions. Rose went so far as to say that Americanization of Catholics had reached the point in the 1930's "that it was questionable whether Catholics could any longer be called a minority group." [15]

The change of attention and emphasis from immigrant status to religious status has been accompanied by a changed attitude toward cultural assimilation. The so-called Americanization movement developed during, and as an aftermath of, the first World War. This was called "imposed acculturation" by Bogardus, who remarks that "in many places it took the form of trying hurriedly to make over Germans and other immigrants into 'Americans.' Immigrant languages and even music were suppressed. Some people assumed that culture was like a coat that could be easily taken off and easily replaced by another one of a different style." [16]

World War II was followed by a de-emphasis on Americanization and an emphasis on cultural pluralism. This concept "assumes that no one culture contains all favorable elements, but that each group that makes up the total American population has unique values, and

13. Charles E. Marden, *Minorities in American Society* (New York: American Book, 1952), p. 388.

14. W. Lloyd Warner and Leo Srole, *The Social Systems of American Ethnic Groups* (New Haven: Yale University Press, 1945), p. 93.

15. Arnold and Caroline Rose, *America Divided* (New York: Knopf, 1948), p. 324. The authors at that time expected the development of new forms of anti-Catholicism.

16. Emory S. Bogardus, "Cultural Pluralism and Acculturation," *Sociology and Social Research*, XXXIV (November-December, 1949), 125-129.

that the nation will be richer and finer in its cultural make-up if it, the country, conserves the best that each group has brought." [17] This explanation is applied quite narrowly to the ethnic groups at a time when these groups have lost their identity and have already largely Americanized their values and patterns. We shall come back later to the question whether cultural pluralism is broad enough to include different religious ideologies.

Whatever we say of Catholicism, as practiced in America today, must be understood in terms of the American culture, which discourages many aspects of "ethnic-group" survival, but which permits religious differentiation. When we talk about the survival and identity of the Catholic population as a social phenomenon, we must emphasize its religious meaning rather than its immigrant status. On the other hand, we do not mean to suggest that the change in immigrant status and the fading out of ethnic differences have so molded Catholics with other Americans that they are hardly distinguishable. It is Herberg's argument that the three religions of America are standing out in sharper relief and that the triple melting pot is replacing the simple older notion of monophasic Americanization.[18]

But this conclusion by no means settles the question of the Americanization of Catholicism. If religion is as important a cultural factor as T. S. Eliot and Ortega y Gasset, and even Toynbee,[19] claim it is, then religion may have an alienating effect upon Catholics that prevents or slows down their Americanization. The question then is whether Catholicism itself is such an alien phenomenon that it clearly distinguishes its adherents from other Americans.

MULTIPLE CATHOLIC MINORITIES

It is a commonplace in sociology that size and solidarity, as well as the culture patterns of a minority group tend to slow down the process of assimilation. If the minority group is large, isolated, and

17. E. George Payne, "Education and Cultural Pluralism," in Brown and Roucek, *Our Racial and National Minorities* (New York: Prentice-Hall, 1937), p. 762. Bogardus gives the concept of cultural pluralism the "nice" name of democratic acculturation.

18. Will Herberg, *Protestant, Catholic, Jew* (New York: Doubleday, 1955), pp. 45-47 *et passim;* also Ruby Jo Kennedy, "Single or Triple Melting Pot?" *American Journal of Sociology,* XLIX, no. 4 (January, 1944).

19. T. S. Eliot, *The Idea of a Christian Society;* Ortega y Gasset, *Concord and Liberty;* Robert C. Angell, *Democracy and Moral Integration,* chap. 2, says that the economic ideology of Marxism has been able to "bring together" people as diverse as the Russians and the Chinese.

solidaristic, its cultural patterns tend to be attributed to the group. But if the minority members mingle freely with out-group members, the individuals tend to conform to majority standards, so that any difference is a personal rather than a group problem. The size of the minority tempers the effect of the dominant culture on any member of the minority.

Unfortunately we have no "pure type" of large Catholic minority in the United States to demonstrate this proposition. The Mexican Catholics of the Southwest and the Irish Catholics of the Northeast have carried ethnic overtones so that in these cases we must talk about the Americanization of the Mexicans and Irish, rather than Americanization of Catholics. The small minority of Catholics in some of the Southeastern States, serves as a better example of this principle. Here we find the scattered Catholics almost totally assimilated to the dominant regional culture on all scores except religion. This regional sub-culture is itself, however, in the process of being Americanized.

The thesis is perhaps best demonstrated among Midwestern Catholics. In this area there has never been a predominantly hyphenated Catholicism. None of the Catholic immigrant groups, Poles, Italians, Germans, Irish, has been large enough or solidaristic enough, to put a peculiar foreign stamp on Catholicism. All of them together have not formed a large and isolated minority that prevented mingling with the dominant non-Catholic majority. Here is an interesting case study in cultural assimilation. Traces of immigrant culture still survive, but their effects tend to be cancelled out as the people of different ethnic strains mingle within the Church, and all of them mingle more and more with non-Catholics. The result is that Midwestern Catholicism has achieved a degree of American maturity not yet approached by Catholics in other parts of the country.

Now we already have a complicated formula for the analysis of Americanization of Catholics. The formula has the following ingredients: the size of the minority, the degree of internal solidarity it exhibits to the dominant majority, and the region of the country in which it exists. There are other ingredients which we shall not consider, like the type of leadership provided by the hierarchy and the way in which the Catholic press interprets Catholicism to other Americans.

THE RANGE OF CATHOLIC VALUES

Let us now assemble the crucial evidence with which we can roughly describe an American Catholicism distinguishable from the

Catholicism of other countries. What kinds of behavior patterns and social relations have been adopted by Catholics largely as a result of their being Americans? Some are quite obvious. Evening devotions, novenas, vespers — customs that were well-fitted for quiet village life, have largely disappeared because they do not fit into the urban family life of Catholics. Practical routines, many of which are measurable, like Mass attendance, reception of Holy Communion, first Friday and first Saturday devotions, are on the increase. They appear to reflect the pragmatic American mentality. The growth of the Christian Family Movement indicates a double adaptation to American culture; it provides one of the few ways in which the layman's voice can be heard, and it fits in quite neatly with the vigorous, general and contemporary American interest in marriage, family, husband-wife relations, and the raising of children.

These few examples are indicative of the involvement of Catholics in American values and behavior patterns, and they may serve as a springboard for a more detailed examination of this adaptation. For purposes of demonstration, we may look at these values on three levels.

A. First, Catholics are participating in at least the externals of the general religious revival now occurring in the United States. At this level we are talking about the popular type of religious behavior that neither irritates non-Catholics, nor isolates the Catholic from the non-Catholic. You are not less American for attending Church every week — in fact, you are urged to do so from roadside billboards, through radio and TV messages. Nobody calls you a foreigner if you have your child baptized and confirmed, and if you receive Communion frequently. These are "good" kinds of behavior; these are the things that respectable people do, each in his own way, and worthy of praise by all good Americans.

Whether or not these practices involve the highest values of Catholics, they certainly involve the values about which Catholics have the greatest certitude and in which non-Catholics have the least interest. They are for the most part the product of rote behavior instilled in childhood. In minor ways they indicate an adaptation to American customs, like the efficiency of getting cars parked and unparked on a Sunday morning, and a Mass celebrated within the space of one hour. The fact that men attend religious services in comparatively large numbers, that Saturday morning is the preferred time for nuptial Masses, and that few people attend funeral Masses or accompany the corpse to the cemetery — these are all forms of adaptation to the exigencies of the American cultural system.

B. At a second level we find certain Catholic values and practices in a state of ambivalence. Here the expectations of the general American culture and the behavior patterns of many non-Catholics are at odds with those of Catholics. The laws of the Church concerning mixed marriage, birth prevention, attendance at Catholic schools, and others, tend to meet head-on the ways of thinking and acting that have developed in our urban, secular, industrial society. The sporadic attempts of the clergy to exert censorship of books and movies among Catholics have sometimes spilled over into the general community. In all of these examples we move out of the circle of those behavior patterns in which "religion is just a private affair."

Here we have cultural conflict, a clash of values, in the minds of Catholics themselves. Here also we have objections from some non-Catholics who feel that their own values and their own way of life are under criticism. The problem for the American Catholic at this level is that he is being pulled in opposite directions; hence the ambivalence. Freedom of individual decision is challenged in the very area where large-scale changes have been taking place in traditional moral and social practices. The impact of the American culture on Catholic values has been greatest here precisely because the old ethnic groups have lost their identity and have been absorbed into the American population.

C. There is, however, a still more confused and unsettled level of cultural change. This is in the area of broad social problems where the Church's teachings have not been spelled out in specific regulations of conduct, where Churchmen are themselves often at odds, and where the American people are disunited. Problems of urban redevelopment, slum clearance, law enforcement, race relations, political parties, management and workers, and similar problems, find the American society divided both in interpretation of values and in approaches to solutions. Here we have the well-known conflict of values about which Myrdal talks.

REGIONAL SUB-CULTURES

Interestingly enough, it is at this level that the pluralism of the American culture is most clearly exemplified, and it is at this level that another factor, besides ethnic and religious adherence, contributes to the confusion. This is the factor of regionalism. We have here what industrial management calls "area practices." In the past, large manufacturers have moved out of so-called "high cost areas," mainly places where labor organizations had won effective demands, to those areas where docile, unorganized workers were available. The wage differential is only one of the practices that have been adapted to the local regional patterns.

As far as Catholics are concerned with these moral and social problems we must probably say that Americanization has been mainly a regional adaptation. The most striking example of this adaptation is found in the Southeastern States where Catholics, including most of the clergy, follow the "area practices" concerning race relations, labor relations, and "States' rights." This identification with local values and mores goes back historically to the slavery question and to the earlier version of states' rights, when the Catholic stand was based not on religion or on ethnic status, but on the regional sub-culture.[20]

The demonstration of this regional influence is so obvious that it hardly need be extended. Catholics share in the anti-Semitism of the Northeast, in the isolationism of the Midwest, in the prejudices against Mexicans in the Southwest. Catholics acted like Californians when the Japanese-Americans were dispossessed and sent to relocation camps, like Texans when the off-shore oil disputes were discussed, and like Ciceronians when Negro families moved into white neighborhoods in Illinois. On this level we are dealing with the moral and social problems on which the American people are confused, and on which Catholics demonstrate their achieved Americanization by sharing in the confusion.

Besides regionalism, one other important factor of adaptation ought to be noted here, the factor of social status. We have said that the degree of Americanization by Catholics cannot be adequately measured by the extent to which Catholics have been distributed throughout the class structure. Nevertheless, it can be said that adaptation can be measured by the extent to which American Catholics share the values and patterns of people in the particular social class to which they belong. As a matter of fact, it is in the physical, geographical region, but especially in the social class, where a person finds himself that this value-sharing is most discernible. Upwardly mobile middle-class Catholic families tend to have the same aspirations, belong to the

20. See Madelein H. Rice, *American Catholic Opinion in the Slavery Controversy* (New York: Columbia University, 1944).

same clubs, have the same frustrations, treat their adolescent children in the same way, hold similar political and economic attitudes, as other upwardly mobile American families in the neighborhood.

We now have some soul-searching questions to ask about the Catholic religious minority and its place in the total American sociocultural system. Except for Puerto Ricans in some large cities, tensions have relaxed between the dominant native and the minority immigrant, and most of the difficulties that once existed among the immigrant groups themselves (especially within the Church) have also subsided. Since ours is a competitive, dynamic culture, does this mean that energy has been released in order to sharpen other cleavages, like that among the major religious bodies, or between the descendants of former ethnics who are now in the middle class and the native Anglo-Saxon descendants who are moving from rural to urban areas, or between urban whites and recently migrated Negroes?

THE NEED FOR GROUP IDENTITY

Since religious differences are permitted, and even encouraged in the United States, can we say that from now on religion will answer the need for group awareness and group adherence that was once supplied by the ethnic groups? Perhaps, the new super-nationalism of the American Way of Life will now provide the "common core of values" and, subsidiary to this, perhaps people will now become loyal to religious values in a way that they used to be loyal to their ethnic values. This may be a partial explanation of the so-called religious revival of our day. Thus it may be that we will develop a strengthened religious pluralism since in almost every other area of urban American life there appears to be a drive for conformity and standardization.

Results of scientific research among groups indicate that there is a deep and authentic need for identification, especially group identification, among modern urban people. The conditions of existence in Riesman's "lonely crowd" may be intolerable over the long run and may sharpen the need for belonging to an established group. The psychological impetus coming from a society in which we seek to "escape from freedom," in Fromm's terminology, and in which we see the evidences of Horney's "neurotic personality" may force us to reach out for a traditional system of values. From this point of view the American religious bodies may be in the process of fulfilling a significant social function.

But let us not exaggerate this potential function as though it were only the ethnic group or only the religious group that can satisfy this personal need for roots and stability. William Whyte tends to sneer a bit at "belongingness" and "togetherness" in modern society, but he also shows the complete dedication and loyalty of the Organization Man to a group that is neither ethnic nor religious.[21] These exaggerations may lead us to overlook the basic reality of our urban secular society: the fact that we live in a multiphasic society with a pluralistic culture. Even the progressional religious functionary has allegiance to groups other than the Church.

Here we have a crucial insight into both the Americanization of Catholicism and the pluralism of the American system. Roughly stated, this insight embraces two propositions. First, cultural pluralism means for the total *society* that there exist numerous different religious, economic, familial, recreational, educational and other institutions. Within each of these there are wide variations and diversities. Second, cultural pluralism means for the *individual* that he enacts institutionalized roles in each of the groups to which he belongs — family, church, business, and so forth. Thus, whether a man is a factory manager or a factory worker, he enacts multiple roles besides his economic or occupational role. Whether a man is a Methodist, or a Catholic, or a Jew, he must be pluralistic in his role-taking in the various groups to which he belongs.

We have heard a great deal about dual allegiance in special contexts, for example, that a man can be loyal to both his union and his company, that a man can be loyal to both his church and his country. It has been pointed out that this is not divided allegiance, but dual and simultaneous allegiance, and it ought to be pointed out that this is only a segment of the individual's adherence to groups. The fact is that any normal urban American has multiple allegiances, or pluralistic loyalties. The inconsistencies of the systems to which he belongs may well affect his social personality, but at the same time it is possible to integrate his personality around an over-all system of values.

UNITY IN DIVERSITY

The whole question of the Americanization of Catholicism, or of the adaptation of Catholicism to a pluralistic sociocultural system,

21. William H. Whyte, Jr., *The Organization Man* (New York: Simon and Schuster, 1956), chaps. 4 and 5. See also chap. 27, where he shows that "The Church of Suburbia" is likewise answering the need for community among the "transients."

hinges around the problem of "unity-in-diversity." One sociologist declared that "the fundamental problem of society is the determination of the manner in which various interests and vitalities in human existence are to be integrated and related to one another and to the whole of social life." [22] Another asks the central question of sociology: "How do complex, urban societies manage to exist as healthy systems; how do they establish and maintain a sufficient level of integration and consensus to maintain order and carry through the necessary accommodations among their heterogeneous people?" [23]

This is a vital question for American Catholics, and the one on which I must conclude this paper. The classic and basic works in the sociology of religion in Western society usually see religion as the answer to the central problem of cultural unity and pluralism.[24] One may deny this, and hold that a political value like democracy, an economic value like capitalism, or a broad philosophy like Soviet socialism, must be the principal integrating factor of Western society. One may even hold that what Durkheim called the "organic solidarity" of highly diverse society will occur because the very inter-dependence of the parts will develop co-operation within the whole.

But if we accept the notion that the sociocultural system is integrated by the highest values held by the people, and that these highest values are contained in religion, then we have a distinctly American problem of religious pluralism. American Catholics seem to accept the notion, "pluralism in everything except religion." American Protestants seem to say "pluralism in everything including religion." A free society like ours resists authoritarian coercion to a basic, integrating, and overarching value system such as the Catholic Church claims to possess. We are now at a point in history when this conflict of viewpoints has to be worked out, and the continued Americanization of Catholicism will depend upon the way in which the solution is attempted.

22. Kenneth W. Underwood, *Protestant and Catholic* (Boston: Beacon Press, 1957), p. 378.
23. J. Milton Yinger, "Social Forces Involved in Group Identification or Withdrawal," unpublished lecture at Arden House Conference on Group Life in America, November 9-12, 1956.
24. Emile Durkheim, *Elementary Forms of the Religious Life* (trans. J. Swain, Glencoe: Free Press, 1934), pp. 10 and 206; also Ernst Troeltsch, *The Social Teaching of the Christian Churches* (trans. V. Wyon, New York: Macmillan, 1931, I, 32, and Joachim Wach, *Sociology of Religion* (Chicago: University of Chicago Press, 1944), pp. 34-35.

Part II

IMMIGRATION AND AMERICAN CATHOLICISM

Thomas T. McAvoy, c.s.c.

Introductory Essay

There is perhaps no element in the culture of the American immigrant about which he has been more sensitive than his religious belief. The importance of this religious sensitivity is perpetuated because in America this religious faith is the one point on which the immigrant cannot be disturbed. There have, of course, been many immigrants who have come to this country in a spirit of rebellion against a religion which had been imposed on them by force in the countries of their origin, but in a sense that rebellion too is an element of religion. Strangely the cause of this religious sensitiveness lies in the almost universal rule that prior to modern times religion was considered a part of government in the sense of a part of the national faith. A religion was maintained if not imposed as part of the public life of most countries from which the American immigrants came. The fact that the United States, while in practice a religious nation, maintained no religion as part of the national life was the most important factor in any discussion of the relation between religion and the immigrant in this country. The second factor in any discussion of the religious life of the immigrant, one which is very much forgotten, is that for practical purposes all the present residents of the United States, except the American Indians, are immigrants either in their own persons or in those of their ancestors, one or several generations back.

Of these two factors governing the religious life of the immigrant, freedom from religious oppression is perhaps the most fundamental in American life, because it is freedom, whether political, religious, social, or economic, that has been the greatest boon offered to the immigrant, at least since the formation of the Constitution. But outside of the Fourth of July orations and occasional appeals in court to the Constitution in individual cases, no one regards this American freedom as anything remarkable. It is true that many Americans get excited when this freedom seems to give unpredicted liberties to some who abuse it, but there is no serious desire by intelligent persons to take away religious freedom.

The second factor in the discussion, the fact that our families are all immigrants, is forgotten more than it is remembered. I suppose that in all human history, any family or group of families that has lived in a region for a while begins to think that the region belongs to them and tries to defend their rights to it in the manner of the family dog defending the campsite on a camping trip. There is no rule that decides when an immigrant ceases to be an immigrant and becomes a native. This may seem unreasonable, since legally these terms are well defined, but socially we speak of immigrants by their place of foreign origin, sometimes after many generations in this country. Sometimes there is a question of language involved, but some of the immigrants dropped their foreign language almost on the moment of arrival but were not thereby accepted as natives. Sometimes there was a question of color and that factor has been the hardest for the white people to overlook, even though the whites were not the first people in the region of the present United States. Certainly the religious faith has been an important factor in differentiating the immigrant from the native, even though, according to existing American laws, such a distinction should be dropped immediately.

It is perhaps well to review some of these points in more detail. A study in full detail of this question would require many volumes, but some elements of the picture must be emphasized before the observer can understand how immigration can be involved in the adaptation of any religious group to a new country. The first point that I would like to emphasize is that, strictly speaking, the fact of immigration cannot be rightly considered a culturally lowering factor because only the native redmen are really natives as far back as we have records. This may seem a contentious statement and perhaps it is, but this fact is important in placing in perspective some of the worst evils of the agitation against immigrants that has appeared at times in the history of the United States. This fact that Americans are nearly all immigrants is also very important because the Constitution does not recognize any form of ancestry, race, or religion as essential for citizenship in the United States. On the question of religion Peter Drucker has emphasized that this does not in any way militate against the fact that the United States is a religious nation, presupposes that its citizens will be religious, and asks God's blessing on all its enterprises. So also there is nothing in the Constitution that says that the citizens of the United States shall be of any race, or of any national ancestry, or possessed of any certain amount of wealth, although it is taken for granted that these citizens of the United States will not only have religious beliefs, but also will have race, social status, and some possessions.

Historically, however, everyone recognizes that the people of the United States whose representatives wrote and approved the Constitution of the United States were real people, mostly of English descent who had been in these regions for at least a generation. The Constitution and the government were not drawn up to take care of an idealized or imaginary people but the real people of the United States. Thus, the first natives — exclusive of the redmen — were for the most part English-speaking, derived mostly from Great Britain, accustomed to English law, to the English language, and to English cultural and political traditions. They certainly did not intend to readopt all these English laws and traditions, and to make clear what they did accept they began to appeal almost from the start to that statement of their rights in the Constitution of the United States and the constitutions of the individual states. This is very important because at times certain lawyers and legal advisers have tried to find in these constitutions guarantees of privileges of race, religion, social distinctions, and economic privileges which are not there. No matter how close the American nation seems to its English ancestor, it is a separate, distinct, and different country of which the chief glory is the liberty guaranteed by law. Any discussion of the rights and privileges of the immigrant as immigrant must presuppose the constitutional freedoms although it will also be concerned with custom, prejudice, and the facts of competition for wealth and privilege which touch very closely on these legal factors but are very distinct from them.

Roman Catholics were among the earliest of these immigrants to what is now the United States. Although they were not recognized by the English law at that time, Roman Catholics did live in England and in English America during our colonial period and were recognized as Englishmen. The confusion between religious and civil rights during the period of the English Reformation, broadly defined, makes it rather difficult to say what kind of Englishmen those Roman Catholics — and other dissenters from the official form of English religion — were, but I think it is quite clear that these English Catholics in Maryland in mid-seventeenth century had in no way ceased to regard themselves as Englishmen. It is very significant that at that time when the noted English Jesuit Father Robert Persons wrote his pamphlet against the migration of English Catholics to Maryland his first argument against the movement was that it would be offensive to their King, the King of England. The desire of Roman Catholics in seventeenth century England to be considered loyal Englishmen is much like the insistence of some present-day American Catholic politicians to be recognized as patriotic Americans.

It is also notable that when the bigots who had taken over the rule of Maryland enacted some very bitter discriminatory laws against Roman Catholics in 1704 and 1706 the worst of these laws were made void by the royal veto of Queen Anne. Further, when during the excitement of the French and Indian wars a double tax was proposed against Roman Catholics, the appeal of the Catholics against the tax, led by Charles Carroll of Carrollton, demanded their rights as Englishmen and as proper members of the Maryland colony according to the laws of the colony. The fact that these Americans of English descent were deprived of some of their liberties because of their Roman Catholic faith was not considered a reason for their ceasing to be Englishmen.

It is not surprising then that among the descendants of these English Catholics of colonial days and among other persons of English descent who have become Roman Catholics in later generations there has appeared at times a feeling of "belonging" that they have in common with non-Catholics of similar English ancestry. In the United States one cannot argue social rank or social prejudices in terms of rights and laws. Social distinctions arise independently of laws and are self-perpetuating because of conditions decided by the members of society — whether strictly local or more general.

These social cleavages and distinctions are very important in understanding the history of American immigration. Thus, one of the most frequent omissions in histories of immigration into the United States has been the story of the English immigrants. In the first place there is nothing in the nature of English culture or law that would make Englishmen better fitted to dominate the United States. On the other hand, no matter how much the non-English peoples are convinced of the superiority of their own language or culture, the facts of history do show that these English in the United States did prosper and that their adaptation of English law and custom was very important if not essential to the continued growth and prosperity of the

English-speaking United States. Part of the story of the continued dominance of these English traditions and language can be explained in the priority of occupation and possession of the land and in shrewd investment, but part of the story of continued English-speaking dominance that has been overlooked has been the continued immigration of other Englishmen throughout the history of the United States. Also, just as some of the Englishmen of colonial days were Roman Catholics, so some of the later English immigrants were also Roman Catholics, although the far greater portion of English-speaking Catholic immigrants to the United States have been from Ireland.

To the English Catholic, the United States offered besides the basic civic freedoms of the Constitution a greater chance for advancement than England granted them. Very few attempts have been made to trace the number and influence of these English Roman Catholic immigrants outside of a few studies of the early Maryland colony. In the later seventeenth century and subsequently, there were small groups of English Catholics who came to Maryland and later sent filial colonies to Bardstown, Kentucky; Nashville, Tennessee; Lancaster, Ohio; Washington, Indiana; and families in other scattered Catholic settlements of the Midwest frontier. Together with the converts of English descent during the nineteenth century these Catholic English immigrants have played an important part in helping the non-English Catholic immigrants to reconcile their religious beliefs with the traditions of a country which was dominantly non-Catholic and whose cultural and political traditions were considered to be Protestant as well as English.

It is comparatively easy today for intelligent persons to say that the confusion of traditions of religion or race with law is ridiculous, but we still have had serious manifestations of this confusion in the twentieth century. But in the first part of the nineteenth century to expect even the full-fledged citizen of the United States to separate civic and national traits from religion would be asking the ordinary American citizen of that day to give up his religion. Despite the falling off of church membership in the United States during the early decades of the nineteenth century, adhering to some form of traditional religion was considered a part of good citizenship. As a matter of fact, the role that some non-English religious leaders took in preventing the Americanization of some of their followers is understandable as action prompted by their fear that Americanization would mean the loss of their religious faith. When colonial Maryland and Pennsylvania, dur-

ing the French and Indian wars, passed laws against the importation
of Irish servants, they were prompted by a fear that these Irish, because they were Catholic, might be traitors and undermine the religious traditions of the colony. Even among the Catholic leaders of
Maryland there was some resistance shown during the second and
third decades of the nineteenth century to the increase of Irish clergymen, because the English and French *emigré* clergymen who were
ministering to them felt that these Irish were lowering the social status
of the Anglo-American Catholics among their English-speaking brethren.

Although some Irish immigrants spoke Gaelic, most of them spoke
the English language and it would probably have been difficult to distinguish the lower class Irishmen from the lower class Englishman or
Scotchman. But in the religious battles of the seventeenth and eighteenth centuries in the English-speaking world English had become
generally equivalent to Protestant and Irish to Roman Catholic. The
Frenchman was generally presumed to be Catholic but after the French
Revolution the practicalness of the Catholicism of the Frenchman had
to be determined individually. So also the religion of the German was
determined mostly by the region from which he and his family took
their departure from Europe. The Italians, the Spanish, and the Austrians were generally presumed to be Roman Catholic. There was very
little reasoning in this confusion of religion and nationality. One might
even go further and say that at a time when religious instruction was
the rare thing the fidelity to religion was too much a matter of patriotism and social consolation. The suggestion occasionally made by
recent historians of immigration that the religious faith was created
by the peasants to enlighten the darkness of their peasantry is a confusion of cause and effect, because it was the faith in the spiritual purpose of man and his eternal destiny that had kept alive hope for a
future amidst man's inhumanity to man. It was natural for the peasant to cling to those religious teachings that had become associated
with the highest aspirations of the downtrodden. It is not remarkable
that when these peasants achieved a better status in the free United
States that their religious institutions prospered with them. It is not
really an accident that church attendance in the United States has
achieved its highest figures in the twentieth century when these poorer
immigrants have likewise achieved their highest economic and social
progress. The complication in this development arises in the adaptation of their earlier beliefs, sometimes encrusted with ignorance and

prejudice, to their new prosperous status. It is in this sense that the problem of the immigrant has been one of the chief problems of religion in the first half of the twentieth century in the United States.

There are a few other general observations which need to be made on this problem. The first and the hardest theory of American freedom to accept is the social equality of all persons no matter what their religious belief, or their race, or their national origin. This equality has never meant that all persons will attain equal social status, but simply that the inequality of social status, if just, must be based upon some other factor than race, religion, or national origin. A businessman likes to talk to businessmen, a scholar to scholars, a sportsman to sportsmen, and a man of one religious persuasion will tend to speak intimately with those who understand his faith, but in all this any supposition that there is an essential social difference between groups of American citizens can only cause dissension and injustice.

A second and harmful notion that has been at times quite common in this country claims that these religious affiliations must manifest themselves in business, in politics, and in other public affairs. No one will deny the desire and even the duty at times of religious leaders to help their followers within legal limits to attain business and social advancements. Sometimes even intellectual advancements are confused with religious leadership and produce unsound and unjust discriminations. There is an old scholastic principle that goodness tends to spread itself and certainly religious goodness tends to do well for all who accept it, but when religious or cultural goods are used to hinder others, or are used as a barrier to prevent the advancement or progress of others then they have ceased to be religious and are more properly called by some secular or even evil name.

Finally in this question of immigrants and religion there is the inherited prejudice of nationality. During much of the nineteenth century many European writers scorned the so-called American nationality regarding it as at best a hybrid. But today that nationality is generally recognized if not always loved throughout the world. Americans generally resent being called material-minded, imperialistic, capitalistic even. As a result Americans should understand better the ridiculous character of the nationalism that dominated much international friction in the first half of the twentieth century. At least our experience in dealing with unfriendly critics abroad should help Americans to cast aside any notions of national superiority based on the country of their ancestors. It is time that Americans realize that very few of these distinctions of language and tradition have anything to do with the mind or the spiritual destiny of man. Names, for instance, in the United States are not a sure guide to nationality, not only because so many of them have been modified for practical purposes, but because they can represent as low as one thirty-second of the ancestry of the bearer. Even when the ancestry of a citizen is purely of one nationality his achievements or failures would usually have been the same had the name or the country of his origin been different.

The question, then, arises about the value of the study of immigrants and the relation between this immigration and religion. The answer of history is to accept the facts and movements of the past as they happened, not as they might or should have happened. The alliance between religion and nationality, between race and religion, and between cultures and religion, have at times been of great importance in good and bad developments in nation and race. The alliance of religion and the hope for freedom in Ireland is a good example of this mutual exchange between religion and tradition. It has likewise been said that the Reformation in France and in Spain took its course according to the faith of the common people. In all these generalizations it is important to distinguish what is religion from what is not, to understand where religious faith has been the strength of the struggling poor or an excuse for domination. And when immigrants have come to the United States, history has the task of disentangling religious activity that is purely social and political from real religion, and of distinguishing where a group were good citizens because of their religion and when they disgraced their religion by using it as an excuse for rebellion or sloth. We are aware today that the old lines of nationality, race, and culture are beginning to disappear. Undoubtedly new lines and barriers are appearing despite the new means of communication. It is important to learn what were the good and the bad barriers of the past and the wrongly built barriers of the present. If a better understanding can be reached about the distinction between religion and nation, there will be some hope that there will be fewer barriers between man and man in the future. Above all it is worthwhile to understand the difference between the highest of national cultures and the religious faith which teaches not merely the national dignity of mankind but his supernatural nature and destiny.

It was possible in the time allotted for the symposium in which most of these papers were read, or in this small volume to include only a few preliminary glances into the problem of immigration and Roman

Catholicism in the American Way of Life. It is a sad fact also that there have not been any serious studies of many immigrant Catholic groups. Furthermore, some of these papers were requested of men who were busy about the practical and important tasks that leave little time for study. This must be borne in mind in weighing the suggestions they have made about the major problem of the Catholic minority in the United States. Dr. DeSantis has, indeed, given us a good introduction into the work that remains to be done. It has been said repeatedly that the third generation of American immigrant peoples is beginning to appreciate the languages and the traditions of their ancestors — and this is generally recognized as a good trend. Many of these third generation immigrants also need a revival of their grandparents' religious faith, a faith, however, that must be intelligently understood. The study of these other languages and other histories promises a cultural good, and it should offer to these young Americans the conclusion that religion is above nationality, above race, above the worship of man himself.

The Immigrant and the City

SAUL D. ALINSKY*

I. The Urban Immigrant

Our explosive atomic mushrooming into a world of new dimensions of time, of distance, communication and power, has come so suddenly that we are caught not just with one foot, but with our head, in the old world; an old world which we knew as recently as a decade ago. Confronted with a bewildering kaleidoscope of a new world in creation, we dimly see the undeniable truth of the living present, but cling to the solid, comfortable, familiar image of the world in which we grew up; the past, the dead past. We exist in the present, but think, act, decide, in fact live, in terms of the past. In truth atomic fission has been accompanied by mental fission. This schizophrenic malady besets many of the leaders of our major institutions, and even the nation, to the point of becoming the prime dilemma of our times. This is our point of departure for our discussion, and we shall return from time to time to this fundamental issue.

The issue of this symposium divides itself into two parts. First the people, the immigrants or newcomers and their needs. Second the community, which is entered by the newcomer or immigrant. Here specific questions arise such as "What can the community and its institutions do for them?" And conversely, "What are the newcomers doing to the community?"

In the past there was the world we knew approximately thirty-five years ago; the world of unrestricted immigration when the United States was traditionally the haven for refugees from persecution, poverty, or both. Many of the major forms of this world of 1924 persisted, at least outwardly, until the past decade. Up to that time our

* Mr. Alinsky is Executive Director of the Industrial Areas Foundation, Chicago, and author of *Reveille for Radicals* and *John L. Lewis, a Biography*.

major cities possessed large national and religious communities which were literally European cultural islands transported and grafted onto the body of the American cities. Here the new immigrants could feel relatively comfortable in a community of familiar language, religion, foods, and neighbors of similar background. Of equal, if not more importance, was the fact that the new immigrants could only afford to live in these low income areas. These national neighborhoods served a significant function in providing a harbor, both economic and cultural, from which the newcomers could occasionally sally forth into the strange, American seas about them. After the immigrants and their children had germinated for some time in this cultural cocoon, absorbing American information and attitudes in their minds and American money in their pockets, they would emerge and take wing into the non-national American society.

These were neighborhoods of change, gradual, slow and easy change, as new migrating national groups replaced the old. A good deal of the talk of today about many of the "stable neighborhoods of the past" involves these national communities. Their doom was sealed with the ending of immigration in 1924. The cutting off of their very life stream clearly signalled the end. It could be reasonably anticipated that these communities would last for another generation, allowing that time for the last arrivals to work and to save their way out into the American scene. This slow death time period was, however, extended by powerful forces which slowed the expected population movement from these communities. The economic depression of the 1930's, followed by the second World War with its acute housing shortage, compelled many to remain.

One last word about these kinds of stable neighborhoods before we begin to discuss the present. Within those small, restricted worlds lived a people by and large temporarily immobilized by fear and suspicion of a strange land; a people subjected to discrimination and exploitation; a people struggling to learn a new language, new customs and new ways of life, and finding most of their reassurance from the security of their national churches, their national this and their national that. Over all hung the spectre of firetraps for homes, dirt, disease, dependency, delinquency and a consequent considerable demoralization. Not a pretty picture of this sort of "stable neighborhood," but when we mourn its disappearance let us at least know whose wake we are attending. Unfortunately memories, like whiskey, mellow with the passing of time, and unpleasant as it is we had bet-

ter sober up and remember these "stable neighborhoods" of that kind
for what they were.

Let us critically examine some of the high points of the past issue
of immigration so that we may have a basis of comparison and a
better understanding of the present problem and its implications.

(1) The urban immigrants of the past have been from all of
the European countries, including the British Isles. At different times
there were heavy concentrations from different nations.

(2) They came to this country at great cost and self-sacrifice, traveling long distances, involving, in many cases, weeks en route.

(3) With few exceptions they were impoverished upon arrival.

(4) None of them were citizens of the United States, and all were
concerned with the various restrictions and penalties involving non-
citizens.

(5) They settled in the low income national communities which
were waiting for them. There was no question about their intrusion
into the general over-all urban scene, as limited by lack of money,
knowledge of language, differences in customs and general fear of this
strange world, they fled to the safe havens of national neighborhoods.

(6) The great bulk of them were unskilled laborers who had been
solicited by American mass industries seeking a supply of cheap, unskilled labor. In many cases these national communities developed
around these particular large industries such as the meat packing industry of Chicago and the steel and coal mining industries in Pennsylvania, Indiana, Ohio, and West Virginia. The location of these
slum national neighborhoods next door to these industries was also
a very desirable element for the immigrant, as he could avoid the
difficulty, confusion and expense of transportation from his home to
his job. Transportation being what it was then resulted in a definite
relationship between place of residence and place of work.

(7) The physical housing of these communities varied from cheap
frame shacks to slum tenements usually owned by outside interests. As
the immigration trends would shift, and people from another national
background would very gradually begin to come into the community,
there might be and in a number of cases were, certain tensions and
conflicts. But the changes were gradual, with no sudden change in
real estate values in either the sale of the houses by the old to the
new or of the income to tenement owners.

(8) A preponderant number of immigrants, particularly from
Slavic nations, were Catholic in religious faith, and the role of the

Roman Catholic Church was that of being a central anchor of security to these immigrants. It was the one familiar part of their life and experience which was the same here as it had been in their native home. In the national churches even their priests spoke their language and practiced the old world customs and traditions. And so to a significant extent the Catholic Church was not only the spiritual fountainhead for the new immigrant, but the place where he went for advice and guidance in all other areas of his life, ranging from his social problems to his political activities. The character of transportation and communication, with the then prevailing propinquity between job and home, resulted in the immigrant spending most of his time in his neighborhood.

This was the situation of the past, and this was primarily the way the problem was met in the past. The issue at that time was not the impact of the immigrant upon the existing community, because the immigrant had his own communities, but simply what could be done to help him, the immigrant, the newcomer.

*   *   *

Now let us turn to the present, the world we live in today. We know that now there has been very little immigration from the European nations, and that when we talk about the newcomers of today and the foreseeable future for the next decade or longer, we are primarily concerned about the major internal population shifts of American citizens from one part of the United States and its Commonwealth to other parts; the mass migration of Negroes from our southern States to our northern cities; the migration of southern rural whites commonly referred to as "hillbillies" to northern cities; the mass movement of Puerto Ricans from the island Commonwealth to the continental mainland, and to a lesser degree the eastward movement of Americans of Mexican ancestry. These vast, internal population shifts constitute today's issue of the newcomer, or of migration and the urban community.

Let us clearly note the differences between these groups and those which preceded them in the past.

The urban newcomers of today, and in a significant sense "immigrants" to an urban culture, are all American citizens. With minor exceptions their distance from home base is a matter of a few hours by air, twenty-four hours by automobile, or overnight by train. Excepting the newly arrived Puerto Ricans they speak English as their native language. They have come north in their search for better living opportunities. They are generally unskilled and of limited formal educational background. With the exception of New York City, where the Puerto Rican migration has been extraordinary in numbers, the major urban newcomers are the Negroes and the southern whites, or the so-called "hillbillies." The great majority of these groups are Protestant in religious faith. They come to a city far different from the urban scene which greeted the immigrants of the past. They arrive in a time of tremendous advances in transportation and communication. In transportation it has meant the breaking of another vital link to the chain binding together the so-called stable community; no longer is it essential, or even desirable, to live adjacent to your place of employment; no longer do we find a significant relationship between the place of physical residence and the place of employment. Developments in both transportation and communications have meant the enormous extension of the horizon of interests as over against the past, when not only the newcomer but the native citizen lived a life which had been relatively circumscribed within their local physical community.

Out of the situation of today is coming a new kind of people; a people who are being exposed to and accepting new areas of interest; new allegiances; new places to look for with reference to counsel and guidance in different areas; a trend towards looking for advice from specialists in specialized fields, and the acceptance of multiple memberships so that no longer does any one institution, whether it be organized labor or organized capital or organized religion, carry the power, the influence or the authority over more than its one particular area of interest and activities.

Every institution in the community now finds itself beset with other interest agencies competing for the attention, and in many cases certain loyalties, of the individual. No single institution today, as has been previously mentioned, whether religious, economic or social, has as many ties to the individual in as many different facets of his life, as they possessed in the past. Specifically, there were the old days when men looked to and accepted the authority and direction of their labor unions in other fields than the direct, specific area — and the same applied to their churches; but those were the old days. These are new people, with multiple minor loyalties to multiple smaller organizations — a life as fluid and mobile as the city itself.

The city is shifting, seething with change, and fearful of the cost of the mass impact of these newcomers upon their communities.

Changes which occur within communities in which the newcomers settle are quick, drastic, sharp, and costly to the previous residents. Here we present our first two premises with reference to the relationship between the urban immigrant of today and the city with its institutions, including the Roman Catholic Church.

(1) The fracturing and almost pulverizing of the previous, simple, relatively organized unity of the individual, his community and his church demands today a unified approach of all of the community institutions working together on those areas of life outside of their particular domain of interest. When the Roman Catholic Church, or any other church, or any other organization, attempts to cope with problems outside of its particular specific functions it must then join forces with every other possible community resource. To try it otherwise would be simply a repeat performance of Don Quixote's tilting with the windmills. The days of isolationism, actually dead for the past generation, have now become so decayed that if the eyes do not see it the nose must smell it. No longer can the Roman Catholic Church, or any church, or any other institution, go it alone when it is dealing with issues outside of its specific area.

(2) The community becomes the only feasible and pragmatic unit for approach to this and other issues. In this vortex of social change it becomes increasingly difficult for even the social unit of the family to successfully fend off the constant changes swirling about it in the pattern of disorganization which is always part of social change. The community must be organized as a social and spiritual matrix if for no other reason than the protection of the family. The Roman Catholic Church must bring its full resources to bear in programs designed to develop the mobilized power of the community in the struggle for order, hope, opportunity and dignity. The community represents that source of energy from which the power can be generated which is so essential for this job.

A significant difference between the representatives of the bulk of the urban newcomers of today, the Negroes and the immigrants of the past is the difference of race. The social distance and barriers between the Negroes and the whites far exceeds the distances which previously separated the American citizens from the European immigrants. This issue presents one of the great current crises to all institutions, and particularly a world-wide organization such as the Roman Catholic Church.

It is simple to dismiss it on an ethical basis with the espousal of the Judeo-Christian concept, but churches are made up of people, with all of their weaknesses, fears, prejudices and the general irrationality of much of human behavior. Those in positions of responsibility owe and bear responsibility to their people and their organization, as well as to the newcomer. Only when one is not in a position of responsibility or being personally threatened can he take to the heights of purity and lash out at the sinners about him. Then, too, one is not restrained by a basic principle of responsible administration, acceptance of the fact that the price of criticism is a constructive alternative. Give those either responsibility or a threatened vested interest and they will react as did Thomas Jefferson. Jefferson, prior to becoming President, contemptuously attacked Washington for action and policies motivated solely out of national self-interest.

The issue becomes one of either continuing the basic segregation pattern and trying to sweep it under the carpet of our conscience, or accepting the fact that segregation is no longer possible. The predominant white attitude basically favors the former, the continuation of segregation in some form or another and the subscribing to a rationale of constantly deploring prejudice in everyone but ourselves, of pious protestations against bigotry in the form of interracial committees, strong denunciations against segregation coming from the annual summit meetings of high administrative circles of various institutions, round and square tables of inter-faith cooperation and other public relations *fol de rol;* then there is always that perennial sanctuary of the status quo, the troubled but grave judgment that this situation can only be resolved through the passage of time, and therefore with profound regret and great relief we table the issue by referring it to the next generation.

Unfortunately for the personal comfort of the present generation these practices of procrastination are no longer available. Forces are loose in our world of today which compel us to work out a moral solution for this issue, the abolition of segregation. Pragmatic considerations of self-interest demand that we assume a moral position (regardless of our aversion to being moral on this issue) and move directly to the development of integrated living in our lifetime. There is no other rational or expedient choice.

Let us take a realistic look at the present status of this much-discussed objective of the integrated community. First, when we strip the evasions and ambiguities away from the publicity about integration, we find that there is no such animal as an integrated community in the United States of America today. There are many communities where Negroes and whites live together, but careful examination discloses them to be communities in a state of transition from white to Negro. Obviously, when a community begins to change, all the whites do not leave at once; it takes time to dispose of property and other arrangements necessary to the move. During the period of this change the prevailing mixed population is wishfully regarded and publicized as being "an integrated community." Our search for the oft mentioned "integrated community" reveals them as either communities in a state of transition, or small, artificial islands of a few idealists practicing a particular personalized pattern; or a situation temporarily operating under economic pressure and disappearing with the removal of that pressure; or conditions whereby there is an absolute degree of control of racial proportions, either residing in a community, or participating in an educational institution such as in the former case a private real estate developer who has control over, who rents or purchases any of the property in the particular community or, in the case of a school, of the control of school districting by a particular authority which would then determine the racial constituency of the school population.

All of the various widely advertised "integrated" programs would fall into one of the above categories. One popular example of integration in housing projects is that prevailing in a major eastern city where there are public housing projects known as middle-income, low dividend housing units. Considerable discussion has centered about the fact that they have a "balanced population." A "balanced population" is one of a number of terms used to describe interracial living. A close hard look at this program reveals the following formula. First a white family is shown an apartment in this project which is very desirable and in which the rent is considerably lower than in a private dwelling. The prospective tenant is then informed that a certain number of Negro neighbors are admitted to this project, and the issue becomes one of "take it or leave it." Under these circumstances most of the white families take it. However, when they move, as soon as they can afford better housing, it is not to an "integrated community."

The story of the low income public housing projects is extremely negative in the sense of the developing of integrated living, and it should be borne in mind that here is a particular situation with a high degree of control.

Occasionally one runs into a community picture which does not seem to fit into the above categories, but upon critical examination the so-called integrated living pattern there is the result of certain power patterns unique to that particular community. One such example is a middle class intellectual community well known for its liberal philosophy and its aversion to any form of violence. Immediately after the legal collapse of segregation, to wit the Supreme Court ruling voiding the legality of the restrictive covenants, Negroes realized that this was one community that they could move into without encountering any acute forms of resistance and a large scale influx began. For a time this community tried to meet the situation by attempting to keep its white residents from fleeing the area, and talking glibly in terms of all of the advantages of interracial living. There was another strong factor here in that a substantial part of the population was directly or indirectly economically dependent upon certain institutions within that community. The situation was finally resolved by the use of an urban re-development program which, while eliminating much of the physically deteriorated sections of the community, also eliminated simultaneously a large portion of its Negro population. The new housing would carry with it substantial controls, both in terms of the high price which would automatically eliminate any of the former low income Negro population, as well as control of renting or selling by a private real estate developer. It will become an integrated community by use of economic controls.

When we think of integration we are compelled to immediately take as our point of departure the essential need for controls. The situation of the pressures and forces involved can best be grasped if we think of the segregated Negro ghetto, with its extremely congested over-population, in terms of a steam boiler with a head of steam far above the danger point. Any puncture or leak in the boiler causes the steam to spurt out, defying any control or attempt to keep it pent up. Any sudden opening in occupancy in a white community is a puncture in the boiler. The first Negro residents in a white community may be (and most are) just as anxious as the white residents to avoid the development of what they had just escaped from, another all Negro, congested area; but they are as powerless as the whites. The monumental driving population pressures for living room pour relentlessly through every crack in the white curtain.

With this in mind we logically approach another factor; the complete acceptance by all interested parties that integration, certainly at this stage of the game, means controlled percentages, balances, or to use an ugly word *Quotas.* Quota is a word which is anathema to any believer in the democratic way of life, and yet every attempt in school and community integration falls back upon the use of some kind of control to keep a situation from becoming all Negro. With few exceptions leaders for integration, both Negro and white, privately agree that only by using a restrictive quota can the Negro make the first break into white communities without the communities following the natural course of the past, of panic, flight of the whites, and the area becoming simply an additional extension of the segregated Negro ghetto. The "balanced population" of the previously referred to middle-income, low dividend housing project in a large eastern city depends entirely upon the use of a quota system. The percentages may vary, from eighty white to twenty Negro, and all the way up to as high as fifty-fifty; but there has to be a controlled mechanism whereby the percentage (I repeat at this time of development) will not result in the whites retreating from the area.

A Gallup Poll report released in March of this year on the issue of the attitude of white parents in the north towards integrated schools found that attitudes were mainly dependent upon the number of Negro children who might attend these schools. Ninety-two per cent of the white parents had no objections to their children attending a school in which a few of the children were colored. The percentage of objecting parents rose sharply with the percentage of Negro children registered at the school, until fifty-eight per cent of the northern parents stated that they would object "where more than half of the children are colored." *Keep in mind that this is the north.*

One of the major leaders of the outstanding national Negro organization fighting prejudice and discrimination lives in a community which is controlled by a private real estate developer. This developer believes in integrated living, and has been able to pursue and implement a policy of a little less than five per cent quota in the particular real estate development which he more or less operates. This Negro leader is in private agreement that this is the only way (under present conditions) that a beginning can be made towards the development of a natural integrated community which would not have any kinds of controls operating except the usual ones of economics and personal preference. Discussions with this Negro leader and other prominent leaders on this particular point usually culminate in the following statement, "We agree that some kind of quota is essential to get moving on developing integrated communities, and we're all for it — that is, *privately;* but publicly we're going to have to attack you because of the principle involved." When they and others are asked whether they know of any other constructive, alternative procedure towards breaking through this present segregated pattern the answer is always one of silence.

With this in mind I would like to relate a discussion which occurred about eight or nine years ago in a private home near a particular parish on the south side of Chicago. Outside in the streets were mobs rioting against a rumor that Negroes were moving into their community. It was well known that the mob leaders, in carrying through their riots, bombing and physical violence, in order to keep Negroes out of "their" community, had the indirect sanction of their local parish. This was a matter of such public record that the death of that particular pastor a few years ago was hailed in the Negro press as one of the great blessings which had come to mankind.

During those particular days I talked to some of the mob leaders. The discussions were frank. At one point I said to them, "Suppose we could have a situation whereby five per cent of your population would be Negro, and a guarantee that that percentage would stay there. Would you then be willing to let them live here peaceably, not segregated but diffused throughout the neighborhood? Would those who were Catholic be welcomed to this church and to all levels of church activity?"

They were restless with hostility, and I repeated, "Remember, I said about five per cent and no more. Would you accept that kind of a situation?" They exchanged confused looks and their hostility was presently replaced by an incredulousness. One of the mob leaders then spoke. "Mister, if we could have about five per cent or even a little bit more than that to live all around the neighborhood but we knew for sure," he looked around and his friends nodded, "and I mean for sure, that that was all there was going to be — you have no idea how we would jump for it! Buy it! It would be heaven! I've had to move two times already, pick up my family, move the kids to other schools (his face hardened), sell and lose a lot of money on my house." He got up and now spoke with a note of finality. "I know that when Negroes start coming into a neighborhood that means the neighborhood's gone; it's going to be all Negro. Yeah, your idea would be a dream. Why, I could start fixing my home and I'd figure this was my home and this is where I was going to live." He laughed, "You know, Mister, you almost sold me a piece of merchandise which don't exist. I'll tell you what I'll do with you; you show me one place, not too far, just *one* in this whole country where you've got something like that and maybe we can talk business."

I sat silent. I did not know of any such place. I do not know now of such a place.

I repeat, what can we do about it? The fact remains that when a Negro, or two Negroes, or three Negroes, or four Negro families move into a white community the ensuing panic, hostility, tensions and all of the unpleasant and unchristian actions which follow are not directed against that one, two, three or four Negro families, but against that which they represent symbolically in the minds of these white people. They represent a forthcoming invasion of the community, and the assumption that this community will become an all Negro area. Is this a fallacious assumption? Unfortunately not, in terms of all past, previous experiences. The fact is that the Negroes in large urban cities are forced to live in the most congested, densest, over-populated areas, in circumstances of building up tremendous pressures which pour into any opening in any neighborhood. Many Negro leaders, even more anxious than certain whites to have integrated communities, know that there is no control over their own people's movements wherever housing opens.

Individual Negro or white organizations, or minor combinations of them, do not possess the power with which to act as a control factor for integration. Many of those in the riots in Chicago's Trumbull Park area were good members of labor unions (parenthetically, also good Catholics in their local church) who in their local union meetings religiously voted for resolution after resolution which denounced and deplored discrimination against Negroes; yet the moment some Negro families moved into a public housing project within their own community they were in the forefront of the welcoming mob greeting them with fire bombs, attacks and terror.

The question which faces us is, "What can we do?" What can any organization do with this problem today? "What can the Roman Catholic Church do?" I believe the starting point must be the total community and the fusing of all the forces in a neighborhood in the hope of coming to realistic grips with this issue.

There is an experiment being launched that we are privileged to be part of. It is beginning in one of the largest cities of this country. It is an all white community of middle class character. It is, more important, a typical community which does not have one tremendous power interest within it such as a combination of extraordinarily large national churches struggling for survival, or a university struggling for survival, but is typical of a great many of the American communities in our national scene.

Here a community organization is being launched in a solid sense. This community, comprising more than 100,000 population, has a number of Catholic parishes (some of the finest in that city) and many Protestant churches. At the present time there is considerable uneasiness at one border of this area, which adjoins a Negro area, as well as to the east where there are signs of coming population changes. The priests and the ministers of this community unite in their fervent public espousal of the Christian ethic, and are privately frantic in their fear that Negroes will enter, with the consequent panic and flight of the whites, leaving the churches as whited sepulchres of a former world. Some of the Protestant ministers have privately said, "We will not tolerate, belong to, support, or have any truck whatsoever with any kind of an organization which aims to keep Negroes out. It is not only unchristian, it is illegal, wrong and immoral." And then, after a pause, "Of course, we are depending upon the Catholic Church and the Irish to do the job for us!"

Not a very promising picture of a community in which to launch a bold new attempt to design a pattern of integration which will work, a way to beat the log-jam. And yet, here is a plan itself in all of its simplicity, a plan about which you will hear nothing at all in three years, for the simple reason that it will have failed; or else it will be the talk of the country, obviously because it has succeeded.

(1) To organize the community around many of its issues in terms of the experience in community organization which we have secured over the past twenty years in almost every conceivable kind of situation, so that the people will have the assurance and the confidence of being part of a mass organization; an organization which possesses the power to implement their desires and to give them a feeling of security that this organization of theirs can cope with and control almost any kind of problem which might face the community.

(2) That this organization will be used as a medium for education to a substantial segment of the population. That they will learn emotionally as well as intellectually that there is only one way to meet this issue.

(3) That they and all of their leadership will be convinced that the percentage formula distributed and diffused through the commu-

nity, a formula ranging in the beginning from say five to seven per cent, is their best and actually their only hope for saving their community.

(4) That Negro families, similar in background, experience and working conditions to the families residing in particular blocks of the community, will be carefully screened, selected and invited into housing which opens up in those particular sectors. This will be "invitation" not "invasion." The inviting whites will feel responsible for them. They will have general community support in this program. The white families will have complete confidence in the power of their organization to hold the lines.

Another factor which will play a positive role here is their own negative fear. These are people who have already been subjected, at least once, to the experience of selling their homes at a loss in the face of a population change-over from white to Negroes. They are fearful of being subjected to this experience again, and its costly aftermath, as well as the fact that they have gotten tired of running. This is a phenomenon which many other white citizens will soon be experiencing. They assume, and rightly so, that if they move from here to another part of the city that sooner or later there will be a repetition of the same sequence of events, and this kind of controlled program offers a possible future of security and stability.

If this controlled program could successfully function in this community then it would unquestionably be the key to opening other communities, prepared by virtue of community organization, to invite a certain percentage of Negro occupancy into their present all-white areas. The important thing here is that this community project carries within it those universalities which are present in all but a minority of American urban communities. The fountainhead of control would be the churches, the social, fraternal, national, labor and business interests of the area; interests which are found in all other communities. The motivating force is the realistic one of self-interest on the part of the present residents. The odds are heavily against the possibility of success, but the stakes are so enormous and the record of failure of other procedures so numerous, that the risk is well worthwhile. We advance this program not only in terms of our own experience with mass organizations and mass reactions, but also because to this date no constructive alternative has been suggested by even the worst critic on the issue of the use of controls for population distribution.

Rollins E. Lambert*

II. The Negro and the Catholic Church

In several ways, the American Negro's situation is far different from that of all the other groups being considered in this symposium.

In the first place, the American Negro is not an immigrant in the ordinary sense of the word, unless we confine our view to the northern States, to which he is an immigrant from the South. The arrival of the Negro in America antedated the general immigration from Europe in the nineteenth century: his reason for making the journey and his condition upon arrival were far different from those of the later travelers to the American shores.

Looking at the Negro in the North as an immigrant from the South, his situation is still different from that of the other subjects of this symposium in that, when he arrives, he is generally not Catholic: the Irish, the Polish, the Italians, many of the Germans, brought their Faith with them. The Negro, in South or North, generally has had little contact with the Catholic Church.

To understand the present situation of the American Negro with relation to the Catholic Church, some knowledge of his history is important. Briefly let us mention some of the most relevant facts.

All American Negroes, of course, are descended, as far as their *Negro* ancestry is concerned, from Africans. There was no Christian evangelization of black Africa before the sixteenth century. When Africa was opened to European contact, it was for business purposes. Europe wanted Africa's gold, ivory, and other exotic products — lion skins, bird feathers, and such. Europe also wanted Africa's men and women for labor in the mines and plantations of the New World.

*Father Rollins E. Lambert, M.A., S.T.L., is a priest of the Archdiocese of Chicago and a contributor to current periodicals.

156

It is an ironic fact that the enslavement of the Negro for work in the New World was the brain-child of a Catholic bishop, Bartholomé de las Casas. It is still more ironic that las Casas made this suggestion out of humanitarian motives: he wanted to spare the American Indians the deadly curse of slave labor, and believed that Africans would be stronger and more durable. In defense of the bishop, we may say that he certainly did not foresee the future inhuman development of Negro slavery, and when its evils became apparent to him, he strenuously protested against them. His objections did not succeed in abolishing the monstrous evil, but they did mitigate some of the circumstances surrounding it, at least where the Catholic faith prevailed.

Slavery in the Catholic colonies was quite a different thing from slavery in the English, Protestant dominions. It is even said that a slave would run away from the latter to embrace the former — if complete freedom were impossible. The reason for this is that the Church, through its priests and bishops, never ceased to defend the basic rights of man to religious instruction and worship, to contract a lasting marriage, and to establish a permanent family. None of these rights was respected in the English colonies, where the Negro slaves were not considered members of the human race.

The slaves in the Catholic colonies were instructed in the Faith and were baptized into it. The few Negroes today who have a Catholic family background of more than one generation can generally claim it for two hundred years or more; the Faith among Negroes is either very new, or else quite old.

Most Negroes, I said before, have had little contact with the Catholic Church. There are several reasons for this.

The bulk of the American Negro population was, prior to World War I, confined to the southern States, which still contain its majority. The South historically has been largely Protestant, as it is today, with the Catholic Church claiming only about four per cent of the general population there. (The Home Missioners of America used to distribute a map showing whole counties in the South which do not have the services of a resident priest; many states had large areas so marked.) Serious missionary efforts to establish the Catholic Church in the South are a recent development, that is, the second quarter of the twentieth century. With the Church generally absent from the South, it is not surprising that Negroes there had little knowledge of or contact with it, except in the two states, Louisiana and Maryland, which at one time were under Catholic control politically.

When he migrated to the North, the Negro generally met with indifference from the Catholic Church and hostility from Catholics. He was isolated socially and often geographically into the Negro "ghetto," from which the established churches, both Catholic and Protestant, generally fled or in which they maintained a precarious existence depending on former members. Most white people were not interested in the Negro's soul any more than they were concerned about his living or working conditions.

It is true that such indifference should not characterize the leadership of the Church, but the bishops had other problems which effectively prevented them from giving the Negro much consideration. It will be brought out, I am sure, in other papers in this symposium, that there was a great shortage of priests to care for the vast numbers of Catholic immigrants from Europe. The priests who came from Europe came to minister to people of a particular nationality, often because of the language problem. Even those who spoke English had their hands full trying to administer the sacraments and build schools and churches to accommodate those who were already Catholic. Perforce, they could not spare time, interest, or money for carrying the faith to those who did not already have it. This, clearly, is a bona fide excuse for the neglect which might be charged to the Church where the northern Negro was concerned.

The hostility on the part of Catholics in northern cities towards the Negroes arriving from the South has another explanation. It was not religious hostility; even if Negroes had been predominantly Catholics, they would still not have been well received, because they were competing for the jobs held by the immigrants from Europe. Moreover, the Negro brought with him a set of mores and folkways which contrasted greatly with those of the groups in possession; his skin color set him apart from them. Consequently, instead of being assimilated into the urban scheme of things, he was set apart as an undesirable element, to be restricted and rejected as much as possible.

Two great names, however, stand out in the Catholic history of the American Negro: Mother Katherine Drexel, who founded a religious order of women specifically to work among Negroes, as well as a college for the higher education of Negro youth. And Father John LaFarge, the Jesuit whose name certainly is known to you as the founder of the Catholic Interracial Council movement, and as the author of several books on the Negro problem. It has been the voices of these two saintly Catholics as much as anything else which has made the American Church conscious of the obligation of doing work among the Negro population.

Such work is not merely an obligation in conscience; it offers the Church the greatest opportunity for its own extension in the United States. The Negro population of the United States is now about thirteen million. Of this number, only three to five per cent belong to the Catholic Church. This means, obviously, that 12½ million Negroes are potentially members. This is a real challenge.

Most Negroes belong to the Baptist Church, with the Methodists running consistently second. As Negroes get more education and develop more social ambition, many of them move to more cultured churches: the Presbyterians, Congregationalists, Episcopalians. In none of these denominations has there been any great effort at integration of Negro and white congregations until the last decade or so. In each case, the Negro branch is completely independent or nearly so.

It may seem strange to a Catholic that change in social status should cause change in religious affiliation. This can be understood only in the light of the history of the Negro churches. In slavery times, social activity of the Negroes was almost exclusively tied up with church activity. It remained so after the Civil War, because even then, religious activity was the only sphere in which the Negro was completely independent of white dominance. This accounts, too, for the multiplicity of "store front" churches in the poorer Negro communities of our large cities. These tiny organizations fill both a religious and social need for their members. With increasing sophistication, resulting from education, Negroes are deserting such churches in favor of the larger, more stable ones; they are turning from the "shouting" type of religious worship, to the more sedate forms. They are demanding a more educated ministry. The silence of most Catholic worship, incidentally, is a reason, though a minor one, for its appeal to some few Negroes. This is a frustrating situation for a priest who, in accord with liturgical trends, is trying to develop active participation of his congregation!

The attraction of the Catholic Church for Negroes is due (under God's grace, of course) principally to two factors: the universality of the Church, and Catholic education. The fact that the Church teaches God's unadulterated truth cannot be discounted, but truth must be beautiful and desirable before a person will be drawn to it. The particular aspect of the truth which draws Negroes is that God founded one Church for all men, whatever their nationality, race, or color.

This truth has been often enunciated with special reference to American Negroes. Pius XI advised the American bishops to pay special attention to the Negro race. Under Pius XII, one of the Roman congregations issued an instruction about the race problem in America. And just last year, the American hierarchy subscribed to a very strong statement condemning racial segregation as immoral and sinful.

The official teaching of Rome and the American hierarchy has been furthered by the Interracial Councils in a number of our large cities, and by the activities of Friendship Houses and other such "semi-official" organs, if one may so call them, of the Church. The interest and kindness of white Catholics individually, too, is responsible for bringing many Negroes into the Church.

The advice given by Rome to the bishops has produced results. Half a century ago or less, it was not uncommon for a bishop to call in a missionary religious order to staff a parish when its neighborhood was taken over by Negroes. This happened in at least three large parishes in Chicago. Such action put the Negro in a special category; it was an extension into religion of the ghetto system. By this I do not mean to imply any lack of zeal or effectiveness in the religious order priests: the work being done today is built on the excellent foundation laid by them. But the Negro work was thereby excluded from the general interest of the diocese and the diocesan clergy. This procedure is no longer followed, at least in the northern States. In Chicago, for example, there are now about sixty parishes which have a considerable number of Negro parishioners; of these, only four are managed by religious orders.

In its practice of universality, the Catholic Church has been gaining a name for itself among Negroes in another respect: it accepts all classes of people. It may appeal more especially to the Negro with some education, but its efforts are directed as well to the poorest, to the recent immigrant in the North, to the sharecropper in the South. The parochial schools are open to children from families of all economic and social levels. Because of this, Catholic missionary work among Negroes has not been branded as something for an elite. Myrdal, in his great work on the American Negro, remarks the fraternal spirit prevailing in Catholic congregations.

The other factor attracting Negroes to the Church is Catholic education. Those of you who attended Catholic schools may not always have appreciated the severity and discipline inflicted by the good Sisters, but it is this which causes many non-Catholic Negro parents to aspire after a Catholic education for their children. There is also an appreciation, however vague it may sometimes be, of the value of *religious* education. You know that most Negroes are forced to live in neighborhoods which expose even small children to vice in all forms. Parents who want to protect their offspring from such influence — since they generally cannot move away from it — do the best thing within their power: they give them religious training, hoping that it will provide an antidote against such a poisonous environment. The Catholic Church, with its system of parochial schools, offers a natural opportunity for this, one which is within the reach of even poor colored families.

In Chicago a system has been developed by which this desire of parents to give their children a Catholic education is reciprocated by an effort of the Church to give its teaching to the parents themselves. In most parishes in colored neighborhoods, a non-Catholic child is accepted in the parochial school only if both parents take a complete course of religious instruction, consisting of about twenty-five classes, each lasting ninety minutes. There can be no compulsory conversion, certainly, but the priests involved have found that many times, once the parents really learn what the Church teaches and demands, they themselves want to be Catholics. Obviously, a great deal of good is done for the parents by the instructions, even when they do not accept the whole teaching of the Church. In my own experience, about 40 per cent of those who take instructions eventually become Catholics.

There remains for us to say a word about the principal obstacles to the conversion of Negroes to the Church.

There was a statement on this subject from headquarters — one of the Sacred Congregations in Rome — a few years ago: the main obstacle, it said, is the attitude of white Catholics themselves. The average Negro will not go where he is not wanted, unless he is on principle fighting a situation. He certainly will not be drawn to a church whose members are hostile to him, in whose activities he cannot participate. Instances could be related of rebuffs at Mass, of non-acceptance in Catholic schools which had many vacant desks, of rejection or segregation in Catholic hospitals, of a color bar in Catholic organizations such as the Knights of Columbus, or parish or diocesan societies. Just as these same situations can result in new conversions, when handled wrongly they can alienate many people of good will.

The other main obstacle to conversion is the law of God about

monogamous marriage. Many prospective converts are living in their
second or third marriage while their first partners are still alive. This
is adultery, according to the divine law, and such persons cannot become Catholics. The saddest aspect of these people is that almost all
of them entered the second marriage in good faith. They were never
taught previously that divorce is contrary to God's law; like most Protestant Americans, they take divorce for granted, and use it when it
seems called for. There are, as you may know, certain privileges regarding remarriage which may be invoked by converts to the faith,
but even using these to the utmost, many Negroes are barred from
membership in the Church until, if they are fortunate, someone's
death solves their problem.

Let me give you, in conclusion, some indications of the growth of
the Negro membership in the Catholic Church. Ten years ago, when
I was ordained, I was the thirty-fifth Negro priest in the United States.
Today there are about seventy-five. The next ten years will see the
number again doubled. Twenty years ago, only one male religious order would accept a Negro candidate, and only one diocese. Now most
orders of men either have Negro candidates or would accept them.
Dioceses all over the country—north, south, east, west, middle-west—
have Negro priests and seminarians. For the Negro girl, twenty years
ago, there was a choice between two orders of colored Sisters. Now
most of the big, nation-wide orders have candidates or professed sisters
who are Negro. There are still a few glaring exceptions, but they will
probably soon disappear.

It has been stated authoritatively that the solution to America's
Negro problem lies with the churches. The Catholic hierarchy, just
last year, stated that "the heart of the race question is moral and
religious. It concerns the rights of man and our attitude toward
our fellow man." Mr. Thurgood Marshall of the NAACP has said
that until consciences are educated by the churches, the integration of
the Negro into American life will not be achieved. The lag is due,
according to Marshall, to the "separate but equal" doctrine which was
American law for a long time. Many people, accepting this law, failed
to see that true justice and true Christian charity demand more. The
Supreme Court has now rejected this norm, and it is up to religious
educators to stimulate the consciences of men to accept and to practice
real justice and charity. The Catholic Church, with its parochial organization, its fraternal, educational, and charitable institutions, is in
an ideal position to make a large contribution here. The Church has

taken the leadership already in this process of education and integration in both North and South. Results are already visible; complete success may be reserved for a future generation to see, but we are moving at a rate that one can be proud of being a Catholic and an American.

What I have said to you in this essay is only a survey covering three hundred years and abounding in generalizations. Perhaps from it, nevertheless, you will realize that the day is arriving when the catholicity of the Church in America will be evidenced not only by its diverse nationalities from Europe, but by numerous dark-skinned members as well.

GILBERT A. CARROLL*

III. The Latin-American
Catholic Immigrant

I propose not to propound social theories but to tell a story. My story starts with a picture of the Puerto Rican in Chicago in 1955. Before World War II the number of Puerto Ricans in Chicago was negligible. After the war a great many migrated to Chicago. I say "migrated" because these people are not immigrants. They come from the Island of Puerto Rico which is a Commonwealth of the United States. They are citizens even as you and I. Legally speaking a Puerto Rican moving to Chicago is no different than a New Yorker moving to South Bend. No visa, no passport is necessary.

But to get back to my story. After the war a large number of Puerto Ricans came to Chicago. In 1955 there were perhaps twenty-five thousand. The cry went up. "Let's do something for the Puerto Rican." This implied that nothing was being done for them in Chicago, which was not true. There were (and are) three Mexican parishes in Chicago where they could hear Spanish sermons, confess in Spanish, etc. Other parishes provided some services in Spanish. The C.Y.O. took an early interest in them, and the Catholic Charities put on a Spanish speaking staff and provided social welfare services. Others helped in other ways. However many felt that the Diocese should have a coordinated program in this area. So, in September of 1955, under the late Cardinal Stritch, the Cardinal's Committee for the Spanish Speaking was formed. Under the leadership of Msgr. Edward M. Burke, Chancellor of the Archdiocese, a group was brought together representing parishes, agencies, and organizations of the Archdiocese. Its purpose was to coordinate the activities of these

* Father Gilbert A. Carroll is coordinator of the Cardinal's Committee for the Spanish Speaking of the Archdiocese of Chicago.

groups and to develop new programs and create new approaches in this field.

The Cardinal's Committee studied and discussed the situation. There were approximately 25,000 Puerto Ricans in Chicago, perhaps 95 per cent of whom were Catholic. However only a small percentage of these were well instructed in their Faith. It is said that only a third had ever been to Confession and made their First Communion. Even in Puerto Rico only about ten per cent attend Sunday Mass and frequent the Sacraments with any degree of regularity. Serious as this situation is in Puerto Rico, it becomes an even more serious problem when we consider that the Puerto Rican in Chicago has left his own familiar Catholic culture to enter a strange, pluralistic, industrialized, and secularized culture with the concomitant problems of urbanization which Mr. Alinsky has treated.

Formerly in the history of Chicago national parishes provided for Catholic immigrant groups coming into the city. The Poles, the Irish, the Germans, etc., each had their own parishes to provide for their spiritual needs. These parishes also helped to develop real communities with sound social values. They helped retain the cultural patterns of their groups. They provided a social structure which brought stability during the transitional period between Europe and America.

The Cardinal's Committee, with the approval of His Eminence, ruled out the national parish as an answer to the problem. In the first place the Puerto Ricans did not and could not bring their priests with them from the Island. There just are not enough priests there. Secondly, the Puerto Ricans were spread too thinly through the city for this to be practical. And of course there were other reasons.

A second possible solution would be to provide spiritual care for these people in whatever parish they happened to be, to encourage them to integrate directly into the parish in which they lived; to encourage them to join the Holy Name Society, the St. Vincent de Paul Society, the Altar and Rosary Society, the Young Ladies Sodality, etc. This solution was also rejected. It was rejected on the ground that it would not work.

The Committee sought a different approach to the situation. We felt that if religious services were made available in Spanish we would still only attract the better-instructed ten per cent of the Catholics. The great majority would be relatively untouched by the Church. And so a plan was devised to try to provide essentially the same sorts of things the national parishes provided in the earlier days.

The Puerto Rican needed a community to which he could belong. He needed a social structure to which he could attach himself. He needed to have something which would foster his pride in himself not only as an American but as a Puerto Rican American. He needed something to help him make the transition from his island home to life in Chicagoland.

The plan, which was accepted, involved the development of a new and different type of organization. It could not work through existing parish organizations such as the Holy Name Society or the Legion of Mary. Nor could it operate through the Knights of Columbus or a similar group. To join such groups a person has to be already committed to lead a Catholic life. This would automatically exclude 90 per cent of the people we wanted to work with. The purpose of this new group was to get to know and work with each other and, hopefully, to develop good social values that would influence the whole Puerto Rican community. This should make the spiritual apostolate a good deal easier.

Now, parenthetically, I must confess to having used some oversimplification to keep from boring you with details. Actually just such an organization had been started in Chicago and seemed to be working, and some of us had a difficult time understanding this different approach.

However in May 1956 I was appointed coordinator of the Cardinal's Committee, Msgr. Burke, the Chancellor, remaining as chairman. Father Leo Mahon, who helped to start the organization we spoke of above, was named my executive assistant for full-time work, since I am attached to the staff of Catholic Charities. An office was opened for carrying out the programs planned by the Committee, and is financed through Catholic Charities.

Our organization is called the Caballeros de San Juan — the Knights of St. John. It is a Catholic organization but the only requirements for membership are that you be Puerto Rican and Catholic. You can belong if you do not attend church. You can belong if you are living in a common-law marriage. The purpose of the club is to form a social structure. Let me explain. If you are an isolated individual in Chicago and not a part of any social structure it doesn't matter much to anyone if you get drunk on Saturday night or live with a woman here when you have a wife back in Puerto Rico. However, if you are part of a community you have friends to whom you must answer for your conduct. You have friends whose opinion of you is important to you.

The Knights of St. John is a grass roots organization. Our staff at present has two full-time Puerto Rican organizers and two part-time. In organizing a club they go from house to house with men in an area inviting others to join. They point out the advantages of being a Knight. The advantages stem from the Club's efforts to meet their basic needs. One of these needs is social. These people need a chance to make friends and to belong to something that gives them identity in a big, cold city like Chicago. Another need is protection. Each club has a lawyer from the Catholic Lawyers Guild who will help them when in trouble. They get an honest lawyer at a very reasonable rate — something easy for us, not so easy for them. They need protection from the police and not only for the occasional bit of poor police work — remember a police station can be a pretty scary place when you are alone and your English fails you in your excitement. The chaplain of each club calls on the local Police Captain. He explains the purposes of the club and offers to help in any way possible. He asks that he or one of the officers of the club be called when a member is involved in a police action. The police have been quite cooperative.

The members have religious needs. While it may not yet be important to all of them to go to church every Sunday, it is important to them that they are Catholic, and deeply so. Religion is not forced on them, but processions, pageants of the three kings, etc., are held.

The Knights of St. John is a men's organization. However, it really includes the whole family, since any celebration that is run includes the women and children. We think it would be a serious mistake to try to organize the women first. The men would never be willing to follow.

To summarize then, each club is organized in a neighborhood. A group of officers is elected and a chaplain appointed. Through their meetings and socials they get to know each other and gradually a social structure among the Puerto Ricans emerges in that area. It becomes a community with social values instead of a number of isolated individuals and families. The club tries to meet their most pressing needs of security (protection), social relations (not just recreation), and religion.

On a city-wide basis we are attempting to build the same sort of community. At present we have eight councils of the Knights of St. John. One of these is located in Waukegan (about forty miles to the north) and the other seven cover the city fairly well. A General Board of Directors (Directiva General) is elected from representatives of the various councils. They plan city-wide events and activities and decide policies affecting the general operation of the clubs. For instance each year they plan and hold a celebration for our patronal feast, St. John the Baptist. Annually they present a plaque to the "Puerto Rican of the Year." In conjunction with this they hold a banquet and dance at one of the large downtown hotels. Two years ago at their annual congress they issued a statement condemning the practice of buying driver's licenses for $25.00 and called upon city officials to do something about it. This caused quite a commotion, but before too long one of our local judges, working with us and the police force, developed a Driver's Training Program given in Spanish and had the examination for a driver's license administered in Spanish.

All of these things, and many I do not have time to mention, add to the prestige of the Knight. They give him a feeling of belonging to a group that is both important and worthwhile. We have about 2,000 active members in the whole organization. We do not expect to bring every Puerto Rican man into active membership in the Society. However we do expect to have an influence on the total Puerto Rican colony through our organization, and believe we are succeeding to some extent.

While the work has just begun, we feel encouraged by the results as we see them. For instance the number attending Sunday Mass had risen from about 1,500 to about 7,000. While this is far from perfect it approaches 25 per cent of the total. This represents a major gain and is far above the record of Puerto Rico, and, as far as we can tell, that of other cities on the mainland. Parish priests are kept busy giving instructions and revalidating marriages. One parish alone has had over four hundred revalidations. Recently three hundred men made a retreat exclusively for Puerto Ricans. The Puerto Ricans view the Church and its leaders as real friends. The Spanish press is friendly. The councils have developed leaders among these men. Our outstanding Knights virtually monopolize leadership roles in the Puerto Rican community.

Perhaps with all this talk of our Knights it may seem that we have neglected traditional apostolic means of working with these people. Spanish courses have been instituted for priests and seminarians. As a result there are over twenty priests who can speak and understand Spanish. Focal parishes were designated in various areas of the city where sermons are preached in Spanish at one Mass on Sunday. Thus the number of churches in Chicago with Sunday sermons in Spanish has risen from 3 to 15. Attendance at Catholic schools has been fostered and released time religious instruction for those attending public schools has been quite successful. Retreats, days of recollection, etc., have been sponsored. So we have not neglected these means of fostering Catholic instruction and practice.

The Cardinal's Committee is concerned with all Latin-American immigrants. Emphasis was placed on the Puerto Rican because of the urgency of the problem. However in Chicagoland there are over twice as many Mexicans, perhaps 70,000. The situation among the Mexicans is very different. Three national parishes, under the direction of the Claretian Fathers, minister to their needs. However, simple observation and a survey by the Committee demonstrated that the Mexican community is quite disorganized, a situation adversely affecting the religious practice of the people and impeding their gradual integration into the Chicago Catholic community. In September 1957 the Cardinal Committee hired a Mexican to form a federation of existing Mexican organizations. There are about thirty-five. This man also does referral work for the Mexican colony. This federation (Illinois Federation of Mexican-Americans) has gradually taken shape but it is still too early to predict how successful it will be. Because of the difference in the problem, we are attempting to organize the Mexicans from the top so to speak — as against the grass-roots type of organizing we did with the Puerto Ricans. The purpose is still the same. To try to bring these people closer together into a real community with good social values.

In two rural areas of the Archdiocese there are Mexican workers, both migrant and resident. At the request of the Committee, two Spanish speaking priests were sent to St. Casimir's Church, Chicago Heights, from which they minister to the needs of some 600 families in the truck-farm area of southeastern Cook County. A highly successful summer school for migrant children was begun there last year.

In the northwestern suburbs, a like number of migrant and resident Mexican families live. For three years now a six-week summer school for two hundred and fifty children has been operated in Arlington Heights. Catechism classes are also conducted throughout the year but as yet no regular services in Spanish have been instituted.

The numbers of South Americans, Central Americans, Cubans, etc., are not great in Chicago. Some have come to our notice through the Knights and through our office. There are not sufficient numbers to develop special programs for them.

At times we have been asked whether, by fostering these organizations, we were not isolating these people from their Chicago neighbors and thus impeding their integration into the Chicago community. Our answer is a practical one. We would be very happy if Puerto Ricans could be directly assimilated into the parishes and neighborhoods in which they reside. However, observation and experience indicate that this just does not happen, except perhaps for a very few. We think that only by uniting themselves through their own groups, by forming their own programs of self-help, by developing leadership from their own members will they be able to take their rightful place in the Chicago community.

This then is my story of the Latin-American in Chicago. It is the story of a challenge that the Archdiocese faced. It is the story of how a committee was formed to work out a practical program to meet this challenge on a diocesan-wide basis. It is the story of how they came up with a different type of program to meet a different type of situation. It is the story of how this approach has worked. It might be interesting to note that other dioceses have shown much interest in our program. With our help a Knights of St. John Council was organized and is doing very well in Gary, Indiana. Of course they are not directly connected with our organization. Other dioceses have sent observers to see how we operate. All in all, we feel, in spite of many shortcomings, that an intelligent approach was used to meet a diocesan problem on a diocesan level.

Complications of Language and Tradition

JUDGE JUVENAL MARCHISIO*

IV. The Italian Catholic
Immigrant

Catholicism is the universal religion of the people of Italy. Less than one-third of one per cent — 82,618 Protestants, 50,000 Jews and two or three thousand others — out of a total population of over 48,-000,000, attest to this fact. The Italian is consequently and unquestionably a Catholic immigrant.

Sailing ships, modern ocean liners, and airplanes, all in their time, have been carrying the children of Italy not only to the United States and the countries that make up the Americas, but to others, including far away New Zealand and Australia. Almost eleven million Italians, living abroad — two million in Brazil, two million in Argentina, one million in France, and more than five million in the United States — have brought with them the heritage of their culture and tradition and, what is more important, the comfort of their Faith.

While referring to the Italian immigrant, we are not unmindful of the millions of other foreign-born and first-generation Americans who, in the simple performance of their daily tasks, have contributed and contribute to the strength, the progress, and the welfare of our nation. Just as the earlier immigrants struggled and toiled to create the United States of America, so do the more recent arrivals continue to add to the sinews that give the country dynamic force for growth and security.

It is important to remember that Italian migration to this and other countries was not prompted by lust for adventure nor by violence done to them, but prompted almost always by a sense of personal dignity and the will to obtain, through work, the right to the necessities of life. The Italian immigrant, here, in America, as elsewhere, seldom abandoned his Faith. Even when he appeared to have

*Judge Juvenal Marchisio is Judge of the Domestic Relations Court of New York City and President of the American Committee on Italian Migration.

172

ignored or neglected it he was still as attached to it as if he had never left his native village. At no time did his belief in God and in the Roman Catholic Church ever waver. At no time was the Protestant Church in America a serious threat to the faith of the Italians — notwithstanding its material inducements. The uncertain existence of Italian Protestant organizations today, after a century of insistent propaganda, needs no elaboration.

There was and still exists a superstition to the effect that one stands high or low on the ladder of humanity in exact proportion to the complexion of his skin. The Anglo-Saxons are tall and fair. Therefore they must be the most highly evolved of the creatures on earth. Scandinavians, Germans are also blond and therefore also highly civilized. And since the English, Danes, Swedes, Norwegians and Germans are mostly Protestant, Protestanism is the chosen religion of nature's elite. The farther south in Europe you go, the darker your skin becomes. An Italian is, therefore, quite far down in the scale of evolution for, in the main, he is dark and somewhat squat in physique — at least according to popular conception. Therefore the Italian and others from Southern Europe are not as good as Englishmen or Swedes. This inferiority is further proved according to this superstition by their religion — Roman Catholic — and, incidentally, their veneration of the Blessed Virgin. Believe it or not, our immigration quotas are based on this outmoded, long-exploded, thoroughly un-Catholic notion of a racial superiority that depends on the color of a man's skin: 65,000 from Great Britain, 5,645 from Italy; 25,814 from Germany, 250 from Spain. This sounds outmoded, but it is, unfortunately, a reality — because our present immigration law says that the value of an immigrant to this country is not to be judged by his moral worth, physical stamina, nor even on the need of this country for his services, but solely on the accident of his place of birth.

The history of immigration does not always make pleasant reading, filled as it is with accounts of prejudice and discrimination, of mistreatment, exploitation, racism, and nativism. Even today, we seldom take an idealistic view of immigration and, in the past hundred and seventy-five years, we seem to have forgotten that the only native American was the American Indian and, though our land was first peopled by the oppressed and the needy, we have to be reminded that it is a duty and a privilege to offer a home to others who are oppressed and in want. Even when immigration to the United States was at its height, Italians and others received, at best, a grudging welcome and there were forces constantly at work to destroy the "melting pot" that is America. To the immigrant, the country, the people, the things around him, all seemed to conspire against him even though he came with his thrift, his industry, and his sense of destiny.

It was not easy for the Italian immigrant to face the America of 75 or 50 years ago — whether as street-cleaner or section-hand, miner, shoemaker, or barber; not easy for the Italian priest, either — he was a little peculiar and funny — he never received many honors from Church or State. It did not matter that the immigrant came with a deep and abiding zeal for the religion into which he had been born because there were those who claimed that his religious fervor would be used to overthrow this country's institutions.

Those who formed the immigration policy did not see that the assimilation of Italians was more rapid than that of many other emigrants, partly because traditionally the Italian has had a tender patriotism rather than a fanatic racialism in his attitude toward his homeland. As a result, Italians who came to this country usually retained their cherished traditions of religious, local or family character, but lost no time in assimilating themselves, whether it be the humble Italian of the lower East Side of New York or the railroad worker whose children went to college though he himself could neither read nor write. Love of work, love of family, honesty, humility, desire to own some property like a home, to till his garden in the backyard, to offer hospitality to the extent that spaghetti and the common pizza have become household words throughout the States — all this was overlooked.

To some reformers, the Italian immigrants, as well as other immigrants, were the source of a municipal squalor and corruption; to some workingmen, they were a drag on wages; to some militant Protestants, they were the tools of Rome. It was alleged in the 1890's and 1900's that the Vatican was ordering subversive Italian immigrants to the United States instead of the Irish because the Irish became Americanized too quickly. Mostly peasants, Italian for the greater part entered the Port of New York where, from the teeming tenements of Mulberry Street, they spread out over the city and, finally, the entire country. Sober, hard-working and thrifty, yet handicapped by a lack of knowledge of the language, they found themselves suddenly uprooted from their Catholic background and put into contact with peoples of many races and of different or no religious convictions.

To meet this challenge was not an easy task for a Church organization which was impoverished. Despite this handicap with a very few exceptions, the Italian immigrant in this country has generally remained loyal to his Church. Even the few Italian anti-clericals, while calumniating the Church for political reasons, have claimed, preposterous as it may seem, to be Catholics.

Some American writers, ignorant of Italian traditions and religious practices, have accused Italian immigrants of superstition and of paganism because they brought with them many religious customs from their native land. These writers err in attributing superstition and paganism for the naming after patron saints thousands of mutual aid societies or of thousands of fishing boats owned by Italians from Massachusetts to Florida, from Washington to Lower California. A visit to Fisherman's Wharf in San Francisco will prove this point. It has been said, with some truth, that the Italian immigrant has not been generous toward his Church. However, he has had very little with which to be generous. His wages were low; his children were many, and a nickel was an important item in the family budget. Later, when he began to enjoy his share of prosperity, he did, and does, his duty like any other Catholic. The beautiful churches, schools, hospitals and homes for the aged they have built throughout the country, under Catholic auspices, attest to their sacrifices and generosity.

Italians do not belong exclusively, as it is believed, to the so-called "new immigration." Italians have been coming to and have settled in the territory that is today the United States of America before any other national group, with the exception of the Spanish. To chronicle all the contributions of Italian Catholics in the discovery and the exploration, the formation, development and progress of the United States is impossible. One can mention only some in passing.

It has been said that if Columbus had not discovered America someone else would have done so — sooner or later. The same thing, of course, is true of most, if not all, other inventions or discoveries in the history of mankind. Columbus was a simple man of faith, inspired not only by the desire for riches and the opportunity to test scientific knowledge, but best of all with the high purpose of bringing to savage people the truths of Christianity. The first thing this fervent Italian Catholic did as he landed was "to kneel down and thank God for the success of the voyage" and to have "a trunk of a tree made into a Cross." Other Italians explored, or helped to explore, our coasts from the Atlantic to the Gulf of Mexico and the Pacific, as well as our interior from Florida to the Mississippi, from Arizona to Kansas, from

Minnesota to Louisiana. Later in the nineteenth century, Italian fur-traders and missionaries were to continue this work of civilization and good will among the Indians of the Northwest. Among those who explored the new world or later added to its embellishment were the Italian Friar Onorato, who set out to explore what is presently New Mexico; Brother Pedro Mingoci who went to what is now Virginia with Father Segura and was one of the eight religious who were killed by Indians on the banks of the River Rappahannock in 1571; eight Italian Jesuits who labored in Lower California in the years 1687 to 1776; Father Bressani, the first man to describe Niagara Falls; the Delieto family, called Duluth, who founded the city that bears their name; Alphonse Tonti, the co-founder of Detroit; Paul Amatis who landed with the first colonists in Charleston, S. C., in 1733; the Italian silk experts who arrived in 1733; Italian teachers of music in the Colonies as early as 1757 including John Palma who gave a concert in Philadelphia; and the first teacher in an American college of the French, Spanish, German and Italian languages — Carlo Bellini, who came to Virginia in 1774. At the outbreak of the Revolution, there were in the Thirteen Colonies thousands of people whose ancestry could be traced directly or indirectly to Italy. Even more important than their number was their quality. Names were changed by clerks or recorders who did not know how to spell them and poor handwriting added to the confusion. A name like Paca at times is found spelled Pecker; Taliaferro as Tolliver; Bressani as Bressany.

Before 1880 there were more Italian priests in the United States than during the next quarter of a century when the millions of immigrants began to land on our shores from Italy. More than one-half of the Italian priests who arrived before 1870 were engaged in educational activities from the District of Columbia to the Pacific Coast, as professors of theology and languages — and even science; some were the presidents or founders of colleges or universities. Others were laying the foundations of the Catholic Church west of the Mississippi and a few were organizing parishes in the East. One of these, Father Balthassar Torelli, officiated at the Church of St. Augustine in Philadelphia in 1806. In the Middle West Joseph Rosati, a Neapolitan, and Samuel Mazzuchelli, a Milanese, were very important clergymen.

Even before many Italian priests began their labors in America, natives of Italy helped to establish some of the first parishes and erect some of the first churches in the United States. In New York, Antonio and Filippo Filicchi became the benefactors of Mother Seton and helped her to establish her order of the Sisters of Charity. Anthony Trapani, a native of Meta, near Naples, was one of the first trustees of St. Peter's Church on Barclay Street. Charles Del Vecchio, a Milanese, was active in the parish of the Old St. Patrick's Cathedral on Mott Street, and was elected vice-president of the New York Catholic Benevolent Society, the first Catholic organization of its kind in the country, in 1816. Old St. Patrick's Cathedral was built by an Italian mason named Morte. In New Jersey, Giovanni Battista Sartori built the first Catholic church in that State, that of St. John the Baptist, at Trenton, in 1814. In Philadelphia, several Italians were active in local parish affairs at the beginning of the nineteenth century. In Louisiana, in Virginia, in Alabama, in South Carolina, Mississippi, Arkansas, Georgia, Indiana, Illinois, and later in California and Colorado are found Italian Catholics during the same period. Father Nicholas Zucchi of the Society of the Faith of Jesus, came to Maryland in 1803. He died at Taneytown, Maryland, in 1845, after serving as prefect at Georgetown College. In 1810, Father B. Torelli and a Father Bonavita were stationed in Philadelphia and New York, respectively, and Father Giovanni Grassi began his labors at Georgetown. Father Grassi, S.J., a native of Bergamo, became president of Georgetown College in 1812. The Lazarists, or Vincentians, from Italy, established their first community in Missouri in 1817. To provide special services for immigrants, Father Moppiatti took care of the Italians at the Church of the Transfiguration in New York in the 1840's and preached sermons in the Italian language. In Philadelphia, Fathers Della Nave and Folchi held religious services for Italian immigrants in 1851 at St. Joseph's Church on Fourth Street and Willing's Alley. Bishop John Baptist Scalabrini is best known for his work in aiding the immigrant and has been called by Pope Pius XII, the "Father of Immigrants." His work has been carried on by the priestly sons of the Pious Society of St. Charles. Mother Francis Cabrini set foot on United States territory when, with a group of six Sisters, she arrived in New York, March 1889. Although she is known to have crossed the ocean twenty-five times during her active lifetime, she made this land her country by adoption and continued the work of charity which she had initiated in Italy and which took form in many great institutions in New York, Chicago, Denver, San Francisco, Seattle, Los Angeles, New Orleans and other communities. The wealth that Mother Cabrini left to the world, and particularly to the United States, embraces both the spiritual and material. More than one hundred and fifty institutions bear her name and thousands of people from the youngest to the oldest are aided yearly in scores of orphanages, hospitals, schools, and convents which house those in need of moral and physical help.

Ninety per cent of Americans of Italian origin reside in the States of New York, Pennsylvania, New Jersey, Massachusetts, Ohio, Illinois, California, Michigan, Connecticut and Rhode Island. Relief statistics demonstrate that the Italian immigrant rarely becomes a burden on the receiving country. Italian immigrants rank high among the immigrant groups in the matter of naturalization. They come, establish themselves, and become American citizens as soon as possible. Italian immigrants are frugal, sober and industrious. A conspicuous characteristic of Italians is their provident disposition to own the homes they live in and to deposit the surplus of their earnings for the growing need of their families and to meet future exigencies. The Italians' adaptation to and solicitude for the land is conspicuous in: a) the development of California's agricultural potentialities; b) Colorado's sugar-beet industry; c) the Northeastern potato and Midwestern wheat belts; d) truck farming. Despite popular belief to the contrary, the record shows that in proportion to numbers, fewer Americans of Italian origin are convicted of felony crime than of any other minority groups. The Italian immigrants' record of loyalty to the United States is unexcelled by any other ethnic group, for it is on the battlefield that all Catholics and Americans of Italian extraction have proved their right to citizenship. In proportion to their numbers, a greater percentage of Americans of Italian origin served in World War II than any other nationality.

It is easy to wave a flag or to profess allegiance — it is not so easy to make the supreme sacrifice. The thousands of Italian-Americans who have died for Old Glory, the dozens of Congressional Medals of Honor and Navy Crosses, the hundreds of Distinguished Service Crosses, the tens of thousands of Purple Hearts, are the most eloquent proof of their loyalty to their country. Let us not forget that not one Italian-American has ever been found guilty of, or has been indicted for, treason to America.

VERY REV. MSGR. ALOYSIUS J. WYCISLO*

V. The Polish Catholic Immigrant

When we speak of Polish Americans we can *ipso facto* speak of Polish Catholics. With very few exceptions, Polish immigrants to the United States have been Roman Catholics, and probably 92 per cent of what is estimated at between five and a half to six million persons of Polish nationality in this country are Catholic. Their antecedents reach back to the first colony in Jamestown, where Poles were brought to engage in a glass and soap-making industry. Poles had a small colonial ancestry between 1608 and 1776. It is estimated that there were over 10,000 Poles here in the period of our national development, when expansion was the keynote and when that same expansion brought on the American Revolution. We are, of course, all familiar with the Polish heroes who participated in that Revolution.

Poles were among the pioneers who opened the West, but their greatest number arrived here toward the end of the nineteenth century and during the first two decades of the twentieth century. They entered the United States with little or no governmental interference and little regulation. They came as suppressed nationalists, convinced that their country would eventually be free, who saw their own language in their native land prohibited or restricted to the home. They came to seek better economic opportunities or, at the behest of relatives and friends, who described in glowing terms the advantages of living in America. The peak of Polish immigration was reached in the year 1912-1913, when it is known that about 175,000 Poles entered the United States.

*Monsignor Aloysius J. Wycislo, formerly member of Archdiocesan Division of Charities of the Archdiocese of Chicago, is Assistant Executive Director of Catholic Relief Services of the National Catholic Welfare Conference.

The drastic measures of our National Origins Act in the 1920's limited Polish immigration to this country to 6,524 persons annually. This figure was arrived at on the basis of what the census of 1920 indicated was the Polish ethnic population in the United States. A figure of one-sixth of one per cent was applied to the number of Poles living in this country. A change in the basic immigration law, popularly referred to as the McCarran-Walter Act of 1952, lessened the number of Poles permitted to enter this country annually to 6,488. After World War II, special legislation for displaced persons and refugees allowed about 100,000 Polish Catholics to enter the United States.

Polish Americans constitute the largest Slavic group in the United States. "Their number brings them just below the Italian figure and makes the Polish minority the second largest in what is referred to as the 'new immigration' and the third largest group as a whole." [1] They are settled predominantly in the region from Wisconsin, east along the Great Lakes, throughout Pennsylvania, into New York State and the New England area. Chicago, with about 600,000, has the largest number of Polish inhabitants, and today, with the influx into that city of displaced persons and refugees, that figure may be higher. Buffalo, Detroit, Milwaukee and Cleveland follow in that order, with from 300,000 to 100,000 Polish Catholics. Here, too, the figures may be higher because of the influx of refugees.

Catholicism, the traditional faith of Poland, has been the most potent force in the shaping of Polish-American life. Poles founded their first parish in the United States in Texas in 1855. Today, American Catholics of Polish background support and maintain about 850 parishes, which are the backbone of the Polish-American community. There are over 2,000 Polish-American priests, most of whom are products of the diocesan seminaries in our country. Seven are members of the Catholic hierarchy in the United States, almost 100 are monsignors, and many of these priests have distinguished themselves in administrative positions in the Church.

More than 500 priests of Polish background belong to religious orders, and there are at least 7,000 nuns. Poles support a large number of educational institutions, day nurseries and homes for the aged and infirm. Even from the foundation entrance to these institutions was not strictly confined to people of Polish background, and today, of course, they serve people of every nationality. As part of the parochial

1. R. A. Schermerhorn, *These Our People* (Boston).

school system, Poles maintain about 585 elementary and 76 high schools. With few exceptions, all these facilities in the educational and welfare fields are Catholic institutions staffed by Americans of Polish ancestry who have held fast to the faith of their fathers.

The Poles, throughout their history, have been a subject people and their religion has been for them a unitive force. The Polish Catholic's adherence to particular practices has tended to set him apart from other American Catholics. This devotion and practice, however, brought about a cohesiveness which seemed very necessary in the early days of settlement. The Pole's strong religious devotion, also a vital part of his cultural background, has had its influence in the development of the Catholic Church in the United States. The differences in customs and in some religious practices among the Polish immigrants were never alien to the substance of the Faith and when these are understood in the light of the Pole's sufferings and needs, they added to the strength of his faith.

In the early days of settlement in the new country, old customs were kept in force. The whole family, for instance, would gather together in the home before a picture of Our Lady and under the leadership of the father, recite their prayers, a custom which Father Patrick Peyton is so ably restoring in our day. The vigil of Christmas Eve has always had particular significance for the Pole. Hay under the tablecloth symbolized the manger in which the Christ child laid, and the breaking and sharing of a blessed wafer followed exchanges of good wishes and forgiveness of grievances. After such private devotion at home, the Polish family went to the Midnight Mass. On Good Friday, parents woke their children with a tap of a branch from a tree, to remind them of Christ's scourging. On Holy Saturday, Easter food was blessed by the pastor or one of his assistants who visited the home. And the lamb made of butter was always a centerpiece on the table for the big feast of Easter.

Religious doctrine and practice among Poles has been so pervasive and has so characterized them, that the Polish Catholic, like some other immigrant groups, has ofttimes been exposed to criticism and ridicule for the way he practiced his faith and sought to preserve it. Usually after he helped build his parish church, the Pole directed his efforts to the building and support of a parochial school not only to assure his children of a Catholic education, but to preserve those Polish customs he considered essential to the preservation of the faith. In the early days it was common practice for Poles even to mortgage their homes in order to help the pastor build a church and school. This author once lived in a parish where he saw the pastor repaying such loans received by a predecessor. Sacrifice of the older immigrants compares well with what enters the Sunday collection basket today.

It has taken generations to recognize the full import of the cultural influence which the practice of the faith and the designs in parochial education have stamped upon the American community. It is recognized today that the community of Catholic institutions, traditions and values that the Pole built blended with American democratic traditions in a way that is now recognized as representing in "microcosm the essence of American cultural and harmonious unity derived from diversity." [2] As a result the children of that "new immigration" are today as welcome in the territorial parish as other Catholics, and in our sprouting suburbia they live, work and pray as do other Americans.

Religion, therefore, for the Pole of a later generation has been an integrating force and has brought him to associate with others in an institution that transcends nationality. External forms among these Poles may still here and there assume some sort of nationalistic expression, yet these are accidental to the substance of the faith. And even these nationalistic expressions can be understood and appreciated when they provide a picture of a community at prayer and a demonstration of the virility of the faith nurtured at the family hearth.

The February 1959 issue of the *Readers' Digest* carries the story of "Mama Krol" who has given America nine children, of whom four are doctors, two engineers, a chemist, an electrical contractor and a dental nurse. When Mary and Alex Krol, a modest Polish couple now in their seventies, were being honored by state and national leaders as an outstanding example of family achievement among the foreign born, "Mama" Krol, in her brief speech of acknowledgement, gave this advice: "Go to Church every Sunday, don't let the children get sassy, and make sure they bring home good report cards." We cannot say that the Krol family is typical but we can say they are a good example of the Polish immigrant Catholic, who held to his mother tongue, had a firm faith and planted a noble heritage of customs and practices into the new rich soil of America.

A new generation of priests is leading the Polish Catholic, formerly so attached to his language and customs, to new acquaintance with the customs and practices of other groups. Among the Polish clergy,

2. Joseph Swastek, *One America* (New York, 1955), p. 156.

particularly of the older generation, it is still a matter of debate as to whether this transition from the old to the new will preserve the faith. It is an undisputed fact that religion and the language through which it was interpreted were, perhaps more than any other factor, responsible for the formation of the Polish-American community. One can hardly critcize the oldsters who decry the loss of language and custom. They firmly believe that when the language was lost — all was lost. Language to them became the cornerstone that would maintain solidarity. When it disappeared, they saw disappearing before them all that was familiar and a reminder of the old country. But a new generation is saying: "We're at home in this language of America, and, young as we are, we have seen customs come and go. Our faith is the faith of our fathers. Its doctrine and practice are the same. We have reshaped our tools to fit the way of life in America. Our fathers have written a glorious page in the history of the Catholic Faith in America. Now, it is our turn to write ours."

It is significant that the second and third generation Pole in the United States, most often Catholics without special ties, came forward with the greatest number of offers of homes and job opportunities for the displaced persons and refugees who formed the latest surge of immigrants to our shores. Here the common bond of faith was expressed in action toward those helpless victims of the recent war, whose language and customs were even alien to those of their sponsors. They welcomed the refugees and strove to arrange their placement and integration in such a way that their adjustment to the American way of life would not be as long and difficult as was that of their forebears.

A common religious heritage gave the newest refugee not only a spiritual, but even a social identification with the new World. This Polish immigrant refugee was luckier than his predecessor of a hundred years ago. He came to a land where the years had indeed refined the process of acceptance and identification. He came to well established churches, schools, and other institutions. His fellow Catholic American "knew the ropes" and would lead him away from the pitfalls that would have labeled him for a longer time as an alien — a foreigner. He led him to the unitive processes of a common faith among Americans of many nationality backgrounds.

About 100,000 Polish displaced persons and refugees came to the United States under special laws of the past decade. Their identification with the Catholic Faith opened doors for them that were not possible for the immigrant of old. From the moment that the Polish Catholic made himself known to the overseas offices of our Catholic resettlement agencies to the moment of his arrival in an American neighborhood, he was assisted in every step of his immigration.

But even for this refugee, the beginnings were hard. For after all,
he did not know the language of his new country, yet he felt at home
because the Church he knew in the homeland was the same Church
here. Some of the customs and traditions were different, but essentially
he recognized the beneficent unity and hospitality of the faith and it
identified him with his sponsor and other Americans interested in his
welfare.

In several dioceses surveys were made, and those revealed that because of the language barrier some refugees placed within the confines
of a territorial parish neglected the sacraments. In the dioceses studied
this was changed. Priests speaking the language of the new immigrant
were brought in from time to time to hear confessions and give talks.
In other places, sponsors themselves went to the trouble of driving the
refugee to a distant church where he would feel at home.

The problem was not as great for the children. They were quickly
enrolled in our parochial schools and lost no time in learning the new
language. Here and there, this learning of the language did retard
their progress in school, but the observers found that generally after a
year refugee children were quite at home in our American institutions. Children were responsible, too, for bringing this knowledgeability
of the new language to the home.

It is also significant that the new refugee immigrant was generally
of a higher intellectual caliber than the immigrant of old. The new
refugees, for the most part, were not peasants. They had come from
the larger cities and towns, where great advances had been made in
education. They brought this knowledge and experience with them.
Where they were placed in communities not of their own nationality
background, observers noticed that they progressed in learning the new
language more quickly and embarked into business and the problems of
making a living much faster than the immigrant of old. Many even
provided new leadership for the older immigrant. Those who were
teachers were quickly absorbed in the schools. Other professionals and
technicians found no difficulty in finding placement in a community
where knowledgeability of two languages was an asset. Writers were
absorbed by a Polish Catholic press which had need of them. Here
supervision was necessary, however, in order that old hatreds and political beliefs would not color the presentation of news to an American
audience.

Some Polish pastors reported that their national parishes took on new life with the influx of the displaced persons and refugees. One pastor in New Jersey claimed that his was a dying parish until some 1,500 displaced persons arrived, and he and his assistant started preaching in Polish all over again.

Another pastor of a "national parish" reported that whereas his teachers were no longer using the Polish language in his school, the influx of refugee children and the need to help them bridge the gap of language necessitated that his teachers embark upon refresher courses in Polish. That same pastor remarked that although parents considered attendance at the parochial school expensive, they were willing to make sacrifices in order that their children not lose the heritage of language and its intimate association with the faith, and also be assured of the continuance of a Catholic tradition in education.

This tradition of Catholic education for their children thus became an accepted fact for Polish Catholic refugees. They came from a country in which the state supported parochial schools. It did not take long for the newcomer to learn that in the United States American Catholics pay for and conduct their own school, from the primary level on through the university. They learned, too, that in the crowded urban areas there was not always room in parochial schools for all the Catholic children and that some were attending public schools. They noted also that it was the parish school which generally had teachers speaking the language their children would understand.

Neither was adult education among these new refugees neglected. The specialized character of this field of education elicited help and advice from Diocesan Resettlement Directors from the national headquarters of the N.C.W.C. The various departments of that organization revised old texts and prepared new material for education in citizenship and language. A Polish civics book in catechism form was issued by the N.C.W.C. and made available to the dioceses. In addition, surveys were made of national and local programs directed toward educating the adult immigrant. Information and material related to such programs was shared with Diocesan Resettlement Directors by the Resettlement Division of Catholic Relief Services — N.C.W.C.

One could go on giving individual instances, but perhaps there stands out in my mind the fact that the refugee immigrant was more adaptable and more quickly integrated than the immigrant who preceded him decades ago.

The Polish Catholic refugee brought with him the habits of a lifetime. He brought a firm faith, tested by an uprooting unheard of in history. He preserved intellectual and aesthetic qualities, despite the demoralization of homelessness and camp life. Planted in the American soil, so well fertilized by his compatriots of old, these inbred practices and attitudes flowered in free soil and will bring about a quicker and more firm adaptation to the American way of life than that of the older immigration.

In order not to cut the refugee away from the sources of his intellectual and spiritual nourishment, the N.C.W.C., in its resettlement program, did much toward integration of the old and the new. Immediately after the bishops formed their National Catholic Resettlement Council, contact was made with Polish organizations interested in the plight of the displaced persons and refugees. Sponsors were sought for Polish refugees. The religious heritage of the faith, as we mentioned earlier, gave them not only a spiritual, but even a social identification with the new world.

Catholic Relief Services - N.C.W.C. made special efforts to acquaint the Polish Catholic refugee with the Catholic Church in the U.S.A. The agency printed a pamphlet in Polish on the history, tradition and practices of the Catholic Church in the United States, and made specific references to such practices in long established Polish communities throughout the country. Such orientation for the new immigrant was a far cry from the unofficial, word-of-mouth orientation that characterized earlier immigration movements to this country.

The Catholic parish, and the lay organizations associated with it, played an important role in helping the Polish refugee settle down in his new community. History seemed to repeat itself. It was the parish around which all activity centered. In this role of a trusted friend, the parish was most often the first link between the refugee and his new neighbor. Even in some areas where Polish displaced persons were placed away from the Polish community, participation in a common and familiar liturgy gave them a sense of belonging. They may not have understood the English sermon, but they did understand the actions of the priest at the altar. Where a pastor or his assistants took a personal interest in their new refugee parishioners, patience, despite the language barrier, paid off. Then again, with the large number of Poles in this country, there was hardly a place where the help of some lay Catholic could not be elicited to interpret for the refugee.

As we indicated earlier in describing the older immigration, so in the newer immigration the Catholic parish for the Pole was an important center for social relations. Here, through parish activities, the

Polish Catholic refugee created new friends and acquaintances, he was encouraged to participate in parochial activities, join parish societies, and, of course, send his children to the parochial school. Many parishes organized special programs of entertainment in which nationals, who were once immigrants themselves, and the new immigrants participated. Through such parish and club activities, old and new immigrants recalled customs long forgotten by the latter, but sparking the memory of a rich heritage which would soon become part of a new environment.

Of the 623 refugee priests who were brought to this country, 137 were Poles. It is significant that only in rare cases were these priests assigned to specific tasks to serve the new immigrants. Most of them had to fulfill needs in dioceses where there was a shortage of priests. Like their fellow immigrants, they had to face the same difficulties of acquiring a new language and new customs. A certain number of them found a warm welcome in national parishes where Polish was still being used. They were a great help to the Polish pastor whose young assistants no longer spoke the Polish language.

Father Rocheau, writing on integration and religious practice in the International Catholic Migration Commission Bulletin, had this to say:

> Religious life does not come under the domain of pure intellect; in the worship that we give to God not only our intelligence comes into play, but our body and soul, our intelligence, our will and our sensitiveness. There is an atmosphere of prayer which one feels but cannot define. Too often this is what the immigrant misses in the churches of his new country.

The priests in the United States who worked and lived with the new Polish immigrants and who sensed this required atmosphere that "one could feel but not define," and who strove to provide for it, were successful in resettling the refugees in their parishes. Refugees stayed with them and sought out and participated in other parochial activities, and it was a joy for them to behold how the blood of new immigrants enriched the faith planted by earlier immigrants. Many such priests could say, "Thine they were and Thou gavest them to Me. I kept them in Thy name: Those that Thou gavest Me I have kept, and none of them is lost" (John 17:12).

COLMAN J. BARRY, O.S.B.*

VI. The German Catholic Immigrant

The Catholic Church in the United States has been in large measure an immigrant institution. The tide of immigration which brought millions of settlers to American shores created a phenomenon for this Church which was unparalleled in its history. Peoples of different races and nationalities, of distinct traditions and prejudices, came individually or in groups to establish new homes in a strange country. Among these varied nationalities the German people occupied a leading place. Immigrant German Catholics of the nineteenth century had a firm loyalty to their religion, sound organizational techniques, and a strong community pattern of worship, culture and social action. From the time of their first Pennsylvania settlements in the mid-eighteenth century, German Catholic leaders had insisted on separate treatment and recognition as a minority group. Their demands in the following century for language rights, national parishes, and proportional representation in the hierarchy were, they maintained, defenses against attack by liberal German Americans after 1848, as well as insurance that their religious faith would be preserved intact.

Simultaneously, leading Catholic churchmen and laymen, following the pioneer example of the first Catholic bishop of the United States, John Carroll, of the colonial Maryland Carroll family, were working to instill devotion to American constitutional and political ideals among immigrant Catholics. Towards the end of the century differences over procedure and practice brought robust Americanizing and German elements into an open conflict. German Catholic leaders and news-

*Father Colman J. Barry, O.S.B., Assistant Professor of History in St. John's University, Collegeville, Minn., is the author of *The Catholic Church and the Germans* (1953), and *Worship and Work, St. John's Abbey and University, 1856-1956* (1956).

188

papers, supported by a large number of French, Polish, and Spanish representatives both in the United States and abroad, accused the Americanizers of striving to break down in a precipitate fashion all traditions and customs among Catholic immigrants. The Americanizers were also accused of causing a loss of religious faith and creating an undue attachment to American secular trends.

On their side the Americanizers, following especially the principles of Orestes Brownson and Isaac Hecker, were wedded to the vision of traditional Catholicism formed in an American democratic mold, and based on a fusion of all national groups. They maintained that free political institutions can be secure only when the people are imbued with religious ideals, that without the religious sanctions so indispensable to democracy, the moral solidarity which makes democratic government possible would be broken. Like Lacordaire, Schlegel, and Wiseman had done in Europe, they wanted to show the necessity of the Catholic religion to the modern world and to impress on Catholics the necessity of their being in tune with the age. Foremost in the ranks of the Americanizers were James Cardinal Gibbons, Archbishop of Baltimore; Archbishop John Ireland of St. Paul, who had been called "the consecrated blizzard of the northwest"; Bishop John J. Keane, rector of the Catholic University of America, and later archbishop of Dubuque; Bishop Denis J. O'Connell, rector of the American College in Rome; the Society of St. Paul the Apostle, or Paulists, which Isaac Hecker had founded; and the majority of the professors at the Catholic University of America in Washington.

This task of creating a religious and national unity among the Catholic immigrants reached a climax during the years after the War Between the States to World War I. German immigration to the United States was given a new impetus after 1865, and Catholics made up an average of over thirty-five per cent of the total German immigration of that period. They totaled around 700,000 in number during the period 1865 to 1900, and became the largest Catholic immigrant group arriving in the States. Between 1830-1870 Irish immigrants had come in largest numbers, up to fifty per cent above the German totals. But by 1865 the Germans had equalled the Irish influx and, from 1870-1890, the Germans led the field until Italian immigration began in earnest in the last decade of the century, and continued as the dominant immigrant movement for many years.

The rapid recovery of the North after 1865, and the advancement of world communication encouraged this movement of Germans to

America. But conditions in Germany itself were, perhaps, a more influential factor in this new and larger tide of immigration. The movement toward unification of the German peoples entailed in its wake political conditions which drove many citizens from their homeland. When heavier taxes and universal military service became the keynote of the new regime, especially after the rise to power of Count Otto von Bismarck; when the small landowners, farm hands, domestic hand workers and shop keepers found they had to abandon their traditional ways of life in a new military-industrial society — many saw their only hope of self-sufficiency and independence in emigration. But more important than these factors for the Catholics of Germany, perhaps, was the *Kulturkampf.* This religious persecution, which reached its peak in Falk's May Laws of 1873, practically annulled papal jurisdiction over German Catholics, abolished religious orders, and fined and deposed resisting German bishops. Although Catholics of the Rhine provinces, Bavaria, and Prussian Poland combined under the leadership of Ludwig Windthorst to wage the Center Party's campaign of "passive resistance," many priests and nuns were forced to flee. A large number of Germany's Catholic laity, wearied by the campaign of vilification in newspapers, and the constant pressure against their faith by their political masters, also turned their eyes toward foreign lands, especially the United States. In 1883 an agent of the *St. Raphaelsverein* in Hamburg asked a Catholic tenant from the Rhineland why he and his family were emigrating to America. He answered:

> My landlord gave us free lodging and 23-30 pfennig a day for wages. For this my whole family had to labor on Sundays as well as weekdays. We were obliged to do our own chores during free hours and on Sunday afternoons. If we asked permission to go to Church on Sunday, the man then abused us . . . every time and said: "You won't always have to be running after the priest if you find yourselves in the alms house." And so I am going to America. My friends write from there that they have such good conditions, and on Sundays as many as want to may go to Church. My children shall not imitate my slavery! [1]

Germans who came after 1865 generally settled in the same regions as earlier German immigrants. As in the eighteenth and early nineteenth centuries German settlers had chosen the best farming land they could find, so in the last half of the nineteenth century they set-

---

1. *St. Raphael's Blatt,* I (January, 1886), 7.

tled in agricultural and metropolitan areas which in time became known as "the German belt." This zone lay between the northern boundaries of Massachusetts and of Maryland, spread westward through the Ohio river basin to the Great Lakes, and then out into the prairie states beyond the Mississippi river. Germans settled in the Mohawk Valley, eastern Pennsylvania, along the shores of the Ohio and Great Lakes, and down the Mississippi to New Orleans. But it was in the triangle embracing Cincinnati, Milwaukee and St. Louis that the German population was especially dense.

Catholic Germans were concerned not only with their material well-being in the new world, but primarily with their spiritual life. This may be deduced from the fact that among their first interests was the erection of a church and a parish school. Fresh from Germany and feeling isolated because of their language differences, the German Catholics from the outset insisted that separate churches were an absolute necessity for themselves. They settled together in colonies whenever possible, often by their own choice, more often under the direction of a German priest or missionary. They desired to have churches of their own in which their traditional religious observances and customs could be carried out, where they could hear sermons in their mother tongue, go to confession as they had learned to confess from early childhood, and take an active part in parish life through their beloved societies. They wanted the order and discipline of parish life as they had known it before coming to the United States. This German attachment to the customs of the fatherland was often misunderstood by their English-speaking neighbors. But the German immigrants felt, that since their new coreligionists, the Irish and English Catholics had no language problem of their own, they could not properly understand the close bond which existed in the German consciousness between the practice of their faith and these traditional customs which were deeply rooted in the centuries-old Catholic culture of the German fatherland.

During the nineteenth century the German Catholic leaders in the United States were insistent upon these special arrangements because they said immigrants were joining German *vereins* where they felt more at home and where they could hear their mother tongue spoken. Editors of the German American press, liberals and freethinkers of the "'48er" type, as well as influential German *vereins* were conducting a concerted campaign to preserve German language and culture in the new world. German Catholics, both in Germany and the United

States, who were judged to be hyphenated Germans because of their allegiance to Rome, realized they would be open to cynical attack if they should diminish their efforts to preserve *das Deutschtum* in the new world. Further, many of the common people among the German Catholics, timid and homesick in a new environment, would be easy prey to such charges.

For these reasons leading German Catholics spoke out for the preservation of German culture, customs and language under the slogan of "Language Saves the Faith." Father Francis X. Weninger, a Jesuit missionary among German immigrants on the frontier, Bishop John Martin Henni of Milwaukee, the first German bishop in the United States, and Bishop John Nepomucene Neumann of Philadelphia all insisted that adoption of the English language and conformity to the American way of life would have to be, to say the least, a slow process for the German immigrant. There were some German Catholic voices raised in protest against this contention. For example, the Redemptorist missionary, Joseph Prost, said: "We are apostles to bring the people to Christ . . . not to maintain or implant a nationality or to spread a language. . . . How laughable it is, therefore, for the German farmers and laborers to establish a *Deutschtum* in America." But such influences were slight compared to that of King Ludwig I of Bavaria, patron of the missions and benefactor of the German Catholics in the United States who advised the first group of German school sisters sent out to America through his munificence: "I shall not forget you, but stay German, German. Do not become English." Or again when he forwarded 10,000 gulden to the Ursuline nuns in St. Louis for their new convent: "I am very, very anxious that only Germans enter the convent as Sisters, and that the instruction should be only in German, both to be perpetual." [2]

The two well-known mission societies, the *Leopoldinen Stiftung* of Austria, and the *Ludwig Missionsverein* of Bavaria, contributed charitable and financial support to German Catholic missions in the United States. But many struggling German parishes did not feel they were receiving enough of these funds which the American bishops were distributing. The burden of erecting cathedrals, churches, rectories, charitable institutions, as well as financing seminaries and schools, was a heavy one, and often the bishops had used these funds, as well as those

2. K. Winkler, "Koenig Ludwig I von Bayern und die deutschen Katholiken in Nordamerika," *Historisch-politische Blaetter fuer das katholische Deutschland,* CLXIX (1922), 706.

from the Lyons Society for the Propagation of the Faith, for non-German and non-French projects. The bishops were also hard put to supply German or German-speaking priests for all of the immigrants, and complaints began to pour into Rome against the administration of the Catholic Church in the United States, with emphasis placed upon the undue influence of the Irish in Church leadership.

John Gilmary Shea, first historian of the Catholic Church in the United States, editor of the New York *Catholic News* and one of the Americanizers, published an article in the *American Catholic Quarterly Review* challenging such German activity. He said that the German Catholic papers were making "the most contemptuous allusions to American and Irish Catholics," and that to foster such national feelings was a great mistake because it would breed animosity. Since the rising generation would be American in feeling the Germans should look upon the United States as their own country. If religion remained a matter of nationality it would expire with that nationality. He wrote:

> Those who labor mainly among Catholics of foreign birth, as well as such Catholics themselves, rarely form a conception of the extent to which we Catholics, as a body, are regarded by the people of this country only as a sort of foreign camp in their midst, who will in time scatter and be lost in the mass of the Protestant, or at least non-Catholic population. Though the census will show that the Catholic far exceeds the foreign population, only part of which is Catholic, it is not easy to convince or disabuse them. Many things which they see and know, keep up the delusion. A Protestant will point to the map and say: "Where are your American Catholics? The whole country is laid off in dioceses, as though you owned it, but how is it that your Popes have never found an American Catholic fit to occupy a see west of the Mississippi and Lake St. Clair? There are thousands of miles where no American-born bishop has ever been seen." [3]

Two German priests of St. Louis, Wilhelm Faerber and Ignatius Wapelhorst, were not slow to take up these charges, and in a German-Catholic theological monthly, *Das Pastoral Blatt,* they branded Shea's article as Nativism and Know-Nothingism. They also charged him with insulting prelates who had labored amid unspeakable hardships when no native-born priests could be found in the West. They insisted that Germans always adapted themselves very quickly to a new environment and added:

3. *American Catholic Quarterly Review,* VIII (July, 1883), 509-529.

Let us allow things quietly to take their course, and to develop
themselves in a natural manner. How in the future the different
nationalities will unite harmoniously in one people, what is to become of the different languages, of the German churches and
schools, will all be arranged later on. Forcible, premature interference is always dangerous. "In nature there is no leap"; this also
holds good in the development of things social, political, and religious. Let us cheerfully permit our descendants to settle those questions. When once immigration has entirely ceased, and there lives
a generation that has been reared up with its priests, the English
language will also be gradually adopted in the churches.[4]

German Catholic leaders in the St. Louis area began at once to
apply these principles in practice. They challenged Archbishop Kenrick's policy in regard to German, Bohemian, and Polish congregations
in that jurisdiction. Kenrick held, because the decrees of the Council
of Trent had been promulgated in the territory of the Louisiana Pur-
chase, that these parishes did not enjoy all the rights and privileges
of English-speaking parishes. They were succursal churches for the
use of their respective nationalities, and that in one given territory
there was to be one parish church, namely the English-speaking church,
despite the fact that the German congregations were larger and more
active than any other parishes of the area. They began a press campaign for equality, and eighty-two priests sent a petition to the Propaganda Congregation in Rome which had been prepared by the Vicar
General of St. Louis, Heinrich Muehlsiepen. Faerber went to Rome
to push the petition personally. Cardinal Simeoni, Prefect of Propaganda, referred the petition to the archbishops of the United States
for their opinions, and it was in this way that they heard of it for the
first time. Cardinal Gibbons told Simeoni that the matter would be
discussed at the forthcoming Third Plenary Council of Baltimore in
1884, and he assigned it to the Committee on New Business, composed
of Archbishops Williams of Boston, Feehan of Chicago and Heiss of
Milwaukee. He stated that he did this because the archbishop of Milwaukee could then have a voice in the discussion. But this committee
reported nothing to the floor on the St. Louis petition, and the Germans present remained silent on the subject throughout all executive
and public sessions. When German Catholics continued to question
this lack of action, Gibbons was not slow to point out that the Ger-

4. The Reverends Wilhelm Faerber and Ignatius Wapelhorst, O.F.M.,
*The Future of Foreign-Born Catholics; and Fears and Hopes for the Catholic
Church and Schools in the United States* (St. Louis, 1884), p. 13.

man leaders present had initiated no discussion when the opportunity was offered to them.

Bishops Gilmour of Cleveland and Moore of St. Augustine took the decrees of this council to Rome for approval, and there they found that petitions and letters had been coming from German Catholics in the United States requesting Rome to safeguard their interests from the aggressions of English-speaking and Irish Catholics. These two bishops prepared a memorial of their own in which they claimed that a spirit of nationalism was being introduced by deliberate effort, that a conflict would result with consequent loss to religion, while Catholics of all nationalities would become ridiculous in the eyes of the non-Catholic population of the United States. If the Germans formed themselves into a distinct nationalizing movement it would be more harmful to their Church than a renewal of the Know-Nothing attacks of thirty years previous.

But almost immediately another organized protest was made in the Milwaukee sector of the "German triangle." After the Baltimore council the Vicar General of Milwaukee, Peter Abbelen, prepared a petition, signed by Archbishop Heiss, which he brought to Rome. Its arguments were strikingly similar to those from St. Louis; he asked Rome to stop forcible Americanization on the part of priests and bishops. But this time the leader among the Americanizers, Archbishop Ireland, was himself on the scene. He and Bishop Keane were at that time in England, on their way to Rome to make arrangements for the founding of the Catholic University of America. When Monsignor O'Connell at the American College informed them by cable of Abbelen's mission they rushed to Rome and the issue was squarely met. They found that a number of curia cardinals were exercising a powerful influence in favor of the Germans. They were the Church historian, Josef Cardinal Hergenroether; the Jesuit, Johann Cardinal Franzelin, and two exiled German archbishops, victims of Bismarck's *Kulturkampf,* Paulus Cardinal Melchers, archbishop of Cologne, and Miecislaus Cardinal Ledochowski, archbishop of Gnesen-Posen. They found that the impression at the Propaganda had been at first entirely in Abbelen's favor, and that it had been proposed to appoint a cardinal protector for the German Catholics in the United States. Ireland and Keane presented a lengthy document to the Propaganda, asking for a delay until the American bishops could be heard. They won their point, and then proceeded to cable all of the archbishops and several bishops at home, warning them of the demands the Germans were making. Gibbons summoned a meeting of the archbishops at Philadelphia so they could, as he said, "state our side of the question, as the German bishops have (surreptitiously) already stated theirs." They forwarded on the next mail boat to Rome a defense of their administration, insisted they were not uprooting old-world customs, but that the process of Americanization had already begun and they were determined that Catholics be a part of it. Many individual bishops sent letters: in one Bishop Gilmour of Cleveland wanted the matter taken directly to Pope Leo XIII, and he declared if something were not done, "within twenty-five years the Church in the Mississippi valley would be bound hand and foot to the wheel of Germanism." Bishop William McCloskey declared:

> If these German prelates are allowed special legislation as Germans, great injury is likely to follow to the interests of religion. We will be looked upon as a German Church in an English-speaking country. Let the Italians fancy a German element in the Church of Italy, riding rough shod over the Italians. How would your Cardinals and the Pope fancy it? [5]

The Congregation of Propaganda gave its decision the following June: since the bishops had been establishing parishes for the respective language groups, the Germans should not demand further privileges; that local bishops should decide whether English or German be used in individual parishes, and that any person had the right to choose an English-speaking parish after he had reached the age of maturity, if he should so desire.

The Americanizers were jubilant that they had won this point, and despite a hot press and pamphlet campaign that was continued by both sides, the matter was terminated at this point.

The German question then took on a second, and quite different, character. For some years a German Catholic layman of extraordinary vision had been working for the spiritual and material welfare of Catholic immigrants as they left European ports. This man, Peter Paul Cahensly, a merchant of Limburg an der Lahn, while pursuing his commercial interests at Hamburg, Bremen, and LeHavre, had become conscious of the thousands of Germans who were leaving these ports for North and South America. After long, tiresome low-class rail journeys, these people arrived exhausted and frightened in a strange port

5. Archives of the Abbey of St. Paul Outside the Walls, Rome: Bishop William McCloskey to Abbot Bernard Smith, Louisville, 16 December 1886.

city, such as LeHavre, without knowledge of the French language. Cahensly watched them fall into the hands of unscrupulous agents, landlords and innkeepers who tricked and robbed them. With the support of the archbishop of Rouen, Henri Bonnechose, he established his first immigrant hotel at LeHavre, persuaded a religious order to take charge, and then began to examine conditions on board ships carrying immigrants to the new world. He made two trips incognito in steerage to Baltimore and New York and recorded his impressions:

A person could climb only with the greatest difficulty to the upper and rear places because of the small amount of free space which was usually barricaded with boxes and trunks. Besides, almost total darkness existed, and I became frightened when I thought that in these small rooms of indescribable disorder and darkness hundreds of people should spend weeks and months. By dividing the sleeping places, difference of sex was almost completely neglected, and it is not surprising that under such circumstances immoral situations developed which defy description.[6]

Cahensly resolved to present his case before the yearly assembly of Catholic societies of Germany, known as the *Katholikentag*. In a short time he had secured official support from the German hierarchy, financial help from the Catholic laity, and a *St. Raphaelsverein* for the protection of German Catholic immigrants was established under the presidency of Prince Karl Isenburg-Birstein of Offenbach. They requested companies such as the *Nord Deutscher Lloyd* to establish immigration regulations, petitioned the French and Belgian governments to set up port authorities, erected immigrant missions at Bremen, Hamburg, Antwerp and LeHavre. They petitioned President Grant to initiate an international immigration commission, and sent a memorial to each of the American Catholic bishops asking them to take an interest in the needs of immigrants and to support their movement. They received no answers from the United States, nor from their own German government, which looked upon emigration as unpatriotic desertion of the fatherland. The government opened a press campaign against the *St. Raphaelsverein,* imprisoned several of their agents, and branded the whole movement as a Catholic effort to spirit their numbers out of Germany. Cahensly was elected a member of the Prussian House of Representatives, and later of the *Reichstag,* and strove

6. Archives of the Diocese of Limburg an der Lahn: Peter Paul Cahensly, "Kirchliche Fuersorge fuer die Auswanderer," p. 18.

through the Center Party to initiate emigration legislation, which the government successfully defeated year after year until 1907, when the Emigration Law of that year came too late to help the large majority of German emigrants.

Pope Leo XIII, however, encouraged Cahensly in his efforts, bestowed honors upon him, and suggested to him that the movement be broadened on an international base. Austrian, Italian, Swiss, Spanish and French St. Raphael Societies were accordingly founded, and Cahensly made a trip to the United States in 1883 to organize an American branch of the movement to help immigrants when they arrived in American ports. Peoples of all nationalities and faiths were admitted in their hostels, cards were attached to their persons so they could be recognized and cared for by agents of the society who met them in North and South American ports. This St. Raphael movement, which began in 1865 and continues today, is a most interesting study in international social action and cooperation, supported entirely by free-will offerings and it seems the first such organized effort in modern times. By 1913 there were 109 St. Raphael agents operating throughout the world: fifteen in Europe, fourteen in Canada, three in Argentina, twenty-two in Brazil, seventeen in Uruguay, twelve each in Africa and Australia, two in Chile, one each in Mexico and Peru, and twenty in the United States.

The St. Raphael immigration movement became a part of the nationality question in the United States in an interesting manner. Cahensly had requested the German Catholics of America to support the movement. After the first rebuff of the St. Louis and Milwaukee petitions, the German Catholic bishops and priests had organized themselves into a *Deutsch-Amerikaner Priester-Verein,* began yearly meetings to pursue their interests, and organized with the German Catholic laity, a yearly American *Katholikentag* as a manifestation of their solidarity and purpose. This movement was looked upon with serious misgivings by American Catholics, and when these German unions swung behind Cahensly a second conflict emerged. Collections were made throughout the United States to erect the Leo House on West 23rd Street in New York to care for incoming immigrants, guide them on their journey, and direct them to Catholic colonies in the West. What was an international movement at its base thus became in the United States a part of the Germanizing effort. Accordingly, when fifty-one representatives of the St. Raphael societies from seven nations met in Lucerne in December of 1890, and submitted a memorial to

Rome asking for definite rights for Catholic immigrants, it was interpreted in the United States as another movement for German particularism. The Lucerne memorialists asked for separate churches for each nationality, priests of the same nationality as their congregations, instruction in the mother tongues, separate parochial schools for each nationality, equal rights for each nationality, and most important of all, proportional representation in the hierarchy for each nationality. Monsignor O'Connell at the American College again warned Archbishop Ireland of what was going on, and together they worked through their friends in the Associated Press to publicize the movement as a German plot by issuing cables to the press from Berlin. Archbishop Ireland also called in the reporters, branded the movement as "Cahenslyism," and forcefully declared:

> What is the most strange feature in this whole Lucerne movement is the impudence of these men in undertaking to meddle under any pretext in the Catholic affairs of America. This is simply unpardonable and all American Catholics will treasure up the affront for future action. We acknowledge the Pope of Rome as our chieftain in spiritual matters and we are glad to receive directions from him, but men in Germany or Switzerland or Ireland must mind their own business and be still as to ours.
>
> Nor is this the most irritating fact in this movement. The inspiration of the work in Europe comes, the dispatch tells us, from a clique in America. . .
>
> Our bishops will be chosen for their offices without regard to their race or their birthplace. The condition for their elevation being their fitness, and for this fitness two things will be required: that they be strong in Catholicity and strong in Americanism.
>
> Indeed, Mr. Cahensly and his supporters are somewhat excusable when they see in Americans naught else, or little else, than foreigners or foreign dominations. This is largely, they perceive, the case in politics. Why should it not be, they ask, in religion? When we will be more American in civil and political matters, there will be fewer petitions from vereins in America and from conferences in Lucerne for the foreignizing of Catholics in America.[7]

The words of the archbishop of St. Paul on this occasion, as on so many others, evoked warm support from non-Catholics. The Lucerne Memorial became an issue of national importance, and the press of

7. New York *Herald,* 31 May 1891.

the nation discussed it, pro and con, while Catholics took sides to such
an extent that Cardinal Gibbons declared it was "his greatest battle."
He was determined that the Catholic Church would continue homogeneous like the nation. He was firmly convinced that nationalist
groups in the Church would tend to become political elements. He
deprecated the introduction of foreign nationalism and class voting
into national politics. He, and the other Americanizers were close
friends of Theodore Roosevelt, Senator Albert Beveridge of Indiana,
William McKinley and Benjamin Harrison, and were part of the
movement toward American national consciousness that was taking
over the center of the stage in national life. The newer immigrant
groups, like the Germans, did not participate at once and so readily
in this growing vision of the so-called "inevitable destiny" of the American people. German Catholics in particular had grown accustomed
in Germany to look upon their government as oppressive, liberal, and
anti-religious, and carried that same prejudice with them to the new
world.

A large majority of American bishops began writing to Rome in
protest against the memorial, and insisted that Gibbons assemble a
refutation and write directly to the Pope. The cardinal was vacation-
ing at Cape May, N. J., at the time, and while returning along the
boardwalk one day he met President Harrison who invited him to
stop at his cottage. There the President discussed the Lucerne Memorial at length with Gibbons, congratulated him on the public stand
he had taken against it, said he would have made a public statement
himself seconding Gibbons' refutation but was afraid he would be accused of interfering in church matters. He told the Cardinal that
he felt the United States was no longer a missionary country, and
of all men the bishops of the church should be in full harmony with
the political institutions and sentiments of the country. Gibbons was
not slow to report this conversation to the papal secretary of state,
Mario Cardinal Rampolla. The decision of Rome on the Lucerne
petition had already been sent, however, and it was exactly as the
Americanizers desired. Leo XIII had stated that the plan was neither
opportune nor necessary, and that existing procedures would continue
according to the proposals of the national episcopate.

Archbishop Ireland was pleased, but at the same time determined
to make a national issue of the affair. He asked his good friend Senator Cushman Kellogg Davis, Republican Senator from Minnesota, to
deliver a speech on the floor of the Senate against foreign interference

in American life. Davis did this on April 22, 1892, and branded the Lucerne Memorial as a prostitution of religious power to political purposes, while making a personal attack on Cahensly as a tool of the German government.

It is on this point specifically that an acquittal is owed in simple justice. To attack Cahensly without checking or at least giving an ear to his clear denials of having arranged a plot; to release manufactured news releases in which his name was associated with a conspiracy; to coin a phrase, playing upon the name of a man who had worked as a pioneer in international social work among immigrants before any American bishops or societies had inaugurated such activity; to associate political intrigue of a Pan-German character with a man who had been at odds since 1871 with his own government over immigrant care — only reveal the emotional intensity of the controversy of these years. At the same time the Lucerne Memorialists cannot be exonerated from an obvious lack of understanding of American conditions, nor from the colonial attitude so apparent in their requests.

The two aspects of the German Catholic problem discussed here, while being fundamental, do not approach a thorough analysis of its eventual outcome. It would, perhaps, be quite interesting to bring in, for example, the ideal of total abstinence which the Irish Americanizers tried to enforce on the Germans who cherished their beer and continental observance of the Sunday; the pressures that were brought to bear on the appointment of English-speaking bishops each time an issue of succession arose in a German-populated diocese; Archbishop Ireland's far-sighted cooperation with the public school system in Faribault and Stillwater which caused Germans, Jesuits, and conservatives among Catholics in the United States to call it an open attack on their cherished parochial school system; the conflict among Germans and Americanizers in the faculties of the Catholic University of America; the role of the first apostolic delegate to the United States, Francesco Cardinal Satolli, and his siding first with the liberals and then with the conservatives; the charges of Liberalism, Modernism and the lack of theological orthodoxy which were hurled at the Americanizers by German Catholic intellectuals; and finally, the events leading up to Pope Leo XIII's tempering encyclical letter on Americanism, *Testem Benevolentiae.*

The German Catholics eventually came to accept the position of the Americanizers, as did the other immigrant groups. Their mother tongue was dying out, American national habits were being assimilated, the United States was becoming recognized by them as a nation. No more protesting memorials were forwarded to Rome, since German parishes gradually became mixed parishes, national parishes slowly gave way to territorial parishes, and the German parishes became distinguished only by a spirit of German Catholicism as practiced by American citizens of German origin. Interest in the appointment of bishops of German ancestry and tongue became an academic question as the American Germans took their place in national life as one of the many elements that went to make up one people.

On the other hand, the Americanizers saw their program accomplished and their ideals fulfilled by this process of German assimilation. Their aims had unquestionably been progressive, but their means were sometimes questionable. The Americanizers on their part, ceased their intemperate charges about a conspiracy and came to realize in time the valuable contribution of Germans to life in the United States. The parochial school system, so vigorously defended by German Catholics, was accepted as a policy of the Church, several points of the Lucerne Memorial and the St. Raphael program, such as colonizing projects and care for immigrants and displaced persons were also incorporated into American Catholic practice. From the German examples of a strong press and vigorous society activity much was learned. The more spirited emphasis on use of the English language was left to time and environment rather than to stern admonitions which were open to misrepresentation and suspicion by immigrants not fully at home in American life. Perhaps, as more and more educators are now saying, the pluralistic linguistic and cultural values of the immigrant groups were recognized and respected too late in American life, and the values which individual nationality groups could contribute from their heritage to the enrichment of American life were not appreciated soon enough.

It is interesting today to watch growing demands for the teaching of foreign languages on all levels of the Catholic educational system. We have been going through a vigorous analysis of the quality of American Catholic intellectual life, and searching questions have been asked about our proportional contribution to cultural life and leadership. The record of German Catholic contributions has been limited, and a rewarding study could be made as to whether too hasty Americanization was a serious cause. Another area that awaits the historian of intellectual and religious life is the nature and character of American Catholic spirituality, or interior life, which has not been touched as yet. Why has there been a slow and reluctant response to the ideals of community worship, of the liturgical movement, of a respect for the Catholic traditions of participation, singing and a Scriptural-centered life? Were immigrant groups such as the Germans swept into the dominant current of the "American" secular cultural patterns? What happened to the ancient Catholic tradition of the arts and crafts in American Catholic life and educational institutions?

I personally think that such aspects of a Christian culture could have developed and received real impetus from immigrant groups like the Germans if they were not up-rooted and shorn of their true identity so rapidly and completely.

Apart from these considerations, the leaders of the Catholic Church in the United States who had encouraged Americanization made a contribution to the nation. Some nine million Catholic immigrants from over twenty countries had come to American shores in the century from 1820-1920. This vast number of settlers, almost half of the total net immigration to the United States of that period, was encouraged to understand and practice American democratic ideals by their new spiritual leaders. Divergent groups of people, like the Germans, were encouraged to amalgamate and adapt themselves. As a result a significant number of Catholic immigrants from Europe learned to live together as Americans.

James P. Shannon*

VII. The Irish Catholic Immigration

Writing in 1880 John Lancaster Spalding, the first bishop of Peoria, reminded the Irish in America that "God's providence can prepare no higher destiny for a people than to make them the witnesses and apostles of the truth as revealed in Christ. And this, as I take it, is the religious mission of the Irish people in the new era upon which the Catholic Church is now entering." Bishop Spalding's luminous prose makes thrilling reading as he describes the apostolic missions of Irish monks and prelates who in earlier centuries had carried the Gospels to Bavaria, Scotland, England, France, Belgium, Germany, Norway, and Iceland. Applying the same concept of Irish destiny in the nineteenth century Cardinal Manning, Archbishop of Westminster, once remarked, "In the Vatican Council (1870) no saint had so many mitred sons as St. Patrick."

In a somewhat more critical but still realistic vein, Evelyn Waugh, with his customary acerbity, has described the fulfillment in America of the prophecy of Bishop Spalding. "The Irish have never suffered a prick of shame in avowing their origins. Indeed the further they move in time and place from their homeland the louder they sing of it. What Europe has lost (in the migration of the Irish people), America has gained. The historic destiny of the Irish is being fulfilled on the other side of the Atlantic, where they have settled in their millions, bringing with them all their ancient grudges and the melancholy of the bogs, but also their hard, ancient wisdom. They alone of the newcomers are never for a moment taken in by the multifarious frauds of modernity. They have been changed from peasants and soldiers into towns-

---

* Father James P. Shannon is President of St. Thomas College, St. Paul, Minnesota and author of *Catholic Colonization in the Western Frontier*, (1957).

men. They have learned some of the superficial habits of 'good citizenship,' but at heart they remain the same adroit and joyless race that broke the hearts of all who ever tried to help them."

In spite of what might be called a congenital lack of sympathy for the Irish, Waugh has more valid insights concerning their place in America than most other commentators I have read.

It is probably worthy of notice that all students of early American Catholic history must rely on the source materials of Herbert Bolton, Reuben Gold Thwaites, and Francis Parkman, no one of whom was a member of the Catholic Church. In more recent times the story of Irish Catholic immigration and settlement has been told by Marcus Hansen, Oscar Handlin, and Carl Wittke, who are respectively a Baptist, a Jew, and a Methodist.

Certainly the splendid scholarly publications of Bolton and Parkman demonstrate that men not of our faith can write accurate and sympathetic accounts of Catholics and Catholic history. To say this, however, is not to admit that Catholics are too close to their own history to be able to describe it accurately. It should be our fond hope that conferences like this symposium will produce some studies of the Catholic immigrant which will deserve to be ranked with the works just mentioned but which will also be distinguished by their Catholic insight and sensibilities.

Even such a sympathetic study of the immigrant as Oscar Handlin's *The Uprooted* accepts the premise that the helpless immigrants "fled to religion as a refuge from the anguish of the world." In a related passage Handlin summarizes the immigrant's view of life on earth as "merely a dreary vestibule through which the Christian entered the life eternal that lay beyond the door of death." Handlin has always been sympathetic to the Catholic Church and well-versed in the more obvious facts of Catholic life; but he does not have, possibly cannot have, a true insight into the intrinsic, as distinguished from the incidental and social, value which the Catholic immigrant attached to his sacred faith.

The more recent study of Carl Wittke, *The Irish In America,* is even more disappointing in its chapter on "The Irish and the Catholic Church." This essay is largely a catalog of facts, biographical and otherwise, about the Catholic Church in America. It offers the discerning reader almost no significant insights into the Irish people or into their characteristic devotion to the Catholic Church.

It is said that more than 20,000,000 Americans today are of Irish origin. There is, unfortunately, no easy way of verifying this interesting opinion. However, it is a fact that more than four and a quarter million Irish immigrants came to the United States in the century preceding our National Origins Act and the establishment of our present quota system for immigrants. Certainly the influence in American society of such an enormous migration must have been considerable. But before such influence can be accurately measured or described, it is necessary that the student of Irish immigration know enough about the history of Ireland and her people to save himself from the pitfalls of that peculiarly durable Irish romanticism which has established itself so firmly in Irish-American circles.

It is my opinion that such recent writers as Sean O'Faolain, Frank O'Connor, Sean O'Casey, and John Millington Synge, have written the books which offer the serious student the insight into Irish history which will train him to distinguish sharply between the stage Irishmen who parade on St. Patrick's Day and the sturdy race of immigrants who have supplied much of the membership and most of the leadership in the Catholic Church in America since the second decade of the nineteenth century.

These writers delineate faithfully the hard life, the abiding sorrows, the fruitless earth, the avenging seas, and the mournful history of modern Ireland. But they also reveal in the grace and beauty of their prose the genius of a people who have always prized the art of rhetoric and the beauties of language more highly than houses or wealth. It is the beginning of wisdom in Irish studies to recognize that *Deirdre of the Sorrows* is closer to the heart of the Irish than is the Limerick-verse of Tammany Hall and Boston.

Since the days of the Stuart wars in Ireland it has never been easy to distinguish between Irish nationalism and Irish Catholicism. Probably the greatest mistake in English history was the decision to identify English rule and the Protestant religion and to force both upon the unwilling Irish peasantry. In their celebrated fight to refuse the rule and the religion of England the Irish people identified the Catholic religion so closely with the Irish nation that the two have been synonymous in popular speech ever since. Even in Brooklyn or Butte today Irish Catholics are prone to suspect that any criticism of Rome is motivated by some hidden antipathy to the Irish.

This sturdy blend of piety and patriotism has not been an unmixed blessing for the Irish in this country, and yet the two influences, reinforcing one another, have helped the Irish bring to fulfillment the religious mission which Bishop Spalding considered their providential assignment. In his view it was part of the plan of God that the Irish should be deprived of even the most elemental material comforts and the political advantages of a free society at home before they were cast on the seas of the world to spread the Catholic religion to other nations. There can be no doubt that in the United States at least this thesis has been verified.

On his trip through this country in 1949 Evelyn Waugh remarked that "there is often a distinct whiff of anticlericalism where Irish priests are in power." But he also recorded his profound conviction that, "To them (the Irish) and to the Germans must go the main credit for the construction of the Church in America. Without them the more sensitive Latins and Slavs would have at first huddled together in obscure congregations, then dispersed and perhaps have been lost to the Faith. The Irish with their truculence and practical good sense have built and paid for the churches, opening new parishes as fast as the population grew; they have staffed the active religious orders and have created a national system of Catholic education."

The day that the Irish immigrant arrived in New York or Boston or Philadelphia, he had the immeasurable advantage of knowing the language of his new land. Centuries before his ancestors had learned to love the Church and the land and had acquired a fondness for the active and challenging life of politics. But years of famine and insecurity on the farm had taught him to suspect the land as an enemy that might betray him. Hence in New York his fond gaze turned toward a new life in the Church or in politics or in business where his native shrewdness would bring its own rewards. If all these avenues failed, he could always turn to the labor gangs on the canals or the western railroads.

The fact that the Irish immigrant feared life on the land kept him from settling in the agrarian South and determined in great part the urban concentration of American Catholics in the eastern and northern cities. Many recent commentators have lamented this imbalance in Catholic settlement in the United States; but the same authors admit that the urban clusters of Irish Catholics were an important influence in the successful "Americanization" of the immigrant masses. It is in one very real sense unfortunate that the Irish settler in this country did adapt himself so readily and eagerly to his new surroundings. All too often he has become a "native American" with such rapidity that he has lost his identity and sometimes his integrity. This rapid assimilation to the American mores has frequently made the Irishman in this country intolerant of later arrivals from other lands whom he quickly labels "foreigners." The Irish in Hartford and San Francisco have still not accepted the Italians who came to America in the present century.

Unlike the German and the French and the Belgian immigrants, the Irish arrivals were for the most part uneducated. Many were even illiterate. They had left such hovels of poverty and misery that it is not surprising for us to discover that they were lacking in any recognizable national culture of their own. Writing in 1881 to describe the arrival in America of some Irish immigrants from Carna in Galway, William J. Onahan said, "The famine was visible in their pinched and emaciated faces, and in the shriveled limbs — they could scarcely be called legs and arms — of the children. Their features were quaint, and the entire company was wretched and squalid. It was a painful revelation to all who witnessed it." The same settlers were refused lodging in American Irish Catholic homes in Minnesota because of their "dirty clothes, rough speech, and offensive manners."

The great glory of these unfortunate migrants will always be their heroic devotion to the Catholic religion. In the years of their greatest suffering at home, they had, like the Jews in exile, learned to love their sacred Faith more deeply and had acquired enormous respect for the person of the priest. It has been remarked that the Irish religion is not a bond with the Church as an organization and still less with the Church as a place, but rather a personal bond between the Irish people and their priests. In penal times there were no churches. The hedge rows served as classrooms and the kitchen table for an altar. And when the priest made his dangerous and infrequent visits to any district, he was received with the courtesy and honor appropriate to the personal envoy of Almighty God. Moved to America, the Irish peasant still had no great desire for splendid churches or impressive ecclesiastical decorations. He knew that the essentials of his religion could be provided in the meanest surroundings by the hands and the words of any priest of Christ. And in the Irish homes there was created an admirable tradition of respect for the priesthood and the religious life. Family prayers frequently asked for the grace of a religious vocation in the family. The history of the Irish in America demonstrates how effectively these prayers have been answered.

It is sometimes said in criticism of the Irish that they have almost a monopoly within the hierarchy of the Catholic Church in the United

States. In our entire history, we have had eleven American Cardinals. All have been of Irish origin. We now have 26 Archdioceses, of which at least 17 are directed by Archbishops of Irish origins. If a defense of these facts concerning the hierarchy is necessary, it should be pointed out that the leaders of the American Church are chosen from the ranks of the clergy and that the national character of this body might well be reflected among the leaders chosen from it.

Another and less complimentary corollary of this Irish strength in the American Church is hidden in the charge that Irish Catholics have brought to America an uncompromising hostility to Protestantism and that Irish Catholics in America tend to consider Protestants as opponents rather than as potential converts. Such judgments as this one can seldom either be verified or disproved. And yet communities which are distinguished by a long tradition of numerous and well-established Irish Catholics often seem to lend some credence to this debatable charge.

I have often wondered whether or not the famous Turner hypothesis concerning the frontier might not be a useful scholarly tool in studying American Catholicism and the regional differences within the Church. Is it possible, for example, that the American environment caused different groups of the same national strain to react differently in different parts of the nation simply because in areas of concentration, large national groups could retain and reinforce their prejudices while in the remote areas of thinner population with many religious groups of equal strength, it was necessary for all denominations to minimize their accidental differences.

If this line of research is pursued, it would lead us to consider the advantages derived by the Irish from settling in communities where they were not numerically dominant and where their ancient prejudices were checked or balanced by the influence of German Catholics or French Catholics or Polish Catholics.

There are some indications that these external pressures on the Irish have been greater in the central portion of the country than on the Atlantic or Pacific Coasts, and that these external pressures have brought out the best in the Irish and the Germans and the Slavic Catholics in the region widely defined as the Mississippi Valley. This line of investigation inevitably suggests the perennial debate on whether or not the Catholics in the Middle West are the most vigorous exponents of Catholicism in this country.

However, even the social demands of living among other groups of Catholics have never been sufficiently strong to bring the Irish-Americans into any kind of large-scale program of united thought and concerted action. History has demonstrated that individual Irish immigrants or their sons could become mayors, governors, generals, and bishops, but that heights demanding group cooperation were never attainable by the Irish in America. Possibly, this fact flows from the tradition of Irish individualism. Whatever the cause or the explanation, the fact seems to be well-established that the Irish in America have never been able to submerge their individual differences in order to achieve a united front on national issues demanding cooperative effort.

In conclusion, I should like to remark that I have deliberately tried in this short paper to raise more questions than I could possibly answer in my allotted span of time. However, I do hope that these remarks, some of them very debatable propositions, would be sufficiently provocative to arouse your interest in discussing them or sufficiently interesting to arouse your curiosity for further study on this subject.

WILLARD E. WIGHT*

VIII. The Native American Catholic, the Immigrant, and Immigration

The immigration of individuals from other nations to what is the present United States has been a characteristic of our history. For purposes of convenience this movement can be divided into five periods. With the establishment of the independence of the thirteen colonies in 1783, the first period closes. From that date to 1830 there was a period of free immigration when no effort was made by the government to control the movement. The years 1830 to 1882 comprise the third period which was mostly one of agitation for some degree of restriction. The fourth period was one of federal control on the basis of individual selection which came to an end in 1924 with group selection as the basis for the fifth period. This paper will deal with the attitude of the native American Catholic in relation to the immigrant and the question of immigration in the third and fourth periods, 1830-1924.[1]

The five decades from 1830 to 1880 were ones in which the subject of immigration was not looked upon as a question of national importance. Despite the agitation of such groups as the Native American Party and the Know-Nothings against the indiscriminate admission of aliens very little was accomplished in the way of legislation on the subject. Immigration was frequently and repeatedly discussed on the floors of Congress, but the absence of legislation may be ascribed

* Professor Willard E. Wight, Ph.D., is a member of the Department of Social Sciences in the Georgia Institute of Technology, Atlanta, and a contributor to historical periodicals.

1. Any student of the relationship between the American Catholic and the immigrant must, as does this writer, record his indebtedness to the pioneer study of John C. Murphy, *An Analysis of the Attitudes of American Catholics toward the Immigrant and the Negro, 1825-1925* (Washington, 1940).

to the fact that the real leaders of the House and Senate seldom had much to say on the issue.

As might be supposed, the call of the Nativist press for the curtailing of immigration met with a varying response from the Catholics of the country. The Cincinnati *Catholic Telegraph* in 1837 objected to the "usual and under some circumstances, even cruel opposition to immigration" in New York City. Even though it admittedly was an evil in some respects, "it should be considered as one which necessarily attends to many advantages connected with an extensive commerce." The treatment received by immigrants moved the editor of the paper to call upon the authorities of the metropolis of commerce of the United States for "a little generosity in erecting suitable buildings on an extensive scale, for the reception of the sick, immediately on their arrival." [2]

The contribution of the immigrant to the growth of the country was frequently cited in refuting the Nativist objection to immigration. A Boston paper pointedly asked:

> Will Americans go into quarries and hew out solid rocks? Will they go into morasses and dykes and creeks of the forest, and hew out and establish a railroad or a continuous canal? . . . . Will the Americans . . . labor in the wasting drudgery of metal foundries, glass furnaces, and other similar occupations, which require the bone and sinew, and robust constitutions, which *Irishmen alone* can bring into such labors? No! they will not do this work. If it depended upon them, it would remain undone.[3]

The editor of a Western Catholic paper believed it was evident that the great public works of the United States, "the foundation and growth of her cities, and the progress of her wealth and greatness" was the work of all her population "the far greater part of which has been formed by immigrants which she received, and by the descendants of the earlier portion of those immigrants." [4]

Appeals were made to the philanthropic beliefs of the founders of

2. Cincinnati *Catholic Telegraph,* September 7, 1837, quoted in Sister Mary Cecilia Paluszak, "The Opinion of the Catholic Telegraph on Contemporary Affairs and Politics, 1831-1871." Unpublished master's thesis, Catholic Univeristy of America, 1940. All further quotations from the Cincinnati *Catholic Telegraph* are from this study.

3. Boston *Reporter,* quoted in Cincinnati *Catholic Telegraph,* February 6, 1845.

4. Cincinnati *Catholic Telegraph,* October 5, 1837.

the nation which held out to the crowded and suffering population of the old world a home in the new. "We are still a generous and confiding people," one Catholic paper proclaimed, "willing to share, with an open heart, and a liberal hand, a portion of that patrimony for which our fathers fought and bled." To have any other feeling "would be unworthy of our country and her institutions, and disgrace the American name." [5]

Despite the advocacy of immigration by some Catholics in this country, there were others who were not blind to the shortcomings of their coreligionists. In New England the Irish were criticized for their lack of cleanliness, and more especially for their disgraceful conduct at funerals and wakes. There were food, tobacco, and liquid refreshments in great quantities at such gatherings so that boisterous laughter, raucous jokes, and even fistic encounters frequently ended a solemn evening.[6] In New York, the *Irish Citizen,* while condemning the Know-Nothing excesses and attacks, fearlessly recorded that "we fear that some [Irish] have been a noisy turbulent and intolerant class, who did no credit to the character of their native country, and were of little benefit to the land of their adoption." [7]

Even with his shortcomings there was an opportunity for the Irishman in America, but only if he exerted himself and was temperate in his habits. John Francis Maguire, himself from Ireland, claimed that he stated "the matured and deliberate verdict of every experienced or observant Irishman from the most exalted dignitary of the Catholic Church to the humblest workman" when he wrote of the Irish in America:

> Any man, no matter who he is, what country he comes from, or what religion he possesses, can get on here, if he is determined to do so; and he will be respected by Americans, if he will only respect himself. If the Irishman is a sober man, there is no fear of him — he cannot fail of success; but if he is too fond of the drink, it is all up with him — he is sure to fail.[8]

While the high-minded American Catholic took his stand beside his immigrant coreligionist in repelling the attacks launched by the

5. *Ibid.,* July 18, 1839.

6. Carl Wittke, *We Who Built America, the Saga of the Immigrant* (New York, 1946), 41.

7. Quoted in Edith Abbot, *Historical Aspects of the Immigration Problem* (Chicago, 1926), 818.

8. John Francis Maguire, *The Irish in America* (New York, 1887), 282.

Nativists and Know-Nothings, there were those who were caught up by the anti-foreign propaganda. "Absurd instances might be told of the sons of Irish Catholic emigrants boasting of their American birth, and expressing their sympathy with the Know-Nothing's hatred of foreigners," wrote a native Irishman. To him such action "was too base an infirmity to touch a generous mind, and those who were affected by it were weak and vain and foolish, and Americans knew them to be such." [9] It was indeed unfortunate that when the victims of Nativism became respectable and prosperous, they, too, began making the old complaints about the newer immigrants though they framed them in new terms.[10]

Even under the attacks of the Know-Nothings, however, the dominant Catholic groups in the United States — the Irish and the Germans — found it difficult to work together. The Irish looked upon the Germans as infidels, foreign anarchists, and universal republicans. Holding this feeling they were unwilling to cooperate with the Germans, and some of the Catholic clergy denounced the Germans with as much fire as the Nativist leaders. The Boston *Pilot* was of the opinion that the effect of the Know-Nothing crusade would be to keep the Germans from getting power and asserted "if the Know-Nothings perform this one good action, posterity will look charitably over the multitude of political crimes committed by that organization of ignorance and bigotry." [11] So deep was the distrust of the German immigrant by the Boston paper that it forgot its traditional position so far as to welcome a decline in immigration and to favor a plan to make naturalization more difficult because this action would reduce the number of radicals and infidels.[12] The feeling was not one-sided as witnesses the opposition of the Wisconsin Germans to a union of foreigners against the Nativists because "it would drive us into a union with Irishmen, those American Croats." [13] At a later date another Catholic paper commented upon the antagonism between the Irish

9. *Ibid.,* 451.
10. Theodore Maynard, *The Catholic Church and the American Idea* (New York, 1953), 161.
11. Boston *Pilot,* July 29, 1854, quoted in Wittke, *We Who Built America,* 488.
12. *Ibid.,* 493; Carl Wittke, *Refugees of Revolution: The German Forty-Eighters in America* (Philadelphia, 1952), 183.
13. Wisconsin *Democrat,* August 17, 1854, quoted in Ernest Brucken, "The Political Activity of Wisconsin Germans, 1854-1860," in *Proceedings* of the State Historical Society of Wisconsin (1901), 196.

and the Italian immigrants and reminded the Irish that they were once in the same position as the Italian. After pointing out that poverty and illiteracy were not confined to the Italian immigrants, the editor cautioned that both Catholic peoples had a great future in the United States if they did not allow ignorance or misunderstanding to provoke ill will between them.[14]

The tendency of the Catholic immigrant to settle in the larger urban centers with his consequent low economic status and crowded living conditions led to a movement to colonize the immigrant in the West. This particular phase of the immigration problem received its greatest attention during the period 1830-1880. The colonization movement owed its strength to the interest of a few individuals. The apogee of colonization was in 1856 with a convention in Buffalo, New York, attended by eighty prominent Catholics, priests and laymen. The primary object of the convention was to organize Catholic colonization on a larger scale. Failure attended this effort when the conditions which inspired it disappeared in a few years and when opposition arose in eastern cities. Archbishop John Hughes of New York staunchly and publicly opposed the colonization movement on the grounds that there was no assurance that the immigrants would improve their condition by moving and because he sincerely feared that they would lose their faith in the West where priests at that time were few in number.[15]

In 1869 an effort was made to revive Catholic colonization on a national scale. The leaders were three Western bishops, John Ireland, James O'Connor and John Spalding, together with two laymen, William J. Onahan and Dillon O'Brien. Bishop Spalding of Peoria, Ill., a descendant of the Maryland Anglo-American group, made the strongest plea for the support of colonization in his book *The Religious Mission of the Irish People*. He clearly delineated the general attitude of the Catholic which was the main reason for the failure of the movement.

> Only here and there, however, was one found who seemed to take interest in the question or to comprehend the urgent need of help-

14. Henry J. Brown, "The Italian Problem in the Catholic Church of the United States, 1880-1890," in *United States Catholic Historical Society Historical Records and Studies*, XXXV (1946), 52.

15. Sister Mary Gilbert Kelly, *Catholic Immigrant Colonization Projects in the United States, 1815-1860* (New York, 1939), 268. A later movement is treated in Sister Mary Evangela Henthorne, *The Irish Catholic Colonization Association of the 1870's* (Champaign, Illinois, 1932).

ing on the movement. Stronger evidence could not be desired on
the dearth of large and enlightened views among wealthy Catholics
on the work and wants of the Church in the United States. Even
the better sort seem to have little idea of anything that reaches beyond a parish charity.[16]

Though there was no widespread interest in the colonization movement, Catholics throughout this period continued to advocate and encourage immigration. Even in the Southern states where the least
immigration had occurred, great efforts were made following the Civil
War to attract those arriving from foreign lands. The need for a thrifty, enterprising population was to be met by attracting immigrants
from Ireland and Germany. Caution was to be exercised in the selection, for only those who would be friendly to Southern interests and
prosperity were to be encouraged. "We must not warm vipers into life
that may sting us when they grow warm." [17] Later a Southern Immigration Association was organized by Cardinal James Gibbons of
Baltimore which attemped through its New York headquarters to divert people from Northern cities to the South.[18]

During the period 1880-1924, the Catholics of the United States
became more aware of the importance of the immigrant and immigration. Editorials from time to time commented upon the large number
of immigrants who were being lost to the Church because of the lack
of interest on the part of the Catholics of the country and such indifference was condemned.[19] Father Francis Kelley, later bishop of
Oklahoma City and Tulsa, in addressing the American Federation of
Catholic Societies in 1915 pointed out that the immigrant could not
be saved without churches, priests, and schools and that all of these
cost money.[20] One writer saw the immigration problem as the most
important, next to that of the parochial schools, with which the Cath-

16. John L. Spalding, *The Religious Mission of the Irish People and Catholic Colonization* (New York, 1880), 195.
17. *Banner of the South,* quoted in Cincinnati *Catholic Telegraph,* August
5, 1868.
18. Rowland T. Berthoff, "Southern Attitudes toward Immigration, 1865-
1914," *Journal of Southern History,* XVIII (August, 1951), 339.
19. Gerald Shaughnessy, *Has the Immigrant Kept the Faith? A Study of
Immigration and Catholic Growth in the United States, 1790-1920* (New
York, 1925), disproved this widely held idea.
20. Francis C. Kelley, "The Church and the Immigrant," *Catholic Mind,*
XIII (September 8, 1915), 481.

olics had to deal and declared that it should be met with "squarely without any seeming clouding of the real facts," for "already we have much to answer for because of our sinful neglect of our immigrants." [21] Another felt that immigration was the most persistent and serious problem and that Catholics should make themselves conversant with the details in order to take effective action through the various Catholic associations. Effective action, it was believed, would include the establishment of private agencies to meet the existing conditions and the passage of state and national legislation on the problem.[22]

The moral obligation of Catholics to help the immigrants was frequently cited. It was the opinion of one journalist that "charity is foiled and philanthropy defeated by the false notion that they who come to these republican shores for domicile are strangers and intruders upon the rights of those who came before them." He advised his readers that they had the "duty of friendly direction and hospitality" for if the immigrant were not like the native in all things, he was useful and willing to be so.[23] More than two decades later the obligation of the native-born was again emphasized. It was the belief of the author that few Catholic college men had devoted any of their time to the immigrant. This was because "American Catholics, themselves descendants of the 'older immigration,' keep themselves strangely aloof from the 'Hunyak' and the 'Dago,' as though these later comers were fit objects for contempt." If there was no other reason for assisting them, admonished the writer, there was the obligation to aid those of their own religion.[24]

Aid to the immigrant by the Catholics was not entirely lacking. Various societies were formed by the national groups represented in the United States to assist those from their country after their arrival. In the period of the old immigration, societies such as the Irish Emigrant Aid Society, founded in 1841, had been established to aid their fellow countrymen. As the various national groups increased in num-

21. "Facts about Immigrants," *America*, XXVIII (November 25, 1922), 133.

22. Louis Budenz, "Some Features of a Constructive Immigration Policy," *Central-Blatt and Social Justice*, VIII (September, 1915), 165.

23. "Leo XIII and the Italian Catholics in the United States," *American Ecclesiastical Review*, I (January 1889), 42, quoted in Murphy, *Attitudes of American Catholics*, 90.

24. Louis Budenz, "Catholics and the Education of Immigrants," *Central-Blatt and Social Justice*, VII (August, 1914), 139.

bers, societies arose to assist the newly arrived immigrant. At Ellis
Island there was assistance for the Irish, Belgian, German, Italian,
Polish, and Spanish to name only the more numerous immigrant
groups. These societies worked independently with little care being
taken to coordinate their efforts.[25]

Not until the establishment of the Bureau of Immigration as a
division of the National Catholic Welfare Conference in 1921 was any
concrete effort made by the Church as a whole to cope with the problems of the immigrant. The new bureau was "to be a clearing house
for matters relating to Catholic immigrants of all nationalities as well
as for questions of immigration and emigration with which the Catholic Church in America" was concerned. Its chief aim was "to safeguard
the faith of Catholic immigrants and also to assist them in becoming
desirable residents of this country by helping them to a knowledge of
its language, its laws and its ideals," and "to give them assistance with
any problems that they might meet." [26]

The chief aim of the Bureau of Immigration reflected an issue
early raised by the countless immigrants reaching these shores — that
of Americanization or, as one writer expressed it, "bringing them to
a better understanding of our American system of government, its relations to those who live under it, their duties and their responsibilities,
as well as their rights." [27] Some believed that the immigrant should
abandon all of his native culture while others felt that even though
many native traits were preserved that the immigrant might still be
a good citizen. In the same vein there were those who advocated that
Americanization be imposed upon the immigrant whether he desired
it or not while others insisted that the use of force would be unsuc-
cessful. The most widely prevailing opinion was that not all interest
in his native country need be renounced and that Americanization
could not be forced. Bishop William Turner of Buffalo expressed the
majority feeling when he told a convention of the Knights of Columbus that the Church did not believe in insulting the racial pride of
the immigrants in order to make Americans of them. "She deplores
the devices of others, devices conceived in hysteria and applied in

25. Bruce M. Mohler, "Immigration an Active Issue," *N.C.W.C. Bulletin,*
(March, 1921), 11-12, quoted in Murphy, *Attitudes of American Catholics,* 92.
26. Murphy, *Attitudes of American Catholics,* 92-94, deals in detail with the
founding and aims of this agency.
27. *Sign,* II (May, 1923), 401-403, quoted in Murphy, *Attitudes of American Catholics,* 88.

petulancy and passion, that would force" on the immigrant population the superficial traits of citizenship.[28]

A convert to Catholicism, Orestes A. Brownson, was one of the
first to raise the issue of Americanizing the Catholic in America. He
had no patience with the ignorance and the opposition to Anglo-
American culture of the immigrant Irish of his native New England.
He wished the Irish to take on as quickly as possible the dominant
culture of their new country.[29] Prelates like Bishop John Ireland,
Cardinal James Gibbons, and Bishop John Spalding urged that all
national differences among Catholics be eliminated through the emphasis upon Americanization. Despite support from the more conservative elements in the Church, the movement whereby each immigrant group would be cared for by priests of their own nationality
fortunately failed. The papacy declined to reverse its historic policy
of employing the speech of the particular country and of drawing its
personnel from the people.[30]

Likewise the Bureau of Immigration of the National Catholic Welfare Conference outlined as the chief objectives of its citizenship program:

> Assistance to the Catholic schools in their work of civic education;
> aiding in the naturalization of the alien resident in the United
> States; stimulating greater civic activity on the part of individual
> Catholics and all organizations of Catholic men and women, and
> giving application and force to the Catholic principles that reli-
> gion supplies the highest and noblest motives for the discharge of
> civic obligations and that our democracy cannot long endure un-
> less all our people are animated by motives of religion in dealing
> with one another.[31]

Indeed, one Catholic writer is of the opinion that the service of the
Church in the assimilation of the Catholic immigrant in the United
States has not often been recognized. "Although it may sound para-
doxical," he writes, "the Church has helped to preserve the individu-

28. *N.C.W.C. Bulletin,* VI (September, 1924), 4, quoted in Murphy,
Attitudes of American Catholics, 110.

29. Thomas T. McAvoy, "Orestes A. Brownson and American History,"
Catholic Historical Review, XL (October, 1954), 262.

30. The definitive study of the extent of the adaptation of Catholic practices to the American way of life is Thomas T. McAvoy, *The Great Crisis in
American Catholic History, 1895-1900* (Chicago, 1957).

31. *N.C.W.C. Bulletin,* V (November, 1923), 10, quoted in Murphy, *Attitudes of American Catholics,* 111-112.

ality of the various national strains, while at the same time trying to build them up into a compact Catholic (and American) body."[32] This great influence of the Church was explained by Bishop Spalding's statement that it was the only moral and civilizing force brought to bear upon the Catholic immigrant.[33]

The large number of immigrants entering the United States in the period following the Civil War, and the threat to labor which many felt as a result of the free admission of so many immigrants served to increase the pressure for a policy of restriction. The decision of the United States Supreme Court in 1875 that the regulation of immigration was a national rather than a state function made the question of restriction of nation-wide rather than of local concern. The movement for restriction which culminated in the passage of the first general immigration law in 1882 was not new but was one which had been current among certain portions of the population for many years and was to reach its culmination in 1924 when the quota system was made permanent.[34] A head tax of fifty cents per person and the exclusion of lunatics, idiots, those likely to become public charges, and convicts was the sum total of the legislation of 1882. In 1891, polygamists and sufferers from dangerous and loathsome diseases were also excluded; and, at the insistence of organized labor, advertising for laborers by companies and the solicitation or encouragement of immigration by transportation companies was also prohibited.

In 1897, Congress passed the first literacy test bill—the most widely discussed method for implementing a restrictive policy in immigration. This measure was vetoed by President Grover Cleveland as were similar measures by Presidents William H. Taft and Woodrow Wilson. In 1917, however, a bill providing for a literacy test for all immigrants over sixteen years of age was passed by Congress over Wilson's veto. This was the fruition of many years of agitation on the part of its proponents.

Catholic opinion on the question of the literacy test was not unanimously for or against such a move, but the majority opinion was in opposition to the test. One writer in a Catholic periodical called attention to the fact that many prominent in our history would have

32. Maynard, *Catholic Church and American Idea*, 299.

33. John L. Spalding, *Catholicism and Apaism,"* *North American Review*, CLIX (September, 1894), 279.

34. Roy L. Garis, *Immigration Restriction* (New York, 1927), treats the history of federal action on immigration in detail.

been barred from entering the country had the test been in force when they arrived.[35] At a later date, Governor Alfred E. Smith of New York, who feelingly defended the immigrants among whom he had lived, asked the Friendly Sons of St. Patrick, "Suppose we had had the literacy test sixty or seventy-five years ago, where would some of us have been today?"[36] In the same vein, Cardinal James Gibbons queried, "What would this country have amounted to as a nation had its founders immediately after the Revolution closed its portals to honest but illiterate immigrants or the sons of immigrants?"[37]

Stressing the fact that the literacy test was based upon a false idea of the value of education, a Catholic writer echoed the reasoning of an earlier era when he forthrightly declared:

> We need them and need millions of them for the gardens and the farms; and for the railway tracks and the city sewer . . . unless we have the bone and sinew and muscle of those foreign illiterates to draw upon, we would soon have very little for fountain pens and typewriters to do. We have in this country no landed peasantry; for each generation of peasants becomes the parents not of other peasants, but of lawyers and doctors and trained nurses.[38]

The divergence of opinion that existed in regard to the literacy test is illustrated in its advocacy by Monsignor John A. Ryan of the Catholic University of America who saw it as the "best single method of restriction." Favoring restriction of immigration on economic grounds, he pointed out that the use of the literacy test was not to guarantee character but was "primarily a method of affecting quantity not quality."[39]

As in the use of the literacy test to restrict immigration, so on the general question of limiting immigration, Catholics were not united in their opinion. It may be said that generally Catholics favored the amendment of immigration laws to keep out lunatics, idiots, criminals, paupers, and such undesirables but beyond that there was a divergence

35. "Notes and Remarks," *Ave Maria*, New Series I (January 23, 1915), 117.

36. *Catholic World*, CXVII (May, 1923), 266.

37. John T. Ellis, *The Life of James Cardinal Gibbons, Archbishop of Baltimore, 1834-1921* (Milwaukee, 1952), 2 vols. II, 534.

38. T. J. Brennan, "The Literacy Test," *Catholic World*, CV (May, 1917), 227.

39. *Fortnightly Review*, XXIII (May 1, 1916), 133-135, quoted in Murphy, *Attitudes of American Catholics*, 101, 107.

of opinion. The question of the supply of labor was raised by one writer who saw that if the immigrant was barred there would be difficulty in finding workers for the menial tasks of society.[40]

Another, basing his arguments upon philanthropic grounds, called upon his listeners at the annual Convention of the American Federation of Catholic Societies to "show the immigrant and the whole world . . . that we are indeed what our positions as Christians demand of us, helpers of those who are oppressed, true friends of the afflicted."[41] In these sentiments he was echoed by the writer who asked, "Have we ceased to be the refuge of the oppressed and the home of the free, shall we deny to immigrants of today what our forefathers sought and received a few decades ago?"[42]

Some believed the opposition to immigration to be based upon the anti-Catholic feeling which had so frequently shown itself in the United States. Analyzing the movement for restriction, one writer found it "closely interrelated to the anti-Catholic agitation," for the opponent of the parochial school was also an opponent of immigration, and those who were opposed to foreigners were also opposed to Catholics holding public office.[43] An editorial in the *Catholic World* on "Catholics and Immigration" took cognizance of this same feeling. It pointed out that had the immigrant stayed in his own country he would have remained a true son of the Church. Since the Church in the United States had not increased in proportion to the number of Catholic immigrants, she "loses by Catholic immigration and so Catholics, merely as Catholics, have no reason to wish to keep up the amount of immigration."[44] Another writer declared that despite the fact that there was a great deal of anti-Catholic sentiment involved in the propaganda favoring the restriction of immigration this fact should not influence the Catholic inasmuch as it was a constructive immigration policy.[45]

The policy of restricting immigration was advocated by Catholic

40. *America*, XXVIII (October 21, 1922), 15.
41. Charles E. Fay, "The Catholic Immigrant," *Catholic Mind*, XIII (September 8, 1915), 502.
42. Frederick Siedenburg, "The Immigration Problem," *Catholic Mind*, XIII (September 8, 1915), 500.
43. John McGuinness, "Is Immigration a Menace to National Unity?" *America* XXVII (July 1, 1922), 249.
44. *Catholic World*, CXVI (January, 1923), 549.
45. Louis Budenz, "Some Features of a Constructive Immigration Policy," *Central-Blatt and Social Justice*, VIII (September, 1915), 164.

writers upon other grounds. The editor of the *Fortnightly Review* claimed in 1913 that the Catholic Church was not in a position to care for the great number who were arriving and the following year found that support for unrestricted entry centered in those who had a special interest in the arrival of unnumbered immigrants — steamship and transportation lines, mill and mine owners, and even "philanthropic organizations whose best asset is the necessity of the immigrant." Carrying his analysis a step farther, he characterized those idealists, who believed restriction to be opposition to some "predestined divine purpose," as logical descendants of those who thought "it flying in the face of Providence to try to check pestilence by sanitation." [46] Another writer favored the restriction of immigration because of the number who were not Americanized. He was certain that those who lived in the nation but were not of it, and "who fail to take on something of the spirit and purpose of America," constituted a danger to the well-being of the country and "are a force to be reckoned with." [47]

Those who favored a restrictive policy of immigration could also base their position on philanthropic grounds as Monsignor John A. Ryan showed. He foresaw that unrestricted immigration would develop in the United States a proletariat and favored restriction as a service to humanity rather than enabling "a comparatively small proportion of the oppressed of Europe to better their condition very slightly." [48] An editorial in the *Catholic World* favored a reasonable limit on the number of immigrants but advocated discrimination on grounds of physical and mental fitness and moral character rather than upon nationality. In answer to a series of articles on "The Immigration Peril" in a popular magazine of wide circulation, the editor further advocated a delay in the period required for naturalization and called upon those concerned to put their houses in order by making social conditions at mines and steel mills and stockyards "as decent, as pleasant and as civilized" as among the Ford Motor Company and Standard Oil employees. [49]

A survey of the attitude of the native American Catholic toward the immigrant and the question of immigration reveals in many in-

46. "The Immigration Problem," *Fortnightly Review*, XXI (1914), 136. quoted in Murphy, *Attitudes of American Catholics*, 100.

47. Eugene Weare, "Our Immigration Problem," *America*, XXIX (April 28, 1923), 32.

48. *Fortnightly Review*, XXIII (May 1, 1916), 133-135, quoted in Murphy, *Attitudes of American Catholics*, 101.

49. *Catholic World*, CXVIII (January, 1924), 554.

stances a wide difference of opinion. During the period 1830-1880 the
continuance of immigration was advocated on the grounds of the contribution of the immigrant and the philanthropic ideals of the country.
While native Catholics were not unaware of the shortcomings of the
immigrant Irish and Germans, real antagonism was felt between the
latter groups. Colonization of the immigrant was fostered by individuals and by organizations but with no great degree of success. Despite
this the continuance of immigration was deemed desirable.

When immigration became a matter of national concern there was
no general agreement among Catholics as to its desirability. Those
who favored its continuance advocated effective action through Catholic associations to assist those of their own nationality as they arrived
in the United States. With the establishment of the National Catholic
Welfare Conference in 1922 with a Bureau of Immigration, nation-
wide direction was given to the Catholic program, especially that of
the Americanization of the immigrant.

Continued agitation for restrictive legislation most frequently took
the form of a literacy test which became required in 1917. Catholic
opinion was not solidly opposed to the establishment of such a requirement for admission to the United States. The opponents of general
restriction of immigration based their appeals upon the need for workers and philanthropic ideals. The inability of the Church to provide
for the hordes arriving as well as philanthropic reasons were cited by
those Catholics who favored some type of restrictive legislation.

VINCENT P. DE SANTIS*

IX. The American Historian Looks at the Catholic Immigrant

More than thirty years ago Marcus L. Hansen wrote his essay entitled, "The History of American Immigration as a Field for Research," [1] in which he suggested a number of problems having to do with immigration and its place in American history. But in the years that have followed, and in spite of the ever-increasing literature on all aspects of American history, only a few of Hansen's ideas have been explored, and most of the problems that he pointed out for possible examination still await investigation. Immigration as a field of study has been neglected by American historians in general, and very much neglected by historians of Catholicism in the United States. In fact, only a few really serious and scientific studies of Catholic immigration exist. Outside of the studies of Thomas N. Brown and Fathers Colman Barry and James P. Shannon one is hard put to find an objective study of the Catholic immigrant by a trained historian. [2] Were it not for scholars like Hansen, Carl Wittke, Oscar Handlin, and Arnold Schreier, whose primary interests are elsewhere than that of American Catholicism, very little would have been done at all about the Catholic immigrant. Thus it is a formidable and hazardous task to deal with a problem about which the evidence is only slightly known.

This is not to say that writers have ignored the Catholic immigrant any more than they have avoided the general question of immigration, for an enormous literature on the latter subject has been built up over the years. But until recently, the field of immigration seldom attracted

* Dr. Vincent P. De Santis is Associate Professor of History in the University of Notre Dame and a contributor to historical periodicals on political history.

1. Marcus Lee Hansen, *The Immigrant in American History* (Cambridge, Mass., 1848), pp. 191-217. This essay first appeared in the *American Historical Review*, XXXII (1926-1927), 500-518.

2. Colman J. Barry, *The Catholic Church and German Americans* (Milwaukee, 1953); James P. Shannon, *Catholic Colonization on the Western Frontier* (New Haven, 1957); Thomas N. Brown, "The Origins and Character of Irish-American Nationalism," *Review of Politics*, XVIII (1956), 327-358.

the trained historian to the point where monographs and special studies on the subject appeared. Yet American historians treated the problem of immigration in their general and special accounts of the history of the United States, and in so doing they set forth certain ideas about the Catholic immigrant that also had wide currency in the popular mind of America in the late nineteenth and early twentieth centuries. This seems all the more interesting and significant in view of the fact that trained scholars should have the same hostility and suspicion about the Catholic immigrant that obtained the strongest foothold among the ignorant and unthinking in America. For in general American historians, who experienced the great flow of Catholic immigrants to the United States in the late nineteenth and early twentieth centuries, were suspicious of them as social and religious innovators and hoped that they would adopt the Anglo-Saxon institutions and way of life.

These attitudes of American historians grew out of a variety of factors. Of chief importance were old stock, Anglo-American, Protestant, and middle or upper class backgrounds. Then, too, the flood of immigration coincided with the increasing industrialization in the United States, and with this came urbanization, slums, poverty, political corruption, and class conflict. In the popular as well as in the scholarly mind these evils seemed more and more the result of the decline of ethnic homogeneity, and the Catholic immigrant became identified with the more unsavory conditions in the country. Finally certain concepts about immigration which were widely and firmly held in America also influenced American historians in making judgments about the Catholic newcomer. One was the belief that the United States was and should remain primarily an Anglo-Saxon and Protestant country. Another was the assumption that labor and class struggles were aspects of European and not American life and that they had been introduced into the United States by the immigrant. Still others were the theories that immigration served to reduce the native birth rate and did not mean a net gain in the population of the country; that it lowered wages, reduced the living standard, and increased crime and diseases and political and social evils. All these ideas helped to prejudice the American historian against the Catholic immigrant, and these prejudices were to be found not only among historians on the Atlantic seaboard but among those on the frontier as well.[3]

Basically then, American historians of the late nineteenth and early

3. Edward N. Saveth, *American Historians and European Immigrants* (New York, 1948), pp. 13-14.

twentieth centuries looked upon the Catholic immigrant as a threat to what they held dear in their own society, and this feeling of insecurity motivated many of their hostile attitudes. Francis Walker, who had established his reputation with the work he had done as chief of the Bureau of Statistics and as Superintendent of the tenth census, also served as professor of history at the Sheffield Scientific School of Yale (1873-1881) before going on to the presidency of the Massachusetts Institute of Technology. He set the scholarly tone of the late nineteenth and early twentieth century about the immigrants from southern and eastern Europe when he wrote in 1899, "They are beaten men from beaten races; representing the worst failures in the struggle for existence. Centuries are against them, as centuries were on the side of those who formerly came to us. They have none of the ideas and aptitudes which fit men to take up readily and easily the problem of self-care and self-government." John Fiske argued that the nation was not obliged, even for humanitarian reasons, to take immigrants of this sort. John W. Burgess described them as "inclined to anarchy and crime," and "in everything which goes to make up folk character, the exact opposite of genuine Americans. It remains to be seen whether Uncle Sam can digest and assimilate such a morsel." Hubert Howe Bancroft, historian of the Pacific Coast, watching the progress of the new immigrants in California politics asked old stock Americans, "is this your boasted republicanism, a government by the people, for the people? Rather a government by wild Irishmen, for wild Irishmen and self-serving labor leaders." [4]

While expressing great faith in the operation of the melting pot, Theodore Roosevelt wrote, "above all the immigrant must learn to talk and think and be the United States." Frederick Jackson Turner, himself a part of the melting pot in the West, regretted that the source of immigration had shifted from northern and western to southern and eastern Europe, and he looked upon Italians, Poles, and Slovaks as "a loss to the social organism of the United States," and as having "struck hard blows since 1880 at the standard of comfort of the American workmen." "The lowering of the standard of comfort. . . the increase in crime and pauperism. . . and the anarchist elements. . . all these and similar problems are presented by the transformation of our immigration," wrote Turner in 1901. Woodrow Wilson, in his capacity of a historian, also objected to the change in the type of immigration late in the nineteenth century. He noted "an alteration in

4. *Ibid.,* pp. 40, 49, 96.

stock which students of affairs marked with an uneasiness." No longer
did men of the "sturdy stocks" or of the "Latin-Gallic stocks," come,
wrote Wilson, for they were replaced by "men of the lowest class from
the south of Italy and men of the meaner sort out of Hungary and
Poland, men out of the ranks where there was neither skill nor energy
nor any initiative of quick intelligence; and they came in numbers
which increased from year to year, as if the countries of the south of
Europe were disburdening themselves of the more sordid and hapless
elements of their population, the men whose standard of life and work
were such as American workmen had never dreamed of hitherto."
John Bach McMaster concluded that the native American looked upon
the sudden and steady flow of Catholic immigrants as a deliberate plot
to subvert free institutions, and Ellis Paxson Oberholtzer observed that
the new immigrants lived "crowded together in ramshackle buildings
in slums like beasts," ate "food that was nauseating to other men,"
and had "revolting and vicious habits." Since they were of the lower
order they repelled those in the higher social scale and those who had
a higher standard of living. Edward Channing believed that the main
source of trouble between Catholics and other Americans "was in the
clannishness of the Irish Roman Catholics. They lived apart by themselves and acted on the advice of their priests. . . ." [5]

Of course there were deviations from this pattern by individual
historians, but in the main the above examples represented the general
opinion of the American historian of the Catholic immigrant in the
late nineteenth and early twentieth centuries. These attitudes have
a twofold significance. One, as we have already noted, they corre-
sponded to the popular beliefs and misconceptions held by so many
Americans about the Catholic immigrant. The other is that regardless
of the subject matter of history, whether the historian emphasized
political, social, or frontier history, the basic attitudes remained the
same.

If a feeling of insecurity helped to motivate some of the hostile
attitudes of historians toward the Catholic immigrant an even greater
feeling of insecurity produced the filiopietistic or ancestor veneration
studies of the immigrant in an effort to bring about a corrective viewpoint in the treatment of him. Now while these writers did much to
open up the field of immigration for research their nationalism and
prejudices were often detrimental to the historiography of the groups
they wrote about. The filiopietists claimed too much for the group

5. *Ibid.*, pp. 115, 128, 130, 142, 187, 190, 198-199.

they wrote about, they too frequently regarded it as an independent entity, and they sought to show that their particular ethnic group was equal to the Anglo-Saxon in terms of achievement and Americanization. Of course they were reacting to the manner in which the trained historian had slighted their group, but in the main, what they produced was a form of nationalist propaganda and ethnic jingoism. In his study of *The Immigrant in American History,* Hansen wrote that, "It is surprising that the English, who have contributed the most to American culture, have been studied the least by students of immigration. There is no English-American historical society, no separate history of the English stock. Discussions of English influence in America are invariably confined to the colonial period and to the legal, economic and social institutions they planted. Such studies ignore the steady inflow of Englishmen that continued all through the nineteenth century. . . ." [6] But this was not the case with studies about Catholic immigrants of non-English origins. So much work went into showing what contributions they made to American life that John Fiske wondered whether they "ever left anything for other people to do." In the opinion of one filiopietist, who wrote about the place of the German element in American history, history ought to be rewritten along "racial or ethnic" lines so that it might perform "its proper function of tracing the causes which form the national character and decide national destiny." While filiopietism had its greatest vogue in the closing decades of the nineteenth and the early ones of the twentieth century, it has by no means died out, for a recent writer with a national audience, recalled the glories of forgotten ethnic heroes and had page after page of such revelations as that "one of Edward R. Stettinius' grandfathers was a Reilly," and that "George Washington was kin to a branch of the McCarthy family." [7]

But in the last thirty years the studies of immigration have produced different and better results than the ones we have already mentioned. In general the contemporary American historians give the Catholic immigrant rather fair treatment — at least fairer than he had between 1880 and 1920. This has resulted in part from the general advance in historical writings in the past several decades — with historians refining and subjecting to intensive research all aspects of American history and with historians using the results of their colleagues in the social sciences. But it has also resulted from the rise of

6. Hansen, *The Immigrant in American History,* pp. 147-148.
7. Saveth, *American Historians and European Immigrants,* pp. 204, 206, 217.

a few trained historians like Hansen, Wittke, Handlin, and Theodore
C. Blegen, who have turned their attention to immigration as a field
of major interest. In so doing they have retrieved immigrant history
from the filiopietists and have produced serious studies which constitute the beginnings of a historiography of immigration. These writers start the story of immigration in Europe and then attempt to find
out how immigrant culture and thought patterns were changed in the
American environment. As Handlin pointed out in his study, *Boston
Immigrants, 1790-1865,* "the character of the environment — the community in its broadest sense — is particularly important in the study
of the contact of dissimilar cultures. It is the field where unfamiliar
groups meet, discover each other, and join in a hard relationship that
results in either acculturation or conflict. . . ." [8]

Yet for all these recent advances and in spite of the prodigious
efforts by the filiopietists, the American historian still knows very little
about the Catholic immigrant. This is all the more distressing for the
historian of modern America when American historians describe the
growth of Catholicism as "the most spectacular development in American religious history after the decades of the eighties," and when they
further point out that "the American Roman Catholic Church was
overwhelmingly recruited from immigrants. . . ." [9] This being the
case the American historian cannot help but stress the absolute necessity of scientific and objective studies about Catholic immigrants by
trained Catholic historians themselves. As already noted, nationalist
propaganda has too frequently distorted the writings of Catholics, especially on the Irish and Poles in the United States. This has probably
resulted from the anxiety and insecurity induced in the children of
Catholic immigrants through their inheritance of discrimination on
the basis of their religious background. But it is very doubtful whether
Catholics are any longer a "despised minority" in the United States,
nor can they justly excuse themselves on the score of serious religious
bigotry. In many ways Catholics have "arrived" in this country, and
it is time they begin to act as mature and responsible people, and
surely it is not mature for them to be writing histories of their particular national groups in any other way than in an honest and straight-
forward manner.

8. Oscar Handlin, *Boston Immigrants, 1790-1865* (Cambridge, Mass., 1941),
pp. vii-viii.
9. Henry Steele Commager, *The American Mind* (New Haven, 1950), p.
189; Harvey Wish, *Society and Thought in Modern America* (New York,
1952), p. 169.

Another matter about the Catholic immigrant that has both amused and irritated historians is his contribution to American culture. Either one of two things happened to him when he mingled in the American social system. He found himself in an entirely American environment in which he soon discarded his old ways and characteristics or he became socially isolated. More often though his lot was cast with hundreds of others who had the same background, and joining hands with them, he developed a society that was neither European or American. "The peasants, in their coming, did not bring with them the social patterns of the Old World," Oscar Handlin tells us. "These could not be imposed on the activities of the New . . . and the environment, in any case, was hostile to the preservation of the village ways. What forms ultimately developed among immigrants were the products of American conditions." [10]

But this is not the picture that one ordinarily gets about the Catholic immigrant and American culture.[11] Too frequently too much space is given to leading individuals, such as politicians, soldiers, writers, and educators and too little to the story of the everyday life of the group in the town, the village, or the city ward, where as Hansen said, "the leaven in the lump can be detected. When a few hundred such studies have been made and compared, we can more confidently say what each group has contributed to the cultural possessions of American society." [12] Too often the accounts of Catholic immigration have failed to understand the heart of the problem here — that immigrant and native culture were dynamic and changing as a result of this interaction. Moreover, it has not been realistic to think of the individual making the contribution as representative of the group culture. In fact his very reasons for achieving success might have come from his casting off the group culture and becoming assimilated. Then, too, in conceiving of the contribution made, the distinction should be made between the immigrant himself and the second and third generation Catholic, which so many writers fail to do. To think of the latter as still an immigrant and to measure his contribution in terms of an ethnic group does not square with the facts, for he was surely an American by this time and had become assimilated to the dominant social and cultural pattern.

10. Hansen, *The Immigrant in American History*, p. 201; Oscar Handlin, *The Uprooted* (Boston, 1951), pp. 170-171.

11. For example see Lawrence M. Flick, "What the American Has Got Out of the Melting Pot from the Catholic," *Catholic Historical Review*, V (1925), 407-430.

12. Hansen, *The Immigrant in American History*, pp. 206-207.

Another aspect of the Catholic immigrant that remains relatively untouched or else misrepresented is that of emigration which as Hansen has pointed out "has been connected with as many phases of European life as immigration has of American life. Freedom to move, desire to move and means to move summarize these phases . . . in short that break-up of the solidarity of the community which, in making the individual mobile, forced him to shift for himself." Nearly all writers of Catholic immigration have had a way of leaving out things that historians would most like to know. What was life like in the agricultural villages? In what kind of homes did the peasants live? What were the cultural influences of these villages and homes? What have been the inheritances in education, art, and government of these immigrants? What about the legal development of the right of emigration, the military obligations affecting emigration, marriage laws, standards of living and birth and death rates in relation to the growth of population in a given region? What about migration to cities, division of the common lands, the transport policies of European railroads, and popular knowledge of America? [13]

But to the American historian the most important as well as the most interesting side of the story of the Catholic immigrant has been his assimilation to the American patterns of life. This has even greater significance in view of the fact that at the same time that the Catholic immigrant was looked upon as a menace to American institutions and way of life he was steadily conforming to them. That this was so obvious seems superfluous to repeat, and yet because of this it has been lost sight of so many times.

The principal reason why so many Americans were suspicious of the Catholic immigrant is that he appeared to segregate himself and thus seemed to be fostering the spirit of disunity and encouraging racialism. But this is what the old stock American feared about the immigrant in general. Yet the country did not develop as many immigrants hoped and many native Americans feared would happen, into a collection of minorities which made national origin, speech, and particular institutions the basis of their allegiance. In fact, today American society is rather uniform — too uniform the critics say — and surely quite different from what it was more than a century ago.

The Catholic Church, in addition to all its other problems, had the unique one of adjusting millions of Irishmen, Germans, Italians, Poles, Czechs, Austrians and others to the American environment. "I

13. *Ibid.*, pp. 192-193.

have in my diocese," said a Bishop, "Germans, Irish, French, Poles, Lithuanians, Czechs-Slovaks, Italians, and Ruthenians." But what about Americans?, he was asked. "Most of them are Americans," he replied, "and we are helping the rest to become so." [14] That this was the case can hardly be disputed, yet most Americans, at the time, would have probably noticed the Bishop's first remark and not his second. Naturally Catholic parishes, which were the social as well as religious centers for the immigrant, seemed many times like foreign chaplaincies, and they kept alive sentiments of affection for the mother countries of their parishioners. But when the colonists came they did precisely the same thing, and there were no serious objections to the sentiments of Presbyterians for Scotland, of Lutherans for Germany and Sweden, or of Episcopalians for England nor to the sentiments still held by many of their descendants.

It is also true that American bishops sent priests to Europe to learn the language of countries from which the immigrants came, and it became the practice of the hierarchy to provide each foreign language group with a priest who could speak its own language. For example in a Hartford, Conn., parish in 1907, ten different languages were used in the services.[15] But the Catholic Church in the United States refused to go beyond this in making concessions to its immigrant communicants, which is all the more amazing when one ponders the conclusion of Aaron Abell that "By the turn of the century [20th], urban immigrants and their children made up fully five-sixths of the Church's swelling membership." [16] While "the parish organization of the Church . . . adjusted itself increasingly to the needs of the newer immigrant," and "enterprising priests" made "their parishes real social centers," [17] the Catholic Church in America retained its homogeneity like the nation.

Cahensylism posed a threat to the homogeneity of American Catholicism and met with defeat. A. S. Will in his life of Cardinal James Gibbons, who worked against Cahensylism, pointed out about the Cardinal that "he was determined that the Church in this country should continue homogeneous like the nation. If the discord of rival

14. Frederick Joseph Kinsman, *Americanism and Catholicism* (New York, 1924), p. 125.
15. J. T. Roche, "A Practical Solution to the Immigrant Problem," *Extension Magazine*, I (May, 1907), 10.
16. Aaron Abell, "The Catholic Church and Social Problems in the World War I Era," *Mid-America*, XXX, New Series, XIX (July, 1948), 139.
17. John O'Grady, *Catholic Charities in the United States: History and Problems* (Washington, D. C., 1930), p. 307.

nationalist aims were definitely introduced, his work would go down a wreck." And Archbishop John Ireland agreed. "The Church of America must be, of course, as Catholic as even in Jerusalem or Rome," he said, "but as far as her garments assume color from local atmosphere, she must be American. Let no one dare paint on her brow with a foreign tint, or pin to her mantle foreign linings." [18] An excellent example of the clear understanding of this point appeared in an article in the June, 1924 issue of *The Homiletic and Pastoral Review* by a foreign-born priest in a "national parish." "The American determination toward a more thorough peaceful amalgamation of the various foreign groups that make up our nation is unmistakable, and it is an unmixed blessing. It is altogether legitimate and cannot be opposed on any valid grounds," he wrote. "Catholics cannot be, and never have been, otherwise than wholeheartedly loyal to America. Foreign Catholics are no exception to this rule. There is danger, however, that if the latter insist overmuch on setting themselves aside in permanently isolated groups, they will contribute to intensify that feeling of distrust," he continued. "There can be no room in the American Republic for colonies of European countries or anything that even remotely amounts to that, such as language groups where a foreign spirit, foreign ideas and foreign customs are clung to tenaciously. There is no need for casting any aspersions on their loyalty. However," maintained this priest, "there is need for serious thought and reform when statistics show that one of our largest national groups — Catholic to the core — has a naturalization record of only 28 per cent, where other national groups have a record of 60 to 72 per cent." [19]

And how has the historian felt about this particular matter? Perhaps what Henry S. Commager has said will suffice. "Whatever conclusion may be drawn from a scrutiny of Catholic doctrine, the fact was that Catholicism had flourished as a major religion for three-quarters of a century without raising serious difficulties except in the imaginations of men and that democratic institutions seemed as sound when the church numbered twenty-four million members as they had been when it counted its communicants by the hundred thousand," wrote Commager. "It might, indeed, be maintained that the Catholic Church was, during this period [since 1880] one of the most effective of all agencies for democracy and Americanization." [20]

18. Commager, *The American Mind*, pp. 193-194.
19. Kinsman, *Americanism and Catholicism*, pp. 127-129.
20. Commager, *The American Mind*, p. 193.

Index

Abbelen, Peter, Vicar General
of Milwaukee,
petitioned against forcible Americanization, 195.
Abell, Aaron,
on the number of urban Catholic immigrants at the turn of the twentieth century, 233-234.
Adler, Mortimer J.,
success of, significant in a Catholic field among non-Catholic students, 61.
Allport, Gordon W.,
has noted that Americans tend to identify themselves in terms of race, ethnicity, and religion, 6.
Americanization,
became the chief problem of Catholics in dealing with the immigrants, 218 ff.;
includes socialization, accommodation, and assimilation, 113-4;
of Catholicism hinges on the problem of unity in diversity, 126-7;
of Catholics cannot be measured by assuming that Catholics possess a sub-culture, 115-6;
of Catholics cannot be measured by class status, 115;
of Catholics not measured by the amount of tension, 114-5;
of religion in America, 13.
Anne, Queen,
vetoed anti-Catholic laws in Maryland, 134.
Anti-Semitism,
seems at low ebb, 10.
Association of Catholic Trade Unionists formed in 1937, assisted in workers' education, 96 ff.

Bancroft, Hubert Howe,
hostile attitude of, toward Irish immigrant, 227.
Bartholomé de las Casas, Bishop,
and Negro slavery, 157.
Beard, Charles A.,
and Stuart Chase, the most vocal

intellectuals in support of economic planning, 81.
Bigotry,
and intolerance of Catholics in secular institutions of higher learning according to Professor C. J. H. Hayes, 64.
Binstock, Louis,
is quoted to illustrate religion when it comes to mean a contentless faith, 17.
Bismarck, Otto von,
policy of, as a factor in German Catholic emigration, 190.
Black, Hugo L.,
and the "wall of separation" doctrine, in the Everson decision, 1947.
Blanshard, Paul,
the nature of the attack of, against the Church, 118.
Blegen, Theodore C.,
helped to rescue immigrant history from the filiopietists, 230.
Bogardus, Emory S.,
on "imposed acculturation" during the Americanization movement of World War I, 119.
Bonnechose, Archbishop Henri,
supported Cahensly on behalf of German immigrants, 197.
Brennan, T. J.,
attack of, on the literacy test, 221.
Brooks, Phillips,
the national mourning accompanying death of, was indicative of the religious complexion of the United States before the turn of the twentieth century, 21.
Brownson, Josephine,
a social settlement worker, 77.
Brownson, Orestes A.,
one of the first to raise the issue of Americanizing the Catholic in America, 219.
Budenz, Louis,
on the immigration problem, 217;
supported restriction of immigration, 222.

235